The Impact of Education

Stephen Pickard | Michael Welker | John Witte (Eds.)

The Impact of Education

On Character Formation, Ethics, and the Communication of Values in Late Modern Pluralistic Societies

EVANGELISCHE VERLAGSANSTALT
Leipzig

The project and the publication were supported by the Alonzo McDonald Agape Foundation and the University of Heidelberg.

Bibliographic information published by the Deutsche Nationalbibliothek
The Deutsche Nationalbibliothek lists this publication in the Deutsche Nationalbibliographie; detailed bibliographic data are available on the Internet at http://dnb.dnb.de.

This book is printed on ageing resistant paper.

Cover: Kai-Michael Gustmann, Leipzig
Cover picture: © persephone3d / www.fotosearch.com
Typesetting: 3w+p, Rimpar
Printing and Binding: Hubert & Co., Göttingen

ISBN 978-3-374-07054-1 // eISBN (PDF) 978-3-374-07055-8
www.eva-leipzig.de

Inhalt

Acknowledgements

This volume was made possible by a generous grant from the McDonald Agape Foundation. We give thanks to President Peter McDonald and the members of the Foundation board for their support. We are grateful to the University of Heidelberg and to our colleagues at the Forschungszentrum Internationale und Interdisziplinäre Theologie (FIIT) in Heidelberg. We also offer thanks for the support and encouragement of colleagues in the Research Centre for Public and Contextual Theology at Charles Sturt University in Canberra. We give thanks for the work on this volume by Dr. Gary S. Hauk, senior editor in the Center for the Study of Law and Religion at Emory University. It was a privilege to learn from each of our chapter authors and to work with our editorial friends at Evangelischen Verlagsanstalt in Leipzig. Warmest thanks to each of them for sharing their time and talents with us so generously.

Preface to the Series

Five hundred years ago, Protestant reformer Martin Luther argued that "three estates" (*drei Stände*) lie at the foundation of a just and orderly society - marital families, religious communities, and political authorities. Parents in the home; pastors in the church; magistrates in the state—these, said Luther, are the three authorities whom God appointed to represent divine justice and mercy in the world, to protect peace and liberty in earthly life. Household, church, and state—these are the three institutional pillars on which to build social systems of education and schooling, charity and social welfare, economy and architecture, art and publication. Family, faith, and freedom—these are the three things that people will die for.

In the half millennium since Luther, historians have uncovered various classical and Christian antecedents to these early Protestant views. And numerous later theorists have propounded all manner of variations and applications of this three-estates theory, many increasingly abstracted from Luther's overtly Christian worldview. Early modern covenant theologians, both Christian and Jewish, described the marital, confessional, and political covenants that God calls human beings to form, each directed to interrelated personal and public ends. Social-contract theorists differentiated the three contracts that humans enter as they move from the state of nature to an organized society protective of their natural rights—the marital contract of husband and wife; the government contract of rulers and citizens; and, for some, the religious contracts of preachers and parishioners. Early anthropologists posited three stages of development of civilization—from family-based tribes and clans, to priest-run theocracies, to fully organized states that embraced all three institutions. Sociologists distinguished three main forms of authority in an organized community—"traditional" authority that begins in the home, "charismatic" authority that is exemplified by the church, and "legal" authority that is rooted in the state. Legal historians outlined three stages of development of legal norms—from the habits and rules of the family, to the customs and canons of religion, to the statutes and codes of the state.

Already a century ago, however, scholars in different fields began to flatten out this hierarchical theory of social institutions and to emphasize the foundational role of other social institutions alongside the family, church, and state in shaping private and public life and character. Sociologists like Max Weber and Talcott Parsons emphasized the shaping powers of "technical rationality" exemplified especially in new industry, scientific education, and market economies. Legal scholars like Otto von Gierke and F. W. Maitland emphasized the critical roles of nonstate legal associations (*Genossenschaften*) in maintaining a just social, political, and legal order historically and today. Catholic subsidiarity theories of Popes Leo XIII and Pius XI emphasized the essential task of mediating social units between the individual and the state to cater the full range of needs, interests, rights, and duties of individuals. Protestant theories of sphere sovereignty, inspired by Abraham Kuyper, argued that not only churches, states, and families but also the social spheres of art, labor, education, economics, agriculture, recreation, and more should enjoy a level of independence from others, especially an overreaching church or state. Various theories of social or structural pluralism, civil society, voluntary associations, the independent sector, multiculturalism, multinormativity, and other such labels have now come to the fore in the ensuing decades –both liberal and conservative, religious and secular, and featuring all manner of methods and logics.

Pluralism of all sorts is now a commonplace of late modern societies. At minimum, this means a multitude of free and equal individuals and a multitude of groups and institutions, each with very different political, moral, religious, and professional interests and orientations. It includes the sundry associations, interest groups, parties, lobbies, and social movements that often rapidly flourish and fade around a common cause, especially when aided by modern technology and various social media. Some see in this texture of plurality an enormous potential for colorful and creative development and a robust expression of human and cultural freedom. Others see a chaotic individualism and radical relativism, which endangers normative education, moral character formation, and effective cultivation of enduring values or virtues.

Pluralism viewed as vague plurality, however, focuses on only one aspect of late modern societies–the equality of individuals, and their almost unlimited freedom to participate peaceably at any time as a respected voice in the moral reasoning and civil interactions of a society. But this view does not adequately recognize that, beneath the shifting cacophony of social forms and norms that constitute modernity, pluralistic societies have heavy normative codes that shape their individual and collective values and morals, preferences and prejudices.

The sources of much of this normative coding and moral education in late modern pluralistic societies are the deep and powerful social systems that are the pillars of every advanced culture. The most powerful and pervasive of these are the social systems of law, religion, politics, science/academy, market, media, family, education, medicine, and national defense. The actual empirical forms of each of these powerful social systems can and do vary greatly, even in the relatively homogeneous societies of the late modern West. But these deeper social systems in one form or another are structurally essential and often normatively decisive in individual and communal lives.

Every advanced society has a comprehensive legal system of justice and order, religious systems of ritual and doctrine, a family system of procreation and love, an economic system of trade and value, a media system of communication and dissemination of news and information, and an educational system of preservation, application, and creation of knowledge and scientific advance. Many advanced societies also have massive systems of science, technology, health care, and national defense with vast influence over and through all of these other social systems. These pervasive social systems lie at the foundation of modern advanced societies, and they anchor the vast pluralities of associations and social interactions that might happen to exist at any given time.

Each of these social systems has internal value systems, institutionalized rationalities, and normative expectations that together help to shape each individual's morality and character. Each of these social spheres, moreover, has its own professionals and experts who shape and implement its internal structures and processes. The normative network created by these social spheres is often harder to grasp today, since late modern pluralistic societies usually do not bring these different value systems to light under the dominance of just one organization, institution, and power. And this normative network has also become more shifting and fragile, especially since traditional social systems like religion and the family have eroded in their durability and power, and other social systems like science, the market, health care, defense, and the media have become more powerful.

The aim of this multiyear project on "Character Formation and Moral Education in Late Modern Pluralistic Societies" is to identify the realities and potentials of these core social systems to provide moral orientation and character formation in our day. What can and should these social spheres, separately and together, do in shaping the moral character of late modern individuals who, by nature, culture, and constitutional norms, are free and equal in dignity and rights? What are and should be the core educational functions and moral responsibilities of each of these social spheres? How can we better understand and better influence the complex interactions among individualism, the normative binding powers of these social systems, and the creativity of civil groups and institutions? How can we map and measure the different hierarchies of values that govern each of these social systems, and that are also interwoven and interconnected in various ways in shaping late modern understandings of the common good? How do we negotiate the boundaries and conflicts between and among these social systems when one encroaches on the other, or imposes its values and rationalities on individuals at the cost of the other social spheres or of the common good? What and where are the intrinsic strengths of each social sphere that should be made more overt in character formation, public education, and the shaping of minds and mentalities?

These are some of the guiding questions at work in this project and in this volume. Our project aims to provide a systematic account of the role of these powerful normative codes operating in the social spheres of law, religion, the family, the market, the media, science and technology, the academy, health care, and defense in the late modern liberal West. Our focus is on selected examples and case studies drawn from Western Europe, North America, South Africa, and Australia, which together provide just enough diversity to test out broader theories of character formation and moral education. Our scholars are drawn from across the academy, with representative voices from the humanities, social sciences, and natural sciences as well as the professions of theology, law, business, medicine, and more. While most of our scholars come from the Protestant and Catholic worlds, our endeavor is to offer comparative insights that will help scholars from any profession or confession. While our laboratory is principally Western liberal societies, the modern forces of globalization will soon make these issues of moral character formation a concern for every culture and region of the world–given the power of global social media, entertainment, and sports; the pervasiveness of global finance, business, trade, and law; and the perennial global worries over food, health care, environmental degradation, and natural disasters.

This volume is focused on the impact of *education* on character formation, ethics, and the communication of values in late modern pluralistic societies. It builds on four volumes already in print on the respective impacts of the market, religion, law, and academic research, and these will soon have a companion volume on the impact of the family. Forthcoming volumes will study the respective impacts of the media, the military/defense system, politics, and health-care systems. A final integrative monograph will distill the main findings of these volumes and outline some constructive responses for late modern pluralistic societies.

Michael Welker, University of Heidelberg
John Witte Jr., Emory University
Stephen Pickard, Charles Sturt University

Introduction

Stephen Pickard

This book investigates the impact of education on the formation of character and the communication of values in late modern pluralistic societies. Scholars from four continents and many different academic fields are involved. While the basic framework for the contributions is informed by Christian traditions, the disciplines cover a significant range, including theology, education, psychology, literature, anthropology, law, and business. This makes for a rich variety of thematic concentrations and perspectives.

While the perspectives and content of the chapters are diverse, a number of themes continually reemerge. First, the authors, perhaps unsurprisingly but none the less importantly, all give voice to the significance of education in its many forms and contexts as a major contributor to the formation of character and the communication of values in late modern pluralistic societies. The educational foundations and trajectories of any given country are pervasive and have a significant reach into the fabric and shape of the society and its values, making education a barometer of the well-being of a people and their culture(s). Thus, a volume on the impact of education is an important addition to this series.

Second, the contributions to this volume point to the contested nature of the role and purpose of education in the formation of character and shaping of values in different contexts. What continually emerges in the essays in this volume is a recognition of the influence of other interests and concerns on policies, programs, and delivery of education. Whether it is the nexus between education and politics, economics and work, or national identity and history, in all these areas and more, the formation of character and values through education is never simple, always inherently fragile, and ever in need of vigilance. In short, it is not a given that education as such can fulfill its purpose as a communicator of values and moral vision for the common good.

Third, the essays in this volume highlight the remarkable potential of informed educational philosophy and policies to foster an environment conducive to forming character and contributing to cultures that value respect, care, and creativity. In this respect, the final three chapters of this volume are of particular note, as they address issues concerning vocation and discernment, the importance of literature, and the call for a radical rethinking of moral education and practice from the perspective of Indigenous and planetary concerns.

The book is divided into three parts covering (a) general issues concerning education with respect to society, values, and character; (b) issues for education and character formation arising from different national contexts; and (c) emergent themes relevant to the contribution of education to forming character and values.

Part One, on *Society, Values, and Character*, begins with a chapter by Anne Stewart, ("What Has Solomon to Do with Google? Old Testament Wisdom Literature and the Mediation of Truth in Modern Pluralistic Societies"). Stewart examines the book of Proverbs as a wisdom system for truth discernment. She argues that such a historical perspective on competing truth claims might have something important to teach our contemporary society, caught as it is in a "contest of information" and "infodemic" related to the spread of misinformation. What is required above all else is discernment among competing voices and truths. This is a timeless human dynamic, albeit made even more challenging by modern media and technology. In short, does Google have the last word, or is there yet an ancient wisdom to fill the void?

Stewart points out that the book of Proverbs says more about character and the gaining of wisdom than any other literature of the Bible. It is an instruction manual for wise living and, as such, a book about education. This includes the young and the old, the neophyte and the sage. Proverbs conveys a sense of urgency, for it has to do with attaining "skills to navigate the world." Nor is the book of Proverbs naïve about the complexities of discernment in the moral world; the book's "aim is to foster wise character in its students, equipping them for living amid the grey hues of moral discernment." In this sense, the book invites "contextual ethical reflection" amid the puzzles and contradictions of life. Stewart is thus clear about the relevance of the book for "the formation of wise character in a context of competing perspectives, truth claims, and moral worldviews." It is apparent from a close reading of Proverbs that we have to do with the "education of desire."

Stewart's discussion of the competing voices of "woman Wisdom" and "strange woman" pierces our contemporary experience of the strange and alluring algorithms of Google and Facebook, with their inbuilt monetizing of desire, ambiguous treatment of information, and tendency to generate division and new tribal networks. A careful reading of Proverbs draws attention to the fact that a contest of truth is at the same time a test of character for a society.

Robert Hefner ("Character Socialization and Diversity in Modern Democracies Today") presses two questions that require precisely the kind of wise discernment that Stewart seeks. He asks: What kind of character education is appropriate for the societies and polities in which we moderns live? And what conditions in society either facilitate or impede the realization of this form of character education and, with it, its ability to influence understandings of the public good? Hefner argues that "efforts to build sustainable consensus on both character education and citizenship" have been hampered by both a radical ethical-religious plurality and what he refers to as "the rise of new forms of social mediation and mobilization," which undermine consensus and generate ethical and social differences for commercial and political purposes. Hefner draws upon the discussions of Charles Taylor and John Rawls on the subject of "overlapping consensus," which is critical "for civic coexistence and the public good." Hefner argues that, notwithstanding serious negative social and ethical consequences for minorities, key features of Christianity have contributed "to the inculcation of genuinely civil habits of the heart, as well as providing theological and ontological grounds for the affirmation of human dignity." The distortions that arise, in Hefner's view, are due to "political entrepreneurs" in civil society who harness popular Christian identities to override the dignity-affirming message of the Christian gospel. Political instrumentalization trumps theological depth. Hefner also highlights the way the Janus-faced capacity for religious socialization can generate exclusive rather than inclusive public ends (as in, for example, France and India). He points out the importance of commitment to the modern values of democratic civility and offers us cogent and urgent reasons to protect our civic and religious education.

Joachim Funke's chapter ("Character Formation from a Psychological Point of View: Search for Values, Search for *Sinn*") examines psychological studies of character formation and values. The emphasis is on the dynamics of development over the course of a human lifespan. This approach, which has been the standard paradigm since the mid-twentieth century, asks about the origins and development of moral values and how they might change. Funke introduces the reader to two different approaches in psychology to the question of character: a narrow one, which associates character with moral attitudes that develop over time like other "faculties," such as cognition, emotion, and language (Jean Piaget and Lawrence Kohlberg); and a broader one, which connects character formation to personality development that involves both stable personal traits and variable states across situations. The latter approach offers greater possibilities for change over time, and education seems to provide the optimum conditions for such change.

Whether or not wisdom might be the result of successful character formation is a moot point. Perhaps character and moral values can be measured. This is an area in which psychologists invest considerable expertise. But what to do with this information, and what insight does it yield for character formation? Another tack involves experimental research in moral dilemmas, though Funke is wary of drawing too much by way of conclusions from such experiments for understanding character formation. In short, it seems that character formation is a complex process that is not particularly accessible by psychological measurement. It seems that the human search for values and *Sinn* (making sense of things) is what makes us human and not robots.

If, as Funke's psychological assessment suggests, character formation and moral disposition are fundamentally matters of individual development in society, then it begs a question: Where, and with whom, does responsibility lie for fostering civic skills and virtues? This question is taken up by Charles Glenn ("Civic Norms and Distinctive Convictions: Finding the Right Balance"). Specifically, Glenn examines the contribution to character formation by nongovernmental schools undergirded by distinctive religious convictions. This matter is clearly controversial, as opponents argue that these kinds of schools constitute a threat to public education's mission "to develop citizens possessing the appropriate dispositions to sustain a well-functioning society." Shared convictions and loyalties that inculcate civic virtues conducive to social and political peace apparently require the banishment of distinctive religious beliefs and convictions of families and communities from the educational process. Underlying this view is what Glenn identifies as the "myth of the common school," associated with the idea of nation forming and social unity via popular schooling. Glenn offers an insightful commentary on the history of this issue, citing Michel Foucault's view that the "state has taken over from the medieval church the role and the techniques of the 'cure of souls,' with pretensions extending well beyond its traditional duties of the maintenance of domestic tranquility and the administration of justice."

Glenn's essay highlights many important issues regarding the role of education for citizenship, the role of governments in such processes, and the dangers of politicizing children's education in ways that thwart the needs of children for a culturally coherent life. He raises fundamental questions about how civic virtue might be developed, and by whom. In the challenging, often fragmenting and highly polarized times in which we live, Glenn sees a critical role for the "vitality of faith-based institutions, including schools, where trust is based upon shared commitments [and] is a precious resource to society at large."

Part Two, *National Contexts*, explores the impact of education on character and moral education in Germany, Australia, South Korea, and the United States. Heike Springhart ("Stabilizing Continuity and Transforming Spirituality: Germany's Democratization after 1945 as an Example of the Impact of Education on Character Formation, the Communication of Values, and the Breakdown of Totalitarianism") is concerned with the potential of religion to contribute to a truly democratic way of life. She examines aspects of Germany's democratization after 1945 in so far as they highlight the role of education in shaping the character and values of a nation in a time of significant transition. In doing so, Springhart identifies various themes—for example, reeducation as a pedagogic program; reeducation as part of the process of comprehensive democratization; and the importance of harnessing "clear areas" (relatively healthy spheres) of society as locations for reeducation.

With respect to this last theme, studies appear to have overlooked the significance of religion and the churches as places of resistance and, hence, "clear areas." Springhart focuses on how religion and the churches played a vital role in the reeducation process, which was strongly influenced by therapeutic models of recovery from social and cultural psychosis. There is a place here for an educational therapeutic designed to shape and strengthen character at both the individual and the national level. Important in this respect is Talcott Parsons's concept of "controlled institutional change," which included a form of religion to help shape a free, democratic society and act as a critical counterpart to the impact of National Socialism. The premise was simple: democracy was primarily a way of life, and healthy social institutions provided a vital component in the process of reeducation and character formation. Springhart shows the extensive international cooperation and shared learning entailed in the reeducation process; draws attention to the significance of and continuing impact of Protestant Academies in postwar Germany as sources of moral and spiritual support; highlights the role of women in the educative and political process in a new German society; and recalls the significance of church-based welfare organizations. Importantly, Springhart underscores the importance of religion in tempering the alienating aspects of change and keeping alive in society questions of meaning and purpose. Overall, we are left with the two complementary ecclesial and theological impulses in the process of education for a democratic way of life: stabilizing continuity and transforming spirituality.

Jo-Anne Reid ("School Education in Australia: Building Character and Reforming the Nation") focuses on the role of school education as a means for reforming national character. The background is the continuing tension between a systemic racism that emerged from Anglo-Saxon colonization in the late eighteenth century and the fact that Australia is one of the most culturally and linguistically diverse societies in the world. Reid argues that "the challenge of shaping a population that will continue to uphold the values of a pluralist society is largely entrusted to the education system, through its national 'civics and citizenship' curriculum." Given the diversity of cultures, races, languages, and values "*schooling* may well be the *only* shared social institution that young people participate in prior to exercising their rights as citizens."

This is a tall order for any education system. It is made even more problematic because Australian education still reflects a set of Christian values contaminated by desires for wealth and status, founded on the "convenient lie of Australia as *terra nullius*," which has been responsible for the emergence of a variety of discriminatory and undemocratic social outcomes. As a consequence, a major task for Australian education is to engage with a "decolonializing curriculum for educating the next generation of young Australians." How well or otherwise this task is undertaken will determine the kind of society–its character and values–that coming generations will inherit and live by. Reid highlights the differences between education within the framework of an essentially British school system and the broader European notions of character building as a social and cultural subject. As Reid makes clear, such a process needs to begin in the earliest years of a child's education.

John Witte Jr. ("Restoring the Value(s) of Religion in American Public Education") draws attention to the easily overlooked fact that the school's influence on character formation is more overt and visible than the more subtle but powerful influences of other major societal systems, such as markets, laws, politics, the media, and so on. His focus is on "the prominent role of modern American state-run public schools in educating modern citizens and the deprecated role of religion in the delivery of this public education." Witte comments on the role of the courts in this latter development and the resultant impoverishment of "the values education and character formation of American students in primary and secondary public schools, and sometimes in public universities, too." The consequences of this diminished place of religion in education have been profound with regard to students' appreciating their own religious beliefs and practices in relation to those of others and promoting the false idea that religion is essentially a matter of private disposition. This loss is particularly serious given the massive industry that education and schooling are in the United States, and it constitutes "a major battleground for constitutional struggles over religious freedom." Witte tracks some of the legal disputes in which religion was pushed further to the margins of public education, and he highlights more recent attempts in the courts to challenge this marginalization on the basis of free speech, freedom of religion, and equal access. Prominent in these battles are critics who argue for the inherent usefulness of religious values in helping to shape the character and outlook of young people preparing to take their place in an open and democratic society.

Witte notes the global resurgence and power of religion, for good and ill. Public-school education ought not ignore this. Witte provides a powerful critique and assessment of public education in the context of current American society and politics.

Chung-Hyun Baik ("An Analysis of the Impacts of the Korean Education System on the Character, Ethics, and Values of Koreans and Its Implications for Late Modern Pluralistic Societies") offers an Asian perspective as a South Korean theologian. Baik comments on the challenges facing a country that places high value on student performance and achievement (particularly in reading, science, and mathematics) yet also registers a high level of student anxiety and unhappiness in the educational process. What are the origins of this tension? What are its implications for the role of education in character development? And, importantly, what correctives are required?

Baik traces the origins of this tension in the history of the Korean education system, noting the early purpose of education in the training of children from ruling aristocratic families to become government officials; later reforms that opened education beyond those from the ruling classes; the further impact of Japanese annexation of Korea, with the result that the Korean education system became subjugated to Japanese imperialism; and post-World War II reforms that nonetheless remained highly politicized, with a focus on anticommunism and an emphasis on education for industrial and economic development.

One consequence of the educational-political link is that the Korean education system is "grounded in meritocracy" based on abilities rather than money or social status. The top priority is for students to serve the purposes of governmental rule, whose achievement is regarded as a sign of not only individual success but also filial duty to one's parents and family. The roots of anxiety are thus sown out of a particular cultural history that prizes both responsible leadership in society and a family centrism and egoistic familism. This culture of success and competition is somewhat at odds with some of the central tenets of Confucianism that encourage loving relations between people and overcoming oneself and governing others well. What this means is that education for the purpose of character development and values has a diminished role in the culture. With increasing cultural and social pluralism, change is taking place. Education for education's sake, as well as its role in shaping character and values for individuals and society, represent a challenge to more entrenched political and historical agendas.

Ashley Berner ("Public Education and Moral Formation in the United States: A View from the Early Twenty-First Century") examines the development of the uniform model for American public education and makes a strong case for an alternative plurality model. Her work has resonances with the offerings of Glenn and Witte in this volume. Berner makes an important and often ignored point that "schools are inherently meaning-making institutions; every component of a school's structure and content is educative for students. Even the omissions–what is unacceptable to discuss–are instructive." Given this reality, the pervasiveness and influence of the uniform model of state control of public education in the United States has proven to be far more problematic than might have been either intended or imagined. Berner traces the emergence of the uniform model as an anxiety-driven response to threats to Protestant hegemony from increased pluralism and diversity. Such uniformity did not imply moral neutrality but rather "reinforced Protestant hegemony," although this hegemony lost considerable force from the mid-twentieth century as courts (as outlined by John Witte in this volume) increasingly moved the country to a more secular model and marginalized the distinctly religious framework of public education. While the past quarter of a century has been marked by increasing diversity and plurality in public education, for the most part the system is captive to the common-school or uniform model.

However, as Berner makes clear, the intent of the uniform model in its secular guise is to inculcate "moral and civic cohesion" across a diverse population. This kind of "civic republicanism" begs the question of which intellectual resources and institutional practices could be broadly acceptable within a heterogeneous society. She notes the lengths to which educators will go to foreclose discussion of fundamental questions concerning values, meaning, and the religious significance of hotly debated ethical issues. The default is to a kind of majority viewpoint associated with what Berner terms a "moral therapeutic deism" and "expressive individualism." What has happened to questions of character formation and moral vision for individuals and a culture? Can a pluralist model of public education gain sufficient traction in the system? Not surprisingly, moral formation remains both contested and controversial.

Part Three, *Emerging Themes*, sets out on a different tack to focus on some areas of emerging and contemporary concern. David Cunningham ("Vocational Exploration as Character Formation: A New Direction for Higher Education") shows how questions that broadly concern vocation are beginning to play a more important role for emerging generations of students in North America and elsewhere. "Students seem to be spending more time thinking about their personal strengths and weaknesses, pondering what will make for a meaningful or purposeful life, and sometimes even using the language of *vocation* or *calling* in their efforts to describe where their lives might be headed." While this vocational turn is only in its infancy, Cunningham (and he is certainly not alone in this) judges this development to be a portent of a preoccupation that will have much wider and more significant implications for the way educative processes contribute to a broader approach to moral formation and civic and social engagements for the common good.

How, then, does reflection on vocation (with its attendant concerns for meaning and purpose) connect with the matter of character formation? Cunningham's chapter offers an insightful examination of the contexts and features of ethics and character formation in higher education in North America. Given the two tracks in higher education in that context–(a) public secular universities that usually steer clear of religious or quasi-religious matters and (b) private institutions that often have a religious foundation–it is not surprising that the latter institutions are most associated with a certain ethical freedom to pursue matters relevant to moral education, character formation, and vocation. This ancient term ("vocation") was reinterpreted by Luther during the Reformation beyond a narrow medieval clericalism to embrace a broad range of human occupations that includes one's work but also domains that are deeply formative of a way of life and a sense of purpose. This richer concept of vocation is being taken up in places of higher education to enable students to explore matters of calling and discernment so that they might live purposefully. In other words, it's not just about their prospective work, but involves moral education and character formation. Cunningham shows how this approach has consequences for personal and community commitments; the cultivation and integration of virtues into career, family, civic life, and leisure; and dealing with experiences of limit and finitude in a world of myriad choices. All of this is grist for the mill of moral development and contribution to the greater good of society. This turn to vocation as a kind of educational experiment has great potential for export into other national contexts.

Irene Pieper ("Character Formation and *Literarische Bildung:* Aims and Potentials in Literature Education") examines the potential of literature as a source and mediator of the educational process and its contribution to character formation and moral development. Pieper's discussion is grounded in the notion of *subjectivation*—a relational process in a sociological environment. This process is operative in the teacher-learner context, where readers encounter texts and learning takes place through co-construction. Pieper finds that the potential of literature to stimulate personal development requires an "environment allowing for co-construction, particularly via communication," which may be provided by family but certainly by formal education at school. In such an environment, literature is inevitably part of a more dynamic process of learning and personal development through the way literature is perceived, discussed, and enjoyed. The reason literature can play such a formative role in moral development is that a great deal "of the literary canon and contemporary literature alike shows a critical stance toward how we live, how societies are shaped or justice questioned, and how the environment is degraded." As literature operates in this manner, the learner's own world is framed, critiqued, and provoked, making possible a personal breakthrough to an expanded understanding of the self in the world and society.

Pieper traces the way this process occurred for young people in the German education system, as the reader moves from moral insight into a broader emancipatory function of literature and a stronger focus on contemporary concerns for identity, both personal and social. Other voices stressed the priority of the aesthetic potential of literature over instrumentalist concerns. The emphasis on personal and moral development, cultural continuity, and identity formation through encounter with literature is the critical matter. Pieper alerts us to the danger that concern for learning outcomes and literacy competency can become decoupled from inquiry into "what particular literary texts have to teach about our various worlds and how they stimulate our imagination." The chapter offers a rich and intricate account of the importance and challenges of literature as a critical aspect in a student's self-understanding of their place and purpose in the world.

Darcia Narvaez ("Resetting Baselines for an Earth-Centered Moral Education") sets out an urgent and radical agenda for moral education against the backdrop of the present existential threat of global destruction. In light of the emergence of a worldwide "Taker" culture, whose origins can be traced to the growth of human civilizations out of nomadic foraging societies over the past ten thousand years, Narvaez poses the question: "What should moral educators do in the face of such a destructive culture, one that is destroying not only humanity's habitat but also the integrity of every ecosystem and that of the planet?" Narvaez responds: "We must examine human baselines, better understand human development, and re-adopt ancestral approaches to living a good life." The alternative to a Taker culture is a "Leaver" culture that resonates with "natural systems as members of the bio-community." Leaver cultures across the world, representing 99 percent of the time that the human genus has existed, "make a more appropriate baseline for determining the goals and methods of moral education." Narvaez addresses the "neurobiology of morality and the vitality of nature-centered morality." She argues for a return to a "sustainable Indigenous wisdom."

Narvaez identifies the hubris of civilized moral education as observed in discussions of morality that "move too quickly into abstractions, reasoning, and right thinking, leaving behind the cultivation of moral *being*, *manner*, and *virtue*." She contrasts ancestral moral development–"evolved nest or evolved developmental niche, EDN," as an extragenetic inheritance–with children of civilized nations, who typically lack many of the evolved-nest components even before birth and arrive at school already less developed "in terms of self-in-nature, lacking self-confidence, and exhibiting various pathologies." Narvaez identifies some critical areas for twenty-first-century moral education to thwart the destructive trajectory toward the self-demise of the human species. The chapter is a powerful clarion call to recover "an earth-centered, nature-respecting moral education." It is a fitting and prophetic chapter to round out a rich and diverse volume.

Part One: Society, Values, and Character

What Has Solomon to Do with Google? Old Testament Wisdom Literature and the Mediation of Truth in Modern Pluralistic Societies

Anne W. Stewart

The conference that occasioned this essay was unfortunately canceled in the wake of the global pandemic. Yet a deadly virus was not the only disease sweeping the globe. Doctors, scientists, leaders, and citizens have been battling not only the novel coronavirus but also a spread of misinformation about its origin, transmission, mitigation, and effects.

In the highly polarized public discourse of many of our countries, the pandemic sparked a contest of information as much as a crisis of public health. In fact, the director general of the World Health Organization (WHO), Tedros Adhanom Ghebreyesus, declared this phenomenon an "infodemic" and called on governments to fight the spread of misinformation.[1] WHO has a team of "myth busters" who work with technology and social media companies, including Google, Facebook, Pinterest, and TikTok, to counter rumors, conspiracy theories, false information, and unfounded medical advice.[2]

The infodemic represents a contest of moral systems. It is not simply a vibrant debate of differing scientific perspectives (though that, too, exists), but instead is the proliferation of verifiably false information that feeds alternative ecosystems of meaning. Conspiracy theories have proliferated in the wake of the virus, with some suggesting that COVID-19 is a bioweapon that was manufactured by U.S. intelligence to wage war on China; others propose that it was purposefully spread by the U.S. and U.K. governments to profit from a vaccine.[3] An infinite variety of

1 "'This Is a Time for Facts, Not Fear,' says WHO Chief as COVID-19 Virus Spreads," *UN News*, Feb. 15, 2020, https://news.un.org/en/story/2020/02/1057481.

2 "Coronavirus Disease (COVID-19) Advice for the Public: Mythbusters," *World Health Organization*, Nov. 23, 2020, https://www.who.int/emergencies/diseases/novel-coronavirus-2019/advice-for-public/myth-busters; see also Matt Richtel, "*W.H.O.* Fights a Pandemic besides Coronavirus: An 'Infodemic,'" *New York Times*, Feb. 6, 2020, https://www.nytimes.com/2020/02/06/health/coronavirus-misinformation-social-media.html.

3 Daniel Jolley and Pia Lamberty, "Coronavirus Is a Breeding Ground for Conspiracy Theories–Here's Why That's a Serious Problem," *The Conversation*, Feb. 28, 2020,

similar themes can be found in many dark corners of the internet. Behind such theories are competing worldviews, founded on divergent pillars of truth. In some moral worlds, the battle of good and evil is set on a geopolitical stage, a contest between East and West. In other moral worlds, it is a conflict between citizens and governments, which are suspected of operating with allegedly nefarious purposes that cannot be trusted.

At the root of such conflict and conspiracy are competing claims of truth. And this contest of truth claims occurs not only on a grand global scale of geopolitical conflict but also in the daily exchange of any human community. In the contemporary world, the forces of marketing and media bombard the consumer with competing truth claims about everything from political ideology to the superior brand of toothpaste. To live in the contemporary world is to be constantly barraged through television, social media, and marketing with a cacophony of voices, all implicitly presenting their version of truth as superior. In other words, daily life in contemporary society presents a complex maze of truth claims that one must navigate, whether one is conscious of it or not.

How is one to discern between the competing voices and truths that consume the airwaves, bandwidths, and very air we breathe? While modern media and technology may exacerbate this challenge, it is a timeless dynamic of human community. An often overlooked conversation partner for these contemporary dynamics is the ancient Israelite wisdom tradition, specifically, the book of Proverbs, which points us to the insight that discerning between competing truths requires and demands the formation of wise character. The book of Proverbs is an ancient instruction manual for the formation of character amid a panoply of competing voices. As such, it offers a helpful point of reflection about the nature of character formation and its role in a society's lively contest of truth.

Character Formation in the Book of Proverbs

The book of Proverbs says more about character than any other book in the Bible. The entire book is built upon profiling the attributes and actions of certain paradigmatic characters. It presents various models of character for the student, some to be emulated–such as the wise, the righteous, and the discerning–and some to be avoided–such as the fool, the wicked, and the senseless. As these characters are presented throughout the book, they embody certain virtues or sometimes vices of character. For example, Proverbs 18:15 proclaims: "The heart of a discerning one acquires knowledge, and the ear of the wise seeks knowledge." Both the discerning person and the wise one possess a certain diligence, for they seek

---

https://theconversation.com/coronavirus-is-a-breeding-ground-for-conspiracy-theories-heres-why-thats-a-serious-problem-132489.

out more knowledge. On the other hand, "As a dog returns to its vomit, so a fool repeats his folly" (Prov. 26:11). Fools also have a certain diligence! But their diligence is persistence in foolishness that is ultimately a character vice. Proverbs is full of such characterizations of the qualities and attributes of the wise, the fool, the righteous, and the wicked.[4]

In its short sayings and longer poems, Proverbs offers a series of observations about the nature of character. The sages who compiled the book, which is traditionally ascribed to Solomon and connected to the royal court,[5] had a highly sophisticated and complex understanding of the human person, and they understood that the cultivation of wise character was about more than gaining knowledge. Wise character has many facets that touch all aspects of life. One's character has implications for how one sees the world and relates to others. It encompasses not only what a person thinks but also her emotions, sense perceptions, and desires.

The book of Proverbs advances itself as an instruction manual for wise living. It begins with a clear articulation of its purpose:

> For learning about wisdom and instruction, for understanding words of insight, for gaining instruction in wise dealing, righteousness, justice, and equity; to teach shrewdness to the simple, knowledge and prudence to the young–Let the wise also hear and gain in learning, and the discerning acquire skill, to understand a proverb and a figure, the words of the wise and their riddles. (Prov. 1:2-6)

Proverbs is a book about education, for young and old, the advanced student and the simpleton. For Proverbs, education is a lifelong pursuit, requiring equal attention from the neophyte and the sage. The book also has an expansive view of the urgency and task of instruction. At stake in this endeavor is not simply the acquisition of knowledge or book learning but, rather, skills to navigate the world.

Proverbs is not naïve about the complexity of discernment in the moral world. Throughout its poems and sayings, the book's aim is to foster wise character in its students, equipping them for living amid the gray hues of moral discernment. Indeed, Proverbs is not an instruction manual with simplistic directions for living.

---

4 For a discussion of character formation in Proverbs, see William P. Brown, *Wisdom's Wonder: Character, Creation, and Crisis in the Bible's Wisdom Literature* (Grand Rapids, MI: Wm. B. Eerdmans, 2014); Anne W. Stewart, *Poetic Ethics in Proverbs: Wisdom Literature and the Shaping of the Moral Self* (New York: Cambridge University Press, 2016).

5 For an analysis of the courtly context of Proverbs, see Christopher B. Ansberry, *Be Wise, My Son, and Make My Heart Glad: An Exploration of the Courtly Nature of the Book of Proverbs*, Beihefte zur Zeitschrift für die alttestamentliche Wissenschaft 422 (Berlin: De Gruyter, 2011).

Rather, the book centers on the formation of wise character in a context of competing perspectives, truth claims, and moral worldviews.[6]

In part, this dynamic is present in the very nature of the literature itself. The bulk of the book is a collection of proverbial sayings, which are, for the most part, not arranged in a clearly delineated structure. Rather, sayings that speak of different situations and even give contradictory advice sit alongside one another. For example, Proverbs 26:4 advises, "Do not answer fools according to their folly, or you will be a fool yourself." This saying clearly advises restraint in the presence of fools and their foolish speech. Yet the very next verse proclaims, "Answer fools according to their folly, or they will be wise in their own eyes" (Prov. 26:5). This saying gives the opposite counsel, warning that failing to address fools will simply leave their foolishness unchecked, in fact risking their further delusion. How, then, should one proceed? Is a fool to be answered or ignored? Of course, the wise reply requires discernment in light of an actual situation, attendant to the context and reality of the particular.

Accordingly, the application of the sayings is never abstract. Rather, the right application of the proverb requires discernment, which relies upon a carefully honed sense of moral deliberation. In this sense, the book acknowledges the ambiguity of life, for different situations call for different actions. Christine Roy Yoder argues that such contradictions serve an important pedagogical function, in that "they call attention to incongruities in the world; they convey that the arena of wisdom is replete with competing discourses, with divergent perspectives on reality and morality."[7] Yoder argues that the existence of contradictory proverbs in the collections teaches something about the nature of the moral self:

> The sages thereby put readers in a position where no single response, no one proverb or perspective, can always work for them. By doing so, they point readers to a reality larger than the proverbs in question: the moral self inevitably holds views that are in conflict with one another and applies those views depending on the immediate circumstances. Readers cannot avoid the relativity of human knowledge–the fact that meaning is contextual.[8]

In this way, the book resists simplistic interpretation; instead, it invites thoroughly contextual ethical reflection. Accordingly, the book of Proverbs is not an in-

---

6 See Anne W. Stewart, "Teaching Complex Ethical Thinking with Proverbs," in *The Cambridge Companion to the Hebrew Bible and Ethics,* ed. Carly L. Crouch (New York: Cambridge University Press, 2021), 241–56.

7 Christine Roy Yoder, "Forming 'Fearers of Yahweh': Repetition and Contradiction as Pedagogy in Proverbs," in *Seeking Out the Wisdom of the Ancients,* ed. Ronald Troxel et al. (Ann Arbor, MI: Winona Lake Eisenbrauns, 2005), 180.

8 Yoder, "Forming 'Fearers of Yahweh,'" 181.

struction manual that proffers truth in a straightforward way. Rather, it suggests a method of discernment that is fundamentally rooted in forming the wise character that is capable of such deliberation.

Character and the Contest of Desire

For Proverbs, the relevant issue is not simply the distinction between wisdom and foolishness, truth and falsehood but, rather, the cultivation of character that facilitates such discernment in the first place. Furthermore, formation of character involves not only appeal to the rational faculties of the intellect but also the education of one's desires. Proverbs suggests two fundamental convictions about the formation of character: first, the things that humans desire shape their character; and, second, humans are constantly confronted by forces seeking to shape character–some for good, and some for ill–and many of these forces appeal to human desires in order to persuade us that their brand of wisdom or model of character is superior. In this sense, character formation is a delicate maze of responding to the right influences and rejecting the wrong ones.

The book of Proverbs creates its own maze of competing voices as a method of schooling the student in discernment. The first nine chapters of the book contain a series of poems that present a variety of voices addressing the student, framed in the overarching instruction provided by the voice of the teacher. For example, Proverbs 1 presents the appeal of a band of thieves, allowing their voices to surface in the midst of the teacher's instruction:

> My child, if sinners entice you do not consent. If they say, "Come with us, let us lie in wait for blood; let us wantonly ambush the innocent; like Sheol let us swallow them alive and whole, like those who go down to the Pit. We shall find all kinds of costly things; we shall fill our houses with booty. Throw in your lot among us; we will all have one purse." My child, do not walk in their way, keep your foot from their paths; for their feet run to evil, and they hurry to shed blood. (Prov. 1:10–16)

By permitting the sinners' voices to address the student directly, the text summons the desires to which they appeal: wealth, the thrill of adventure, and the camaraderie and acceptance of belonging in the group. Yet the framework of the teacher's instruction provides a context and interpretation to this imaginative exercise, educating the student that indulging these desires with this company ultimately leads to death.[9]

---

[9] For an analysis of the teacher's discourse in Proverbs 1–9, see Carol A. Newsom, "Woman and the Discourse of Patriarchal Wisdom: A Study of Proverbs 1–9," in *Gender and Difference in Ancient Israel*, ed. P. Day (Minneapolis, MN: Augsburg Fortress, 1989), 142–60.

Throughout the first nine chapters of the book, Proverbs presents a contest between the voices of two women who equally seek to shape the character of the student. One of these women is Wisdom personified, who seeks to shape character by offering the student various things he desires, like health, wealth, and security. In Proverbs 8, woman Wisdom proclaims: "I love those who love me, and those who seek me diligently find me. Riches and honor are with me, enduring prosperity. My fruit is better than gold, even fine gold, and my yield than choice silver. I walk in the way of righteousness, along the paths of justice, endowing with wealth those who love me, and filling their treasuries" (Prov. 8:17–21). Wisdom's love promises delight and prosperity.

But Wisdom has a negative counterpart, who is equally, if not more, attractive and appealing. She is foolishness personified, and she, too, seeks to shape the character of the youth by appealing to the things he desires. The direct appeal of this "strange woman" holds similar themes to woman Wisdom's own call. The strange woman is described with alluring language, enticing the youth and calling out to him directly: "She seizes him and kisses him, and with impudent face she says to him, ... 'Now I have come out to meet you, to seek you eagerly, and I have found you! ... Come, let us take our fill of love until morning; let us delight ourselves with love'" (Prov. 7:10–13, 18). As the voices of woman Wisdom and the strange woman reverberate throughout the book, competing for the student's attention, they appeal not just to *reason* but also to emotion, desire, and the breadth of the student's senses.[10] They present the student with two contrasting models, which require discernment to choose the wiser course.

At times, the competing voices the student encounters are remarkably similar, even identical. In Proverbs 9, for example, two nearly indistinguishable entreaties–with diametrically opposed outcomes–are presented. First, woman Wisdom addresses the simpleton and promises a nourishing meal, leading toward insight and abundant life: "[Wisdom] calls from the highest places in the town, 'You that are simple, turn in here!' To those without sense she says, 'Come eat of my bread and drink of the wine I have mixed. Lay aside immaturity, and live, and walk in the way of insight'" (Prov. 9:3b–6). Woman Wisdom calls from a place of prominence and offers good things. Yet immediately we hear another voice, also calling from the high places: "[The foolish woman sits] on a seat at the high places of the town, calling to those who pass by, who are going straight on their way, 'You who are simple, turn in here!' And to those without sense she says, 'Stolen water is sweet, and bread eaten in secret is pleasant' (Prov. 9:14b–17). This woman mirrors the language of woman Wisdom exactly, "You that are simple, turn in here!" She, too, promises a fine meal, yet the premise of her invitation is based in secrecy

10 See Christine Roy Yoder, "The Shaping of Erotic Desire in Proverbs 1–9," in *Saving Desire: The Seduction of Christian Theology*, ed. J. Henriksen and L. Shults (Grand Rapids, MI: Wm. B. Eerdmans), 2011, 148–62.

and deceit. The chapter ends with a proclamation of the consequence of dining with the foolish woman: "[T]hey do not know that the dead are there, that her guests are in the depths of Sheol" (Prov. 9:18).

According to the book of Proverbs, what is at stake in the formation of character is the ability to discern between and properly order the competing voices, appeals, and desires that one encounters in the world. This ability is complicated by the fact that these voices can often sound remarkably similar, yet discerning between them is a matter of life and death.

Search Results and the Search for Wisdom

In contemporary society, we often rely upon technology to order and present the competing voices in our world. Google's algorithms, for example, determine the search results that one receives to any query. The order by which those options are presented is determined not only by their perceived relevance to the search but also by the financial incentive of paid advertising and a vast trove of personal information about individual users that the company has collected and stored. The results of my Google search will be based, in part, on what Google knows that I desire, based on my past shopping and searching history. And it will be informed by the things that Google's advertisers *want* me to desire–and to purchase.

The book of Proverbs might draw our attention to the fact that character is being shaped and formed by the very presentation of these voices. They appeal to the consumer's delights and desires–whether for material goods, social standing, or the endorphin rush of click bait. In so doing, they seek to shape emotion and behavior.

Moreover, discerning among these voices requires mature and wise character, the ability to read situations rightly and to perceive the implications of various appeals, for there may be wholesome or nefarious purposes beneath the surface. Thus, the teacher of Proverbs admonishes the student that although some appeals seem sweet and smooth, they are in fact bitter and sharp:

> My child, be attentive to my wisdom; incline your ear to my understanding, so that you may hold on to prudence, and your lips may guard knowledge. For the lips of a strange woman drip honey, and her speech is smoother than oil; but in the end she is bitter as wormwood, sharp as a two-edged sword. Her feet go down to death; her steps follow the path to Sheol. She does not keep straight to the path of life; her ways wander, and she does not know it. (Prov. 5:1-6)

Google and its counterparts are not exactly analogous to the conception of the "strange woman" in Proverbs. Yet the teacher of Proverbs points to a dynamic that is equally vibrant in contemporary society and exacerbated by the forces of technology. The voices present to us on the superhighway of information require discernment to test the nature of the truths they present and the capacity to read between the lines of the appeals they offer, for they may not always be as desirable as they first appear on the surface. After all, not only is Google marketing to our desires, it is marketing the consumer herself, collecting extensive data about the user's demographics, geography, and preferences that will aid companies in marketing their products. As the adage says, if you are not paying for the product, you *are* the product. One wonders if the teacher of Proverbs might counsel contemporary students that while their search results appear with sweet ease, in the end they may exact sharp costs in data and privacy.

Community and Character, Friendship and Facebook

For Proverbs, the community is a central element in the formation of character and the development of faculties of discernment. One cannot find wisdom alone; rather, it can be pursued only in the company of others. As Proverbs 15:22 advises, "Without counsel plans go wrong, but with many advisors they succeed." Yet the company one keeps also requires discernment, for listening to the wrong counsel can of course lead one astray: "Whoever walks with the wise becomes wise, but the companion of fools suffers harm" (Prov. 13:20). The friends and companions we seek both mirror and shape our character, for "just as water reflects the face, so one human heart reflects another" (Prov. 27:19).

No force in the current era accelerates this dynamic more rapidly than social networking. Facebook and other social-networking platforms are a powerful force in the contemporary world. These platforms are designed to organize and order the community of voices to which we are exposed. Facebook creator Mark Zuckerberg once said that the idea of Facebook is to create more transparency in the world, to let you see who your friends really are. He noted, "I think as humans we fundamentally parse the world through the people and relationships we have around us. So at its core, what we're trying to do [at Facebook] is map out all of those trust relationships, [called] friendships."[11] Facebook's vision is to parse the world through people and networks of relationships, in the conviction that these relationships shape the way we see the world and the way we see ourselves. In some respects, this is similar to the idea we find in Proverbs that one's companions shape one's character and are often indicative of one's character.

Yet Facebook does not order and display these friendships without partiality. Rather, its algorithms determine the content with which individual users are

---

11 Lev Grossman, "Person of the Year 2010," *Time Magazine* Dec. 15, 2010, http://content.time.com/time/specials/packages/article/0,28804,2036683_2037183_2037185,00.html.

most likely to interact, thus leading users to spend more time and engagement on the platform. The company explains that the information and posts displayed on an individual's news feed "are ranked in the order we believe you'll be most interested in seeing them. ... The News Feed algorithms prioritize posts that are predicted to spark conversations among people, whether because of format ... or because the posts were shared by people, groups or Pages you interact with frequently."[12] This kind of curation of information is purported to be a service to make the user's time on Facebook "more meaningful" and better able to "bring people closer together."[13] Facebook presents itself as a vehicle for knitting together the relational fabric of society.

However, curating information this way can also have a dark side. In fact, Facebook and other social networking platforms have accelerated the velocity of polarization in contemporary society, rending apart what they have vowed to bring together. The way in which these platforms incentivize user engagement can reward and foster inflammatory speech. For example, a 2017 Pew Research Study found that social-media posts that expressed "indignant disagreement" received nearly twice as many "likes" and "shares" and three times as many comments as other content on Facebook.[14] The algorithm feeds a vicious cycle, for it elevates such posts that spark engagement with more exposure to other users, which, in turn, generates even more engagement. Moreover, the platform suggests similar content to its users, thus feeding and reinforcing the preferences, opinions, and perspectives that one endorses. The result is the digital construction and proliferation of competing moral systems. In effect, the circle of one's digital "friends" is both broadened and narrowed at the same time, as the user is shown more and more of the kind of content to which he reacts.

While at its most benign level this dynamic can result in a user spending hours watching endless loops of cute animal videos, this phenomenon can have devastating consequences for society, at its most dire level fueling extremism and real-world violence. For example, in 2018 the United Nations report on genocide in Myanmar attributed a large role to Facebook in facilitating the spread of hate

---

12 "No, Your News Feed Is Not Limited to Posts from 26 Friends," Facebook blog post, Feb. 6, 2019, https://about.fb.com/news/2019/02/inside-feed-facebook-26-friends-algorithm-myth/.

13 Adam Mosseri, "Bringing People Closer Together," Facebook blog post, Jan. 11, 2018, https://about.fb.com/news/2018/01/news-feed-fyi-bringing-people-closer-together/.

14 See Pew Research Center, Feb. 2017, "Partisan Conflict and Congressional Outreach," https://www.pewresearch.org/politics/2017/02/23/partisan-conflict-and-congressional-outreach/. See also Jonathan Haidt and Tobias Rose-Stockwell, "The Dark Psychology of Social Networks," *The Atlantic*, Dec. 2019, https://www.theatlantic.com/magazine/archive/2019/12/social-media-democracy/600763/.

speech and false information that ultimately led to mass ethnic cleansing.[15] Similar dynamics have factored into allegations of manipulation of public opinion around national elections and the spread of misinformation about the current pandemic and public-health crisis. These factors have led to a highly fraught and contentious public conversation about the role of technology companies and social-networking platforms in the dissemination of information–and *mis*information–in society.

Character Formation and the Mediation of Truth

The ancient wisdom of Proverbs is timely in an age characterized by a lively contest of truth and a constant barrage of competing voices. Proverbs highlights the fact that the voices confronting us daily–and the digital platforms that order and amplify them–are shaping our collective character. In turn, they require discernment about their ultimate aims and effects. The book underscores the stakes of character formation for individuals and society as a whole, for discerning rightly among these voices has consequences for the moral health of the entire community. The aim of character formation is to acquire the ability to see the world rightly, in accord with truth and order. Yet character can also be malformed, distorting one's ability to distinguish truth from falsehood.

For Proverbs, the conception of truth has a theological orientation, rooted in God's own wisdom and ordering of the world. Consequently, falsehood is one of the greatest threats to the community, for it threatens the sense of divine order. Thus, Proverbs prizes the consistency between appearance and reality. Proverbs 11:1, for example, states: "a false balance is an abomination to the LORD, but an accurate weight is his delight." On the surface, this statement is simply about measurements, but it also relates to the sages' vision of order in the world. The world works because one can rely on the accuracy of weights and measures. The integrity of the currency, in this case, is vital to the functioning of the community. For financial exchange to work, people must trust the reliability of the system. For this reason, "differing weights are an abomination to the LORD, and false scales are not good" (Prov. 20:23).

Similarly, a person's integrity is the consistency of her character, and human integrity is equally essential for a healthy community. The ability to rely on the integrity of one's neighbors fosters trust and allows the community to function smoothly. Conversely, those who willfully deceive or foster discrepancies between who they are and who they appear to be are destructive. They cause the

15 "Report of Independent International Fact-Finding Mission on Myanmar," Aug. 27, 2018, https://www.ohchr.org/EN/HRBodies/HRC/MyanmarFFM/Pages/ReportoftheMyanmarFFM.aspx.

erosion of community bonds. Thus, the sages condemn those who appear falsely or who present themselves as different than they really are, and they praise those who can see the true character of a person, as in Proverbs 28:11: "The rich person is wise in his own eyes, but a discerning pauper can see through him." The ability to distinguish truth from falsehood is finally about the health of the community's life together.

This brings us back to where we started, and the crisis of truth currently surging across the globe in the form of the pandemic's infodemic, which has severe consequences for the physical, mental, and moral health of society. While Proverbs does not offer a prescription for the contemporary form of this malady, it points to the dynamics of competing voices clamoring for a hearing and urges discernment about the desires to which they appeal. Proverbs suggests that a contest of truth is in many ways a test of character within the community.

Character Socialization and Diversity in Modern Democracies Today

Robert W. Hefner

Any discussion of the challenge of character education and citizenship in late modern democracies must address several key issues. Among the two most vexing are: What kind of character education is appropriate for the societies and polities in which we moderns live? And what conditions in society either facilitate or impede the realization of this form of character education and, with it, its ability to influence understandings of the public good?

These are the issues on which I focus in this essay. In doing so, I draw on my own and others' research on character education and citizen recognition in modern democracies, both in the West and in non-Western settings. My core thesis is that efforts to build a sustainable consensus on both character education and citizenship have been made more difficult by two contemporary trends: the growing ethical-religious plurality found in most late modern societies, and, more serious yet, the rise of new forms of social mediation and mobilization that, rather than bridging pluralities through the construction of an overlapping consensus, instrumentalize and exacerbate ethical and social differences for the purpose of commercial or political gain.

Our Present Predicament

Several years ago, in a chapter published in a volume on the boundaries of modern toleration, the well-known Canadian philosopher and ethicist Charles Taylor observed, "our present predicament is for the most part rather different than the one which generated" the traditions of political community and solidarity once commonplace in Western societies.[1] He went on to explain that, whereas, in an earlier age, political authority in the West and many other states "was defined and

---

1 Charles Taylor, "How to Define Secularism," in *Boundaries of Toleration*, ed. Alfred Stepan and Charles Taylor (New York: Columbia University Press, 2014), 59–78, at 61.

justified in cosmic-religious terms,"[2] today Western societies have become so culturally diverse as to make any shared political theology impossible. In "the kinds of societies in which we are now living in the West, the first feature that strikes us is the wide diversity not only of religious views but also of those that involve no religion."[3] It is in these unsettled circumstances "that contemporary democracies, as they progressively diversify, will have to undergo redefinitions of their historical identities, which may be far-reaching and painful."[4] On what grounds, then, are we to reach agreement on critical matters like citizenship and social justice? Taylor's answer to this question is sociologically underspecified but nonetheless noteworthy. Rather than building on a deeply shared religious cosmology, "We are condemned to live an overlapping consensus."[5]

Taylor's reference to an overlapping consensus invokes, of course, the American liberal political philosopher John Rawls and his ideas on justice in liberal societies. In Rawls's hugely influential account, modern citizens are not just utility-seeking monads; to interact and cooperate, they require some measure of ethical agreement on matters of justice and the public good. However, Rawls observed, in light of the ethical and religious plurality that characterizes modern democracies, we can no longer assume that this overlapping consensus builds on some deep collective consciousness like that once provided by religion or some other (in Rawls's phrase) "comprehensive doctrine."[6] Where citizens reach agreement in such an overlapping manner, each will subscribe to some core concept of justice "internal to" or otherwise grounded on her or his own comprehensive doctrine.

Although the ontological grounds for endorsing these core social values may vary, Rawls, like Taylor, makes clear that he believes that having such an overlapping consensus remains vital for civic coexistence and the public good. Rawls was not a sociologist of public ethics, however, and he provided few details on just what social processes facilitate the emergence of such an overlapping consensus. He conceded that citizens in some societies may have too little in common to develop a shared conception of justice or the public good. But he also implied that in modern Western societies, a sufficiently shared culture of citizenship and social trust had emerged so as to sustain an overlapping consensus. Charles Taylor places his hope in a similar process. However–and, again, without sociological elaboration–he does so while making clear that, far more than Rawls, he worries that much of the edifice for such a consensus has collapsed under the weight of our societies' growing ethical-religious plurality. Though socially necessary, the

---

2 Ibid., 68.

3 Ibid., 63.

4 Ibid., 68.

5 Ibid., 70.

6 John Rawls, *Political Liberalism* (New York: Columbia University Press, 2005).

requisite "redefinitions of ... historical identities ... may be far-reaching and painful."

I agree with the basic premise of Taylor's account, but I fear that it oversimplifies the causes and depth of our late modern moral predicament, with the result that his prescriptions for ethical improvement are likewise too simple. In both his essay on secularism and his monumental article a generation earlier on "The Politics of Recognition,"[7] Taylor attributes much of our plight to the loss of shared worldviews and comprehensive doctrines or, as in the *Multiculturalism* volume, to the passing of an earlier social order based on social hierarchy and honor.

> I am using *honor* in the ancien régime sense in which it is intrinsically linked to inequalities. ... As against this notion of honor, we have the modern notion of dignity, now used in a universalist and egalitarian sense. ... The underlying premise here is that everyone shares in it. It is obvious that this concept of dignity is the only one compatible with a democratic society.[8]

Taylor's narrative about the disappearance of shared lifeways and the social hierarchies on which they were grounded is, of course, a familiar one in the theological and social sciences. But I fear that its sociology is incomplete, in a way that makes it difficult to diagnose what may be required to bring about the painful redefinitions of historical identities about which he so eloquently writes. To explain this point, let me turn for a moment to another historical dimension of religion and citizenship in Western liberal societies, one that does not feature in Taylor's account of our contemporary predicament, and that may provide us with some better clues as to how to overcome our plight.

The issue to which I am referring is one raised in several recent studies of Christianity's role in the creation and socialization of citizen ethics in modern liberal democracies, including an article written by the Israel-based political scientist Jonathan Fox.[9] In that essay, Fox reviews a broad range of facts about relations of state, society, and religion around the world, this time in Christian-majority democracies in Western Europe, Latin America, and Eastern Europe. Fox points out that about thirty of the forty countries that meet his criteria for being Christian-majority and stable democracies managed to develop their democracies under circumstances where the state favored either one Christian church (40 percent of the sample) or several Christian denominations (and, more rarely, Judaism as well) over other religions. He thus demonstrates that an American-style "separa-

7 Charles Taylor, "The Politics of Recognition," in *Multiculturalism and "The Politics of Recognition": An Essay*, ed. Amy Gutmann (Princeton: Princeton University Press, 1992).

8 Ibid., 27.

9 Jonathan Fox, "Separation of Religion and State in Stable Christian Democracies: Fact or Myth?," *Journal of Law, Religion and State* 1 (2012): 60–94.

tion of church and state" is *not* a prerequisite for democracy to emerge. But when one looks more closely, the character-shaping effects of Christianity in these democracies reveal themselves to have exclusive as well as positive impact. In 87.5 percent of Fox's Christian democratic sample, course instruction in Christianity is offered in public schools; however, only a tiny minority among the Christian democracies offer non-Christian students the option of instruction in their religions. More ominously, Fox notes, "religious discrimination is ubiquitous in Christian democracies," as expressed in restrictions on the ability of minorities to build places of worship, bring in foreign clergy, or otherwise enjoy a freedom of religious expression on par with that of their Christian fellow citizens.[10]

In his 2009 history of secularism and society in modern France, Turkey, and the United States, the San Diego-based political scientist Ahmet Kuru sheds a similar light on the Janus-faced influence of religious institutions on citizen socialization, this time with regard to Protestantism and democracy in the United States. Kuru recognizes and celebrates the argument presented almost two centuries ago by the renowned French writer Alexis de Tocqueville, that at the dawn of the republic, participation in congregational life was one of the first institutions of American democracy. In particular, Tocqueville observed, it was in congregational worship that small-town Americans learned the "habits of the heart" required for self-government and broadly participatory leadership.

Drawing on historical and sociological studies, however, Kuru reminds us that some American Protestants in the nineteenth and early twentieth centuries drew on these same socializing experiences to assert a less inclusive claim in American public life. They invoked their Christian identity to argue that all citizens who were non-Protestant and nonwhite were in fact not full and equal American citizens. Notwithstanding the First Amendment's strict separation of church and state, then, "Protestant quasi-establishment"[11] became the informal reality of American civil religion from the early 1800 s onward. A generic, King-James-Bible-based variety of Protestantism was mandated in public-school curricula, with the express aim of "acculturating students with non-denominational Protestantism"; "the public schools' curricula were rife with material that Catholics and Jews found offensive."[12] As the Catholic proportion of the population swelled from thirty-five thousand in 1780 to three million in 1860, anti-Catholic and anti-Semitic nativism surged as well. When Catholics responded to Protestant bias in public schools by appealing for state funding for their own schools, Protestants replied by pressing for a constitutional amendment banning funding to "sectar-

---

10 Ibid., 86.

11 Ahmet T. Kuru, *Secularism and State Policies toward Religion: The United States, France, and Turkey* (Cambridge: Cambridge University Press, 2009), 78.

12 Ibid., 85.

ian" schools.[13] Outside the state, in civil society, the nativist surge took an even more exclusive turn, as extremist groups like the Ku Klux Klan unleashed an epidemic of violence.[14] Between 1880 and 1920, as the Catholic population grew to more than seventeen million people (of some ninety-two million total), official supports for Protestant quasi establishment were challenged and gradually dismantled. But informal discrimination and violence remained widespread, now often targeting African Americans and non-Christian minorities as well as Catholics.

By my reading, none of these reminders of the uncivil side of religion's character-shaping role detract from the fact that key features of Christianity in the modern West contributed to the inculcation of genuinely civil habits of the heart, as well as providing theological and ontological grounds for the affirmation of human dignity. For example, even in the mid- to late nineteenth century, nonnativist currents in American Protestantism played a central role in the struggle against slavery and its Jim Crow legacy in the American South; similar currents contributed vitally to the struggle for women's and, later, African American civil rights.

This complexity acknowledged, these examples offer general lessons on how ethical socializations experienced in religious lifeworlds can shape public ethics in diverse ways, sometimes inclusively but other times exclusively. The first lesson is that, even as some theological characteristics of lived Christianity may provide a richly encumbered grounding for human equality, other features of religious social life can be drawn up into a crude identity politics that promotes a citizenship differentiated along religious, racial, or gender lines. Consistent with a key premise of the FIIT project at the University of Heidelberg that is the basis of this volume, we can recognize in this phenomenon the important fact that normative communication and moral education in modern pluralistic societies are pervasive features of our modern life, linked in turn to powerful social systems like government, law, religion, and the market. The fact that congregational Protestantism in nineteenth-century America was Janus-faced in its attitude-shaping effects was not the result of some deep current in Protestant theology. It instead showed that under certain circumstances political entrepreneurs in "civil" society were able to mobilize popular Christian identities in such a way as to override the dignity-affirming message of the Christian gospel. Political instrumentalization trumped theological depth.

In a recent study, African American sociologist Jean Beaman has provided a vivid analysis of a related instrumentalization of religious identities, this one in contemporary France. As we are all well aware, in France since the 1990 s, far-right nativists, many of them previously indifferent to Catholic realities, have

13 Ibid., 86.

14 Rory McVeigh, *The Rise of the Ku Klux Klan: Right-Wing Movements and National Politics* (Minneapolis: University of Minnesota Press, 2009).

learned to play a racialized and pseudo-Catholic identity politics. In so doing, they have pressed for a "differentiated citizenship" that excludes Muslims and racial minorities on the grounds that a true French person is Catholic and white.[15] It goes without saying that in recent years a similar, populist, and identarian mobilization of Christian and racial identities has featured in far-right politics in the United States.

We can and should go a bit farther afield, however, so as to more clearly appreciate that the Janus-faced nature of religion and character education is not something peculiar to Christianity or Western democracies. In India, the world's largest democracy, the rise of the majoritarian and xenophobic movement known as *Hindutva* (Hindu nationhood) has been the single most dramatic feature of national politics since the 1990 s. It is important to recognize, however, that the Hindutva phenomenon was not the result of a conservative Hindu movement mobilizing *against* electoral democracy; "the movement has grown and come to power largely by obeying the procedures of parliamentary democracy."[16] So Hindutva has played by the rules of the democratic game. But it has done so in an exclusive and majoritarian manner, through the efforts of gifted political entrepreneurs deploying majoritarian sentiments against Muslims, Christians, and other minorities.

The Hindutva example speaks to a public ethical phenomenon seen in other late modern democracies. In many such societies, nativist politicians have learned to play by the procedural norms of electoral democracy. They do so today often in conjunction with a skillful use of social media, which allow a more targeted and segmentary rather than inclusive messaging. These political entrepreneurs unleash their social messaging not for the purpose of socializing a more inclusive variety of "democratic civility," with its trademark affirmations of liberty, equality, and solidarity across difference.[17] They aim, instead, to redirect religious identities toward the socialization of a public culture that is majoritarian, exclusivist, and illiberal with regard to the rights and identities of social minorities.[18] Majoritarian movements in places like India, Myanmar, France, and

15 Jean Beaman, "Citizenship as Cultural: Towards a Theory of Cultural Citizenship," *Sociology Compass* 10 (2016): 849–57.

16 Thomas Blom Hansen, *The Saffron Wave: Democracy and Hindu Nationalism in Modern India* (Princeton: Princeton University Press, 1999).

17 See Robert W. Hefner, *Democratic Civility: The History and Cross-Cultural Possibility of a Modern Political Ideal* (New Brunswick, NJ: Rutgers University Press, 1998).

18 See Gregor Fitzi, Jürgen Mackert, and Bryan S. Turner, *Populism and the Crisis of Democracy,* Vol. 1, *Concepts and Theory* (London: Routledge, 2019). And in an Indian setting, Thomas Blom Hansen, "Democracy against the Law: Reflections on India's Illiberal Democracy," in *Majoritarian State: How Hindu Nationalism Is Changing India,* ed. Angana P.

the United States *do* aspire to craft citizens with subjectivities more "encumbered" than the isolated monads of Kantian or libertarian liberalism. However, the encumbrances they seek to create do not aim to deepen commitments to an inclusive citizenship. They aim, instead, to stoke resentments against minorities and elites said to be indifferent to the values and interests of the majority.

Ethical Prioritization in Civic Education

What final lessons can we learn from these examples of the Janus-faced capacity for religious socialization to be put to exclusive rather than inclusive public ends? At their most basic level, these examples confirm the central premise of the Heidelberg project: that, whether in the West or elsewhere, late modern societies and polities are not just or even primarily assemblies of free and equal individuals making rational choices on the bases of values and preferences of their making alone. As the Harvard ethical philosopher Michael Sandel has tirelessly argued for more than a generation, actors in all societies are "encumbered" by the attachments and identifications constitutive of their social being.[19] The examples I have featured in this essay also underscore that the social encumbrances and solidarities latent in one social field, such as congregational life in nineteenth-century America, can be repurposed by actors in another social field, such as national politics. When this occurs, the ethical socializations operative in one domain may be put to ends antithetical to the values embraced by some adherents to those same normative traditions.

Processes like these, involving the capture and repurposing of one cultural and institutional assemblage by another more powerful entity, have long featured in Jürgen Habermas's analysis of capitalism and power's colonization of modern lifeworlds.[20] My sense, however, is that comparative analysis from around the world indicates that contests for hegemony and instrumentalization of this sort are even more pervasive than Habermas's classic model implies, and its effects are deployed toward ends far more varied than the interests of capital and power alone. Moreover, and most critically for our purposes here, however destructive processes like these might be, the social domains they reconstruct remain replete with ethical norms and socializations. As organizers of the Heidelberg project af-

---

Chatterji, Thomas Blom Hansen, and Christophe Jaffrelot (Oxford: Oxford University Press, 2019), 19–39, at 21.

19 See Michael J. Sandel, "The Procedural Republic and the Unencumbered Self," *Political Theory* 12, no. 1 (1984): 81–96.

20 For a recent visitation of the Habermas thesis, see Timo Jutten, "The Colonization Thesis: Habermas on Reification," *International Journal of Philosophical Studies* 19, no. 5 (2011): 701–27.

firm, late modern pluralistic societies never see their varied value currents brought fully under the control of just one institution, social class, or political grouping. And even where societies repurpose or transform the values operative in some social field, they do not abolish normative regulations but bring new ones and new ethical debates into existence.

A third and final lesson from these examples is equally simple but no less important. It is that in modern societies characterized by the agonistic plurality of ethical currents, actors committed to the modern values of democratic civility (liberty, equality, and solidarity across difference) still exist. Indeed, in some areas of social life–human rights, gender relations, environmental issues, the rights of minorities–such actors have at times demonstrated an uncanny resilience. These actors, movements, and institutions survive, of course, in societies marked by a plethora of powers and social institutions, and an agonistic plurality of ethical registers and socializations. In such circumstances, the possibilities for the proponents of democratic civility to achieve hegemonic influence across a broad swath of society may well be slim. But these same circumstances underscore another simple but important lesson. In agonistic circumstances like these, educators and other proponents of the values of democratic civility have a clear guide for what is to be done: they must do all that they can to carve out and protect the relative autonomy of the religious and educational fields, so as to preempt the capture and repurposing of their institutions by other, more powerful agents in society.

Inasmuch as modern societies are not unions of autonomous individuals but social formations with their own hierarchies and powers, the protection of civic and religious education from such hegemonizing powers may be difficult or at times impossible. But the guardianship and flourishing of just such spheres of independent socialization and deliberation are vitally necessary if the inclusive deliberations at the heart of modern democratic life are to survive.

If I am not mistaken, it is just this sort of public ethical protection and *prioritization* that Charles Taylor had in mind when he warned against the "festishization" of certain civic practices–such as, he argued, the banning of headscarves from French schools on the grounds that these violate republican principles. Taylor rightly counsels that we need to think long and hard about our ethical priorities, and what social and institutional measures most effectively realize their aims. Taylor also emphasizes the importance of developing policies and institutions whose "purposes or reference points" can serve as a true "bulwark of their freedom and/or the locus of their national/cultural expressions."[21]

These reference points–expressed in both word and acts of ethical exemplarity–are an often-overlooked feature of ethical socialization in late modern democracies. I end my remarks here by observing that their social urgency is all the

21 Taylor, "How to Define Secularism," 66.

greater in an age of Twitter rage and exclusions, an age when even offices at the very heart of our democracies appear to have been captured by the proponents of new forms of illiberal exclusion.

Character Formation from a Psychological Point of View: Search for Values, Search for *Sinn*[1]

Joachim Funke

Introduction

Have you ever asked yourself where your values come from, where your character stems from? The easy answer might be: from your parents and from the culture you are living in. However, this answer is a bit superficial and needs a more in-depth look.

From a psychological perspective, human development can be seen as a steady process from the moment of conception to the last moment at the hour of death. Developmental psychology analyzes how all human attributes unfold during the stream of life. Part of this psychological perspective is an analysis of the lifespan development of character. The special subdiscipline is called moral development, and it deals with questions like the following: How do moral values develop? Where do they come from? How can they be changed? This lifespan perspective on human development has become the standard paradigm in developmental psychology within the last eighty years. It started with the book *Der menschliche Lebenslauf als psychologisches Problem* (The human course of life as a psychological problem) by Charlotte Bühler (1933) and culminated in the book *Life-Span Developmental Psychology* by Paul Baltes, Hayne Reese, and John Nesselroade (1977).[2]

---

1 I am grateful to Dr. Marlene Endepohls for her careful reading of and commenting on a draft of this chapter. The German word *Sinn* is often translated into English as "sense," but it has richer connotations that suggest "meaning," "consciousness," "mind," "preference," and "taste."

2 Charlotte Bühler, *Der Menschliche Lebenslauf Als Psychologisches Problem* (Leipzig: Hirzel, 1933). Paul B. Baltes, Hayne W. Reese, and John R. Nesselroade, *Life-Span Developmental Psychology: Introduction to Research Methods* (Hillsdale, NJ: Lawrence Erlbaum, 1977).

What Is Character?

Two potential understandings of what constitutes character are presented here: a narrow one, which connects character to moral attitudes and sees character formation as moral development, is compared to a broader view, which connects character formation to personality development.

The narrow view sees character formation as the construction of a kind of psychological "faculty" (like the faculties of cognition, emotion, motivation, language, and so on) that develops over time, with discrete levels. This view is represented mainly by the ideas of Lawrence Kohlberg, who proposed a famous model of moral "stages" (levels) that are passed through from childhood through adolescence. Depending on the course of development, persons end up in one of six postulated levels. I present Kohlberg's approach in more detail below.

A broader view takes a different stance. In this view, character is embedded in a larger understanding of personality. According to Cornelia Wrzus and Brent Roberts, "personality constitutes characteristics that reflect relatively enduring patterns of typical cognition, emotion, motivation, and behavior in which individuals differ from others of the same culture or subpopulation."[3]

Within research on personality, the term "character" sounds old-fashioned and represents a trait approach to personality. Modern views take an interactionist perspective: personality is a mixture of (more permanent, stable) *traits* that characterize a person and (more transient, variable) *states* that vary across situations.[4]

Classical (Narrow) View: Progression through Stages

The classical (narrow) view on moral development was established by the Swiss psychologist Jean Piaget (1896–1980) and his American colleague Lawrence Kohlberg (1927–87). They saw the process of moral development as an ordered progression through developmental stages. During each stage, a specific rule describes the respective behavior. In the classical view, stages are connected to certain age periods.

3 Cornelia Wrzus and Brent W. Roberts, "Processes of Personality Development in Adulthood: The TESSERA Framework," *Personality and Social Psychology Review* 21, no. 3 (2017): 253–77, https://doi.org/10.1177/1088868316652279, p. 254.

4 Norman S. Endler and Jean M. Edwards, "Interactionism in Personality in the Twentieth Century," *Personality and Individual Differences* 7, no. 3 (1986): 379–84, https://doi.org/10.1037/h0036598; and David Magnusson, "Personality in an Interactional Paradigm of Research," *Zeitschrift Für Differentielle und Diagnostische Psychologie* 1, no. 1 (1980): 17–34.

To assess the actual stage of moral development, Kohlberg used vignettes like the famous "Heinz dilemma."[5] This dilemma presents a woman in Europe near death from a very bad disease, a special kind of cancer. There was one drug that doctors thought might save her, a form of radium that a druggist in the same town had recently discovered. The drug was expensive to make, but the druggist was charging ten times what the drug cost him to manufacture. He paid two hundred dollars for the radium and charged two thousand dollars for a small dose. The sick woman's husband, Heinz, went to everyone he knew to borrow the money, but he could get together only about a thousand dollars, half of what the druggist was charging. He told the druggist that his wife was dying and asked him to sell it more cheaply or let him pay later. But the druggist said, "No, I discovered the drug and I'm going to make money from it." Heinz, desperate, broke into the man's store to steal the drug for his wife.

Subjects were asked to read this vignette and write down their answers to these questions: Should the husband have done what he did? Was it right or wrong? Is your decision that it is right (or wrong) objectively correct, is it morally universal, or is it your personal opinion?

Based on the answers to these questions, subjects were classified into one of three levels. Level 1, preconventional morality, contains no personal code of morality. Instead, the moral code follows the standards of adults. The consequences of following or breaking their rules are most important. Level 2, conventional morality, is the stage where the moral standards of valued adult role models are internalized. Authority is internalized but not questioned. Moral reasoning is based on the norms of the group to which the person belongs. Level 3, postconventional morality, is the stage where individual judgment of moral dilemmas relies on self-chosen principles. Moral reasoning is based on individual rights and justice. According to Kohlberg, this level of moral reasoning is as far as most people get.

Following Saul McLeod,[6] we can note some known problems with the Kohlberg approach to the development of moral reasoning. First, dilemmas lack ecological validity (that is, they are, in a sense, artificial). The Heinz dilemma (stealing a drug to save the life of his wife) does not reflect the life experience of the ten-to-sixteen-year-old subjects whom Kohlberg studied. Second, one might criticize the hypothetical settings: no real consequences will follow the decisions (low-stakes instead of high-stakes testing[7]). Third, there was biased sampling: accord-

---

5 Lawrence Kohlberg, *Essays on Moral Development* (San Francisco: Harper & Row, 1981), 12.

6 Saul McLeod, "Kohlberg's Stages of Moral Development," *Simply Psychology*, 2013, https://www.simplypsychology.org/kohlberg.html.

7 Paul R. Sackett, Matthew J. Bornemann, and Brian S. Connelly, "High-Stakes Testing in Higher Education and Employment: Appraising the Evidence for Validity and Fairness," *American Psychologist* 63 (2008): 215–27.

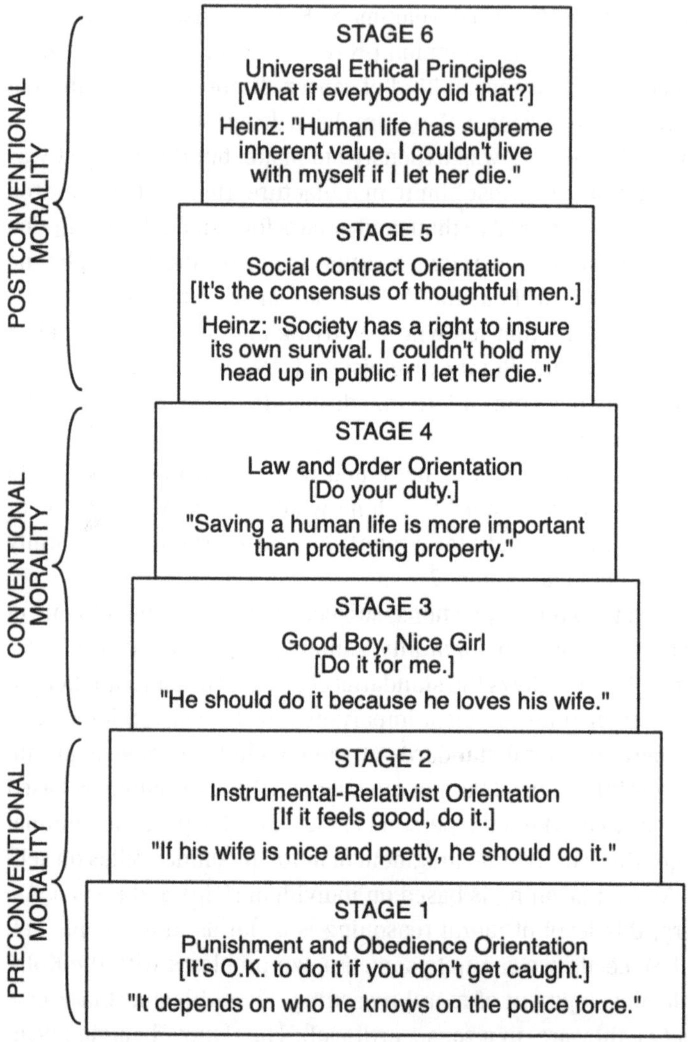

Figure 1: The six stages of moral development, according to Lawrence Kohlberg. Source: http://commons.wikimedia.org/wiki/File:Kohlberg_Model_of_Moral_Development.png.

ing to Carol Gilligan, Kohlberg's samples were all male subjects and represented an "androcentric" definition of morality (most important are the principles of law and justice rather than compassion and care).[8] Fourth, a cross-sectional study design was used instead of longitudinal designs, which would better reflect the de-

8 Carol Gilligan, "In a Different Voice: Women's Conceptions of Self and of Morality," *Harvard Educational Review* 47 (1977): 481–517.

velopmental process. Nevertheless, Kohlberg's model serves as a reference in many approaches and should be seen as a starting point for improvements.

Broader View: Character Formation as Personality Development

To change moral values, we have to change the core of a person. That means that we have to change her or his personality. To change personality is not easy, but it occurs. One simple way is aging: whereas younger people–according to Wrzus and Roberts–increase their "Big Five" scores in the four dimensions of agreeableness, conscientiousness, emotional stability, and social dominance,[9] older people show a reversed pattern, with longitudinal decreases in agreeableness, conscientiousness, emotional stability, and openness.[10] Other opportunities for trait changes often occur together with significant life events (life transitions, changes in personal relationships, work experiences). However, a direct influence on these types of events is not possible. In this broader view of character formation, education seems to be most important.[11] No wonder that in modern times, even computer games are seen as training instruments for moral sensitivity.[12]

---

9 Richard E. Lucas and M. Brent Donnellan, "Personality Development across the Life Span: Longitudinal Analyses with a National Sample from Germany," *Journal of Personality and Social Psychology* 101, no. 4 (2011): 847-61, https://doi.org/10.1037/a0024298; Brent W. Roberts, Kate E. Walton, and Wolfgang Viechtbauer, "Patterns of Mean-Level Change in Personality Traits across the Life Course: A Meta-Analysis of Longitudinal Studies," *Psychological Bulletin* 132, no. 1 (2006): 1-25, https://doi.org/10.1037/0033-2909.132.1.1; Brent W. Roberts and Daniel K Mroczek, "Personality Trait Change in Adulthood," *Current Directions in Psychological Science* 17 (2008): 31-35.

10 Anne Ingeborg Berg and Boo Johansson, "Personality Change in the Oldest-Old: Is It a Matter of Compromised Health and Functioning?" *Journal of Personality* 82, no. 1 (2014): 25-31. https://doi.org/10.1111/jopy.12030; Christian Kandler et al., "Patterns and Sources of Personality Development in Old Age," *Journal of Personality and Social Psychology* 109, no. 1 (2015): 175-91. https://doi.org/10.1037/pspp0000028; Lucas and Donnellan; René Mõttus et al., "Correlates of Personality Trait Levels and Their Changes in Very Old Age: The Lothian Birth Cohort 1921," *Journal of Research in Personality* 46, no. 3 (2012): 271-78, https://doi.org/10.1016/j.jrp.2012.02.004.

11 Bart Engelen et al., "Exemplars and Nudges: Combining Two Strategies for Moral Education," *Journal of Moral Education* 47, no. 3 (2018): 346-65, https://doi.org/10.1080/03057240.2017.1396966.

12 Johannes Katsarov et al., "Training Moral Sensitivity through Video Games: A Review of Suitable Game Mechanisms," *Games and Culture* 14, no. 4 (2019): 344-66, https://doi.org/10.1177/1555412017719344.

Moral Values: World Studies

How are moral values distributed on Earth? In an exciting study run by a group of anthropologists, Oliver Curry, Daniel Mullins, and Harvey Whitehouse examined sixty societies around the world for the prevalence of seven forms of cooperative behaviors–helping kin, helping one's group, reciprocating, being brave, deferring to superiors, dividing disputed resources, and respecting prior possession.[13] The background idea was to test their theory of "morality-as-cooperation." This theory is based on assumptions from evolutionary biology and game theory and asserts "that morality consists of a collection of biological and cultural solutions to the problems of cooperation recurrent in human social life."[14] The theory predicts cooperative behavior in seven domains and postulates that these seven moral values will be universal. To test their predictions, the three anthropologists made a "content analysis of the ethnographic record" of sixty societies distributed over the world (see Figure 2). Data come from the six regions of the globe: Sub-Saharan Africa, Circum-Mediterranean, East Eurasia, Insular Pacific, North America, and South America.

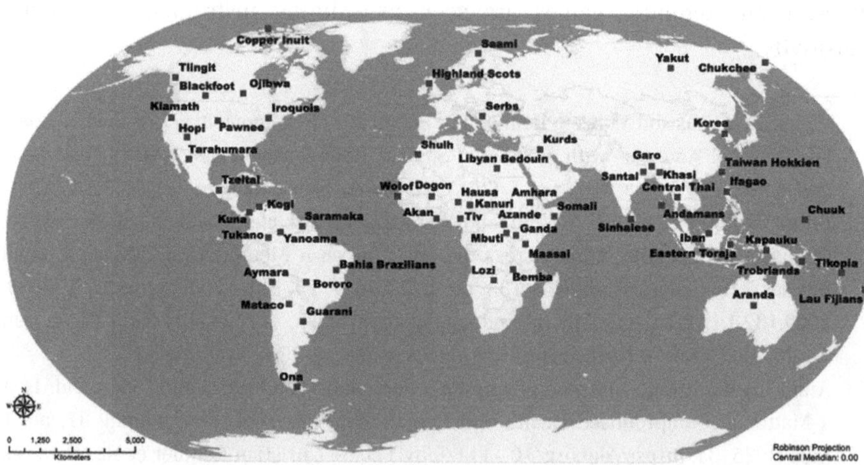

Figure 2: The 60 societies analyzed in the study from Curry, Mullins, and Whitehouse.[15]

---

13 Oliver Scott Curry, Daniel Austin Mullins, and Harvey Whitehouse, "Is It Good to Cooperate? Testing the Theory of Morality-as-Cooperation in 60 Societies," *Current Anthropology* 60, no. 1 (2019): 47–69, https://doi.org/10.1086/701478.

14 Ibid., 48.

15 Ibid., 53.

They carefully rated data from a huge archive of twelve hundred selected pages from the digital version of the Human Relations Area Files. This archive contains thousands of full-text ethnographies. According to a codebook, the authors selected examples for the following seven areas of morality noted above. As a result of this analysis, 961 out of 962 relevant text paragraphs valued these cooperative behaviors positively. The one exception was a negative evaluation that came from the Chuuk, in Central America, and concerns property issues: "to steal openly from others is admirable in that it shows a person's dominance and demonstrates that he is not intimidated by the aggressive powers of others."[16] The authors conclude: "As such, these results provide strong support for the theory of morality-as-cooperation, and no support for the more extreme versions of moral relativism."[17] The cross-cultural survey contains a lot of interesting points, but people in Western industrialized countries might follow different moral principles than people in foraging societies.

Similarly, Shalom Schwartz explored the universality of value systems by drawing samples from twenty countries, mostly consisting of school teachers and university students.[18] Schwartz based his work on the assumption that eleven basic value types can be found all over the world, within all cultural regions. These basic ("universal") values are self-direction, stimulation, hedonism, achievement, power, security, conformity, tradition, spirituality, benevolence, and universalism (see Figure 3). Interestingly, he separates instrumental values (the "means" in a means-end relation) from terminal ones (the "end states").

His approach follows the tradition of Hofstede[19] and does not contain a developmental perspective. Thus, it does not contribute much to the question of character formation.

Character Formation and the Genesis of Wisdom

One of the long-term results of character formation can be seen in the development of wisdom. Barbara Tuchman defined wisdom as "the exercise of judgment

16 Ibid., 54.

17 Ibid., 55.

18 Shalom H. Schwartz, "Universals in the Content and Structure of Values: Theoretical Advances and Empirical Tests in 20 Countries," *Advances in Experimental Social Psychology* 25 (1992): 1–65, https://doi.org/10.1016/S0065-2601(08)60281-6.

19 Geert Hofstede, *Culture's Consequences: Comparing Values, Behaviors, Institutions, and Organizations across Nations*, 2nd ed. (Thousand Oaks, CA: Sage Publications, 2001).

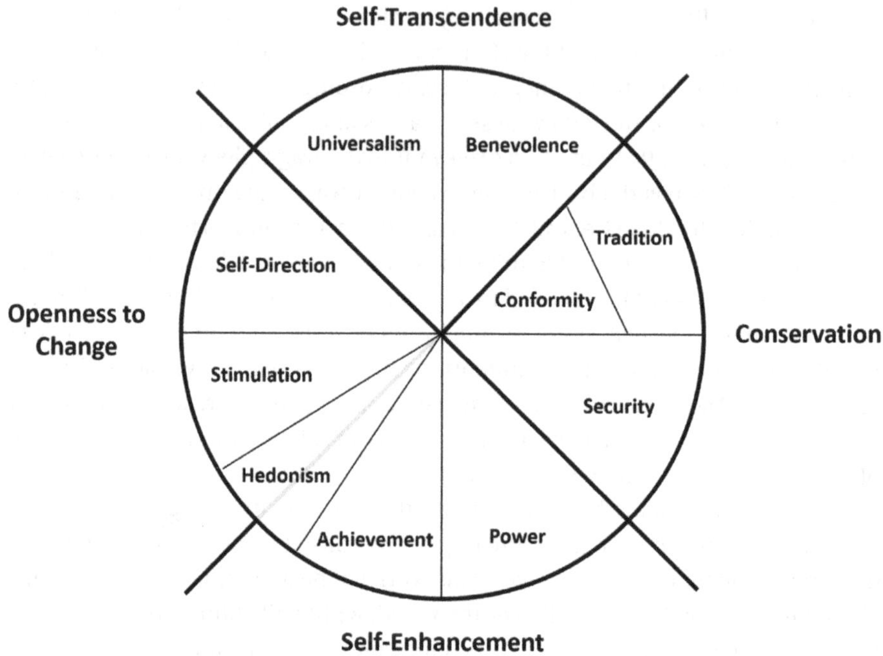

Figure 3: The basic values, according to Schwartz, sorted into four main classes (Source: https://medium.com/bits-and-behavior/measuring-values-and-culture-264205035c87).

acting on experience, common sense and available information."[20] Is wisdom the result of successful character formation? What do we know about the connection?

In a recent article, Judith Glück presents twelve definitions of wisdom.[21] Only one of them mentions "values" explicitly, namely the "balance theory of wisdom" presented by Robert Sternberg.[22] According to that theory, wise people know–besides having other competencies–that different people can have different values. This idea of "value relativism" in wise persons is also one of the five criteria for wisdom within the Berlin Wisdom Paradigm.[23] However, to know that there are

---

20 Barbara W. Tuchman, *The March of Folly: From Troy to Vietnam* (New York: Ballantine Books, 1984).

21 Judith Glück, "Wisdom," in *The Psychology of Human Thought*, ed. Robert J. Sternberg and Joachim Funke, 307–26 (Heidelberg: Heidelberg University Publishing, 2019), https://books.ub.uni-heidelberg.de/index.php/heiup/catalog/book/470, p. 310, table 16.1.

22 Robert J. Sternberg, "A Balance Theory of Wisdom" *Review of General Psychology* 2, no. 4 (1998): 347–65.

23 See, for example, Paul B. Baltes and Ursula M. Staudinger, "Wisdom: A Metaheuristic (Pragmatic) to Orchestrate Mind and Virtue toward Excellence," *American Psychologist* 55 (2000): 122–36.

different perspectives on dilemmas does not imply that one has clear moral values –it is a kind of metaknowledge, free of any special content.

Similarly, Andreas Fischer argues for a context-free view of wisdom and sees it as "independent of one's values and context."[24] On the other hand: Fischer has collected twelve propositions that were commonly attributed to wise men from four different cultures (Socrates, Jesus, Confucius, and the Buddha). Those four wise persons show significant parallels concerning certain wise content (for example, Proposition 10: "Good people (and children) make good company"). Once again, however, there is no idea about how to acquire these pieces of wisdom. We all know that simply reading those "wise" propositions will not make us a wise person instantly.

Measuring Character and Moral Values

Psychologists are known for their expertise in measuring dispositions.[25] So they also develop ideas on how to measure morality and character.

Based on the narrow perspective, the Heinz dilemma presented earlier represents an item from the Moral Judgments Scale (MJS) developed and used by Kohlberg. It allows subjects to write open answers. A bit more standardized is the Defining Issues Test (DIT) that also presents moral dilemmas but requires a categorical answer instead of free text. As Erica Giammarco reports,[26] there are also dilemma-free assessments–such as the Ethics Position Questionnaire,[27] the Visions of Morality Scale[28]–and self-reports, such as the Moral Foundations Questionnaire,[29] the Moral Justification Scale,[30] the Measure of Moral Orientation,[31] and the Moral Orientation Scale.[32]

---

24 Andreas Fischer, "Wisdom–The Answer to All the Questions Really Worth Asking," *International Journal of Humanities and Social Science* 5, no. 9 (2015): 73–83.

25 For a critical view, see Stephen Jay Gould, *The Mismeasure of Man*, rev. expanded ed. (New York: W. W. Norton, 1996).

26 Erica A. Giammarco, "The Measurement of Individual Differences in Morality," *Personality and Individual Differences* 88 (Jan. 2016): 26–34, https://doi.org/10.1016/j.paid.2015.08.039.

27 Donelson R. Forsyth, "A Taxonomy of Ethical Ideologies," *Journal of Personality and Social Psychology* 39, no. 1 (1980): 175–84.

28 Charles M. Shelton and Dan P. McAdams, "In Search of an Everyday Morality: The Development of a Measure," *Adolescence* 25 (1990): 923–43.

29 Jesse Graham, Jonathan Haidt, and Brian A. Nosek, "Liberals and Conservatives Rely on Different Sets of Moral Foundations," *Journal of Personality and Social Psychology* 96, no. 5 (2009): 1029–46, https://doi.org/10.1037/a0015141.

Coming from the broader view (presented above), the measurement of character implies the measurement of personality. The "Big Five" inventories (for example, BFI, HEXACO-PI-R, and NEO-PI-R[33]) measure the following personality attributes (character) via questionnaires: (1) extroversion (the degree to which one is active, assertive, talkative); (2) neuroticism (the degree to which one is anxious, depressed, irritable); (3) agreeableness (whether one is generous, gentle, kind); (4) conscientiousness (whether one is dutiful, organized, reliable); and (5) openness to experience (whether one is creative, imaginative, introspective). The current state of affairs concerning this trait approach can be found in a recent review by Paul Costa, Robert McCrae, and Corinna Löckenhoff.[34]

Moral Dilemmas in Experimental Research: Trolley Experiments

In recent years, the analysis of moral dilemmas has shown interesting results in moral decision-making. Dries Bostyn and colleagues describe the trolley-style dilemmas as follows:

> In their archetypal formulation, these dilemmas require participants to imagine a runaway trolley train on a deadly collision course with a group of unsuspecting victims. Participants are asked whether they would consider it morally appropriate to save the group but sacrifice a single innocent bystander by pulling a lever to divert the trolley to another track, where it would kill only the single bystander.[35]

---

30 Linda S. Gump, Richard C. Baker, and Samuel Roll, "The Moral Justification Scale: Reliability and Validity of a New Measure of Care and Justice Orientations," *Adolescence* 35 (2000): 67–76.

31 D. L. Liddell, C. Halpin, and W. G. Halpin, "The Measure of Moral Orientation: Measuring the Ethics of Care and Justice," *Journal of College Student Development* 33 (1992): 325–30.

32 Nancy Yacker and Sharon L. Weinberg, "Care and Justice Moral Orientation: A Scale for Its Assessment," *Journal of Personality Assessment* 55, nos. 1–2 (1990): 18–27, https://doi.org/10.1080/00223891.1990.9674043.

33 BFI = Big Five Inventory; HEXACO-PI-R = HEXACO Personality Inventory-Revised, HEXACO being the acronym for the six dimensions of Honesty-Humility (H), Emotionality (E), Extroversion (X), Agreeableness (A), Conscientiousness (C), and Openness to Experience (O); NEO-PI-R = Revised NEO Personality Inventory.

34 Paul T. Costa, Robert R. McCrae, and Corinna E. Löckenhoff, "Personality across the Life Span," *Annual Review of Psychology* 70 (2019): 423–48, https://doi.org/10.1146/annurev-psych-010418-103244.

35 Dries H. Bostyn, Sybren Sevenhant, and Arne Roets, "Of Mice, Men, and Trolleys: Hypothetical Judgment versus Real-Life Behavior in Trolley-Style Moral Dilemmas," *Psychological Science* 29, no. 7 (2018): 1084–93, https://doi.org/10.1177/0956797617752640.

For some time, it was an open question whether these hypothetical moral judgments have anything to do with real-life moral decision-making. Nevertheless, with the advent of self-driving autonomous cars, these hypothetical situations have become very realistic. Artificial moral agents have already been developed by computer scientists.[36]

What are the fundamental insights from experiments with trolley-style dilemmas? It seems that subjects follow a utilitarian perspective to save the most lives possible.[37] What can we learn about character formation from these studies? Due to the highly artificial (that is, not real) situation that has to be imagined, I have doubts about the validity of these studies. I do not believe that we can learn a lot about human character from these highly unnatural settings. It is a bit like insights from Milgram's famous experiment on obedience, in which volunteer teacher subjects had to electrically shock learner subjects for their errors on a memory task with increasing degrees of shock until reaching deadly intensities. Recent interpretations of the experimental situation argue that the experimental setup says more about the willingness of the subjects to fulfill the requests of a demanding experimenter ("engaged followership") than about obedience.[38] Likewise, trolley dilemmas might tell us about something other than moral decisions.

Conclusion

Character formation is a complex process that is not easily accessible to psychological measurement. One thing seems to be sure: "Moral reasoning is developmental."[39] Moreover, humans are always searching for sense and meaning–even in senseless written words, we try to find a message. We see things that are not present (visual illusion); we hear things that are not spoken (phonological

36 For a review of these developments, see José-Antonio Cervantes et al., "Artificial Moral Agents: A Survey of the Current Status," *Science and Engineering Ethics* 26, no. 2 (2020): 501–32, https://doi.org/10.1007/s11948-019-00151-x.

37 See, for example, Joshua D. Greene et al., "Cognitive Load Selectively Interferes with Utilitarian Moral Judgment." *Cognition* 107, no. 3 (2008): 1144–54, https://doi.org/10.1016/j.cognition.2007.11.004.

38 S. Alexander Haslam, Stephen D. Reicher, and Megan E. Birney, "Questioning Authority: New Perspectives on Milgram's 'Obedience' Research and Its Implications for Intergroup Relations," *Current Opinion in Psychology* 11 (Oct. 2016): 6–9, https://doi.org/10.1016/j.copsyc.2016.03.007.

39 Melanie Killen and Kelly Lynn Mulvey, "Challenging a Dual-Process Approach to Moral Reasoning: Adolescents and Adults Evaluations of Trolley Car Situations," *Monographs of the Society for Research in Child Development* 83, no. 3 (2018): 110–23, https://doi.org/10.1111/mono.12380, at 112.

gap); we feel things that are not there (rubber hand illusion); we remember stories that were not told.[40]

We, as human beings, are not robots that require error-free programming and need perfect input; we construct the world around us in such a way that it makes sense to us, even if the input is ambiguous. It has been argued that humans develop "cargo cults" when they do not understand the deeper meaning of certain rituals.[41] Richard Feynman used this term to describe puzzling rituals that rely on a misunderstanding of otherwise meaningful actions. Humans search for sense, but at the same time, humans search for values: what action is right and should be done more often, what actions are wrong and should be reduced in their frequency? It will be an endless story–but one that sharply discriminates humans from machines. The search for values and the search for *Sinn:* it makes us human.

40 Sir Frederick Bartlett was the first to show that human memory is schematic in the sense of adding elements to a "nonsense" story in order to make it understandable; see Frederic C. Bartlett, *Remembering: A study in Experimental and Social Psychology* (Cambridge: Cambridge University Press, 1932).

41 Richard Feynman, "Cargo Cult Science," *Engineering and Science* 37, no. 7 (1974): 10–13.

Civic Norms and Distinctive Convictions: Finding the Right Balance

Charles L. Glenn

Introduction

A quarter century ago, Mary Ann Glendon warned that the "deteriorating circumstances of child-raising households in the United States amount to a major national crisis," which she associated with the pressing "problem of politics–how to foster in the nation's citizens the skills and virtues that are essential to the maintenance of our democratic regime."[1] Recent experience around the 2020 U.S. presidential election shows how prescient she was, and how urgent it is to answer her question satisfactorily.

Is the fostering of civic skills and virtues a task for the state or for families and the civil society institutions in which they participate? Are social order and political compromise threatened if parents choose to entrust their children to faith-based schools, schools that in some or many respects offer an alternative understanding of the requirements of faithful citizenship?

Apart from such outliers as Cuba and North Korea, almost every country in the world allows parents to send their children to nonstate schools; in many cases, government provides full or partial funding in support of these choices.[2] The opportunity to select a nongovernment school is generally based on the right of parents "to choose for their children schools, other than those established by the public authorities, which conform to such minimum educational standards as may be laid down or approved by the State and to ensure the religious and moral

---

1 Mary Ann Glendon, "Forgotten Questions," in *Seedbeds of Virtue: Sources of Competence, Character, and Citizenship in American Society*, ed. Mary Ann Glendon and David Blankenhorn (Lanham, MD: Madison Books, 1995), 1 f.

2 Charles L. Glenn and Jan De Groof, eds., *Balancing Freedom, Autonomy, and Accountability in Education*, vols. 1-4 (Nijmegen: Wolf Legal Publishing, 2012). Available also at https://edpolicy.education.jhu.edu/global-pluralism/.

education of their children in conformity with their own convictions,"[3] though in some countries this had already been achieved through long and bitter political struggles.[4]

More recently, some reformers have argued that parental choice of schools can stimulate healthy competition and make room for educational experimentation and accountability,[5] a claim that has given rise to a flood of research, pro and con, which we will not seek to assess. Putting aside the question of measurable instructional outcomes, there is a fundamental policy question: does the existence –and, in the United States at present, rapid expansion–of alternatives to government-operated schools represent a threat to the mission of public education (broadly conceived) to develop citizens possessing the appropriate dispositions to sustain a well-functioning society and political order?

This is the charge brought against school-choice policies by their opponents in the public-school establishment. According to the "civic republican" argument for a government monopoly on popular schooling, it is only by banishing from the formal educational process the distinctive convictions held by families and civil-society groups that social unity and civic virtue can be achieved. Elite independent schools based on humanistic norms or alternative pedagogies are seldom criticized, but nongovernment schools informed by strongly held religious convictions, whether Catholic, evangelical, Orthodox Jewish, or Islamic, are considered by much elite opinion to represent a threat to essential civic norms. Is there really a fundamental tension between strongly held religious beliefs and education for good citizenship?

The Myth of the Common School

What I have called the "myth of the Common School"[6] continues to shape how many people think about education and to define policy debates. It does so powerfully in the United States, despite the fact that it was never more than a myth, a story told persuasively by elite reformer Horace Mann and his emulators, but always frustrated by the stubborn localism and particularism of American life. The

---

3 United Nations, International Covenant on Economic, Social, and Cultural Rights (1966), https://www.ohchr.org/en/professionalinterest/pages/cescr.aspx, Article 13.3.

4 See Charles L. Glenn, *Contrasting Models of State and School: A Comparative Historical Study of Parental Choice and State Control* (New York: Continuum, 2011).

5 Milton Friedman, "The Role of Government in Education," in *Economics and the Public Interest,* ed. Robert Solo (New Brunswick, NJ: Rutgers University Press, 1955), and many subsequent authors.

6 Charles L. Glenn, *The Myth of the Common School* (Amherst: University of Massachusetts Press, 1988).

essence of this myth has been the conviction that a monopoly of popular schooling under government management is required to inculcate in each rising generation a set of shared convictions and loyalties, those civic virtues essential to social as well as political tranquility. The corollary of this conviction is that social peace and patriotic commitment are in danger if a significant proportion of a nation's youth fail to experience this shared indoctrination.

To advocates of the common school, this danger has seemed particularly acute if these youth, rather than simply left in ignorance, are educated to perspectives and convictions that challenge some of those promoted by government-sponsored common schooling. Notably, the education provided by Catholic schools in France[7] and the United States[8] in the nineteenth (and to some extent throughout the twentieth) century was considered by leading supporters of their republican governments as deeply subversive; that suspicion has been extended to evangelical, Orthodox Jewish, and Islamic schools in contemporary American policy debates.[9]

The project of nation-formation through popular schooling began in Prussia and other German states in the seventeenth and eighteenth centuries[10] and was adopted in France and the United States starting in the 1830 s.[11] It spread to Italy, Spain, and parts of Latin America later in the nineteenth century. In the postcolonial period of the 1950 s and after, it became the norm (not always implemented effectively) in new nations seeking to create shared identity among often diverse peoples.

Rousseau, echoing Plato's *Republic* (which he called "the most beautiful educational treatise ever written"), argued that an authoritarian government, enforcing its decrees by police power and other means, would never be sufficiently sta-

7 René Rémond, *L'Anticléricalisme en France* (Paris: Éditions Complexe, 1985); Yves Bruley, ed., *1905: La séparation des églises et de l'état: Les textes fondateurs* (Paris: Perrin, 2004).

8 Horace Bushnell, *Life and Letters* (New York: Harper and Brothers, 1880); Josiah Strong, *Our Country* (1891), ed. Jurgen Herbst (Cambridge, MA: Harvard University Press, 1963); Paul Blanshard, *Religion and the Schools: The Great Controversy* (Boston: Beacon Press, 1963).

9 Jason Bedrick, Jay P. Greene, and Matthew H. Lee, eds., *Religious Liberty and Education* (Lanham, MD: Rowman & Littlefield, 2020).

10 See Glenn, *Contrasting Models of State and School*; Ludwig Fertig, *Zeitgeist und Erziehungskunst: Eine Einführing in die Kulturgeschichte der Erziehung in Deutschland von 1600 bis 1900* (Darmstadt: Wissenschaftliche Buchgesellschaft, 1984); Peter Lundgreen, *Sozialgeschichte der deutschen Schule im Überblick, Teil I: 1770–1918* (Göttingen: Vandenhoeck & Ruprecht, 1980); Klaus Deppermann, *Der hallesche Pietismus und der preußische Staat unter Friedrich III* (Göttingen: Vandenhoeck & Ruprecht, 1961).

11 See Glenn, *Myth of the Common School.*

ble or adequate to its mission; what was needed was a regime capable of shaping the innermost thoughts of its subjects. The chosen instrument for achieving this would be education under the control of the state, since "education is of still greater importance to the State than to the fathers" of children, and "is certainly ... the most important business of the State" (*Discourse on Political Economy*, 1755).[12] In *Considerations on the Government of Poland* (1773), Rousseau insisted that "it is education that must give the souls of the people a national form, and so shape their opinions and their tastes that they become patriots as much by inclination and passion as by necessity."[13]

The purpose of such popular schooling was to form well-behaved and, above all, loyal citizens out of diverse populations and thus facilitate the tasks of government and the strength of the nation. Philosopher François Guizot, serving as France's minister of education after the Revolution of 1830, wrote that "the great problem of modern societies is the government of minds" and declared that this would be achieved through enlisting village schoolmasters as agents of the state.[14] Or, as Risorgimento leader Massimo d'Azeglio famously said a generation later, "Now that Italy has been created; it is necessary to create Italians."[15]

Despite American education reformer Horace Mann's admiration for Prussian schools (which he visited on his honeymoon), this nation-building educational agenda did not prevail in the United States apart from those urban areas experiencing heavy immigration.[16] For these, typically, a leading nineteenth-century economist emphasized "how important it is that we cherish our educational system, in order that this oncoming generation of the children of the foreign-born may be brought under its influence. It must be of such a character as to fit the pupils for the duties of citizenship."[17]

12 Jean-Jacques Rousseau, *The Social Contract and Discourses*, trans. G. D. H. Cole (London: Everyman, 1993), 148.

13 Rousseau, *The Minor Educational Writings of Jean Jacques Rousseau*, trans. William Boyd (New York: Teachers College Press, 1962), 97.

14 Glenn, *Myth of the Common School*, 34–37; Jacques Billard, *De l'école à la République: Guizot et Victor Cousin* (Paris: Presses Universitaires de France, 1998); Pierre Rosanvallon, *Le moment Guizot* (Paris: Gallimard, 1985).

15 Although usually attributed to him thus, this saying first appears in negative form in his memoirs *I miei ricordi* (1867): "Pur troppo s'è fatta l'Italia, ma non si fanno gli Italiani." Simonetta Soldani and Gabriele Turi, *Fare gli italiani: Scuola e culture nell'Italia contemporanea. I. La nascita dello Stato nazionale* (Bologna: Il Mulino, 1993), 17.

16 David Tyack, *The One Best System: A History of American Urban Education* (Cambridge, MA: Harvard University Press, 1974).

17 Richmond Mayo-Smith, "Assimilation of Nationalities in the United States. II," *Political Science Quarterly* 9, no. 4 (Dec. 1894): 649–70, at 664.

In most of the country, however, local schools, established and funded by local citizens, taught as much literacy and numeracy as was judged necessary to meet local needs and, along with those skills, a common morality reflecting that of the sponsoring community. School readers by Samuel Goodrich (writing under the pen name Peter Parley), Noah Webster, William McGuffey, and a host of others offered lessons in history and geography that provided glimpses of a world beyond the village or farm, embedded in a generalized Protestant worldview, but these privately published and locally chosen readers were not government prescribed.

It was only in the twentieth century that American public schooling became the massively bureaucratic enterprise that we know today, led by an emergent class of specialists in "administrative science." The process included the consolidation of school districts from nearly 130,000 in 1931 to fewer than 16,000 in 1987, and the consequent abandonment of what had been the most extensive form of local democracy in the world. Leaders in education strongly supported such consolidation, as well as the extension of state regulation, as a way to buffer schools from what they considered the unprogressive influence of parents and other local voters. All these forces combined to reduce the influence of parents and concerned citizens over what was taught and what values were conveyed in public schools, though without replacing it with a cohesive *morale républicaine*, as in prewar France.[18]

Those who have defined and redefined the purposes of schooling in the United States over the past century have been the relatively small "clerisy," the "intellectuals and scholars dedicated to the state precisely as their medieval forebears were to the church."[19] Michel Foucault described how the state has taken over from the medieval church the role and the techniques of the "cure of souls," with pretensions extending well beyond its traditional duties of the maintenance of domestic tranquility and the administration of justice.[20] Orestes Brownson, a hundred years earlier, had already warned that the efforts of his contemporary Horace Mann "would create a modern form of priesthood by setting up an educational establishment empowered to impose the 'opinions now dominant' on the common schools. 'We may as well have a religion established by law,' Brownson maintained, 'as a system of education.'"[21]

18 Jean Baubérot, *La morale laïque contre l'ordre moral* (Paris: Éditions du Seuil, 1997); Laurence Loeffel, *La question du fondement de la morale laïque sous la IIIe République (1870–1914)* (Paris: Presses Universitaires de France, 2000).

19 Robert Nisbet, *Twilight of Authority* (New York: Oxford University Press, 1975), 5.

20 Irena Rosenthal, "The Dutch Pastorate: Pluralism Without Pain?," in *Education in Conflict*, ed. Ina ter Avest (Münster: Waxmann, 2009), 63.

21 Christopher Lasch, *The Revolt of the Elites and the Betrayal of Democracy* (New York: W. W. Norton, 1995), 65.

American legal tradition as it has developed since 1839, when Brownson wrote, has been similarly cautious about assertions of government control over the beliefs and loyalties that children form through their school experience: a standard text asserts that "the Constitution and relevant cases strongly suggest that the formation of opinions, attitudes, values and beliefs should largely be in private hands and not governmentally controlled."[22]

Often justified by the need to find a remedy to the breakdown of the family and of the local community, the extension of government's role into such domains tends instead to exacerbate the conditions that it pretends to alleviate. While many of the measures taken on behalf of the "secular pastorate"–improved sanitation, for example–sought only to improve the bodies of citizens, the reformers could not resist seeking to improve their souls as well. This has led to constantly renewed conflict over schools. As philosopher Nicholas Wolterstorff warns, "the public school, if it attempts to inculcate moral principles beyond those of the most elementary, essential, and inevitable housekeeping sort, will almost certainly violate the conscientious convictions of various of its constituents."[23]

Current Debates

The bitterness of current debates in several Western democracies over a whole range of cultural matters derives in substantial part from the drive by government, impelled by the logic of bureaucratic procedure, to reduce the infinite variety of human life–including choices about how and for what ends to live–to routinized categories for treatment in standardized ways. As government has taken on a larger and larger role, it inevitably makes decisions and adopts policies that trespass upon matters about which citizens differ profoundly.

Such tensions develop above all between public schools and the human-level institutions of family, congregation, and voluntary association that teach, model, and reinforce habits of moral obligation. The Cato Institute has usefully been keeping track of hundreds of school controversies each year across the United States.[24] It is in such local settings that moral issues have traditionally been confronted and resolved; the new intrusiveness of government increasingly incapacitates this arena of discussion, compromise, and decision.

---

22 Tyll Van Geel, *Authority to Control the School Program* (Lexington, MA: D. C. Heath and Company, 1976), 19.

23 Nicholas P. Wolterstorff, *Educating for Life: Reflections on Christian Teaching and Learning*, ed. Gloria Goris Stronks and Clarence W. Joldersma (Grand Rapids, MI: Baker Academic, 2002), 200 f.

24 See Cato Institute, "Public Schooling Battle Map," https://www.cato.org/education-fight-map.

In particular, the myth of the public school as the unique agent of social unity and progress serves as a pretext for deploring the existence of alternative schools that express distinctive understandings of the requirements for a flourishing human life, understandings at once too deep and too radical to be included in a public-school curriculum.

There is, of course, a place for expertise in various aspects of pedagogy and resource management, but should we defer to experts in determining the goals of education? Is there a scientific consensus on the nature of the Good Life, of the human flourishing that education should promote? Or is that something for parents to decide with respect to their own children, and for the voluntary associations to which they may choose to entrust those children to determine?

The role of experts in defining the goals of education on a supposedly scientific basis goes back about a hundred years, to the Progressive Era. From this perspective, schools that have a different agenda, especially if that entails the development of the religion-based perspective critical of some actions of the state, are perceived as a threat to a vital national interest of nurturing loyal citizens. This perception can lead to strongly hostile reactions by government toward such alternative education, and not only under authoritarian or totalitarian regimes.

It can in fact be difficult to draw a clear line between the educational intentions of what has been called an "activist tutorial state" and those of a totalitarian regime, though of course the power to carry out such intentions differs very greatly. We need to set aside our knowledge of how badly totalitarian regimes turned out and remember that Lenin and Mussolini were greatly admired by liberal intellectuals in North America and Western Europe in the 1920 s. Their regimes claimed to be effectively addressing issues that the liberal democracies seemed unable to confront, not least through the intrusive public schooling that John Dewey so admired in Soviet Russia.[25]

In fact, studies of the effects of totalitarian schooling report that it tends to produce in many students quiet alienation and cynicism rather than the intended whole-hearted loyalty to the regime,[26] but this is beyond our present theme. More to the point, as we will see, is that even under democratic regimes, the notion of education for citizenship risks negating or at best minimizing the benefits that children gain from becoming self-fulfilled individuals who can choose from among various visions of the good life under the guidance of their family and cultural community. Indeed, the notion presents a frightening image of children as

---

25 John Dewey, "Impressions of Soviet Russia, III: A New World in the Making" (1928), in *John Dewey: The Later Works, 1925–1953, 3: 1927–1928*, ed. Jo Ann Boydston (Carbondale: Southern Illinois University Press, 1988).

26 Oskar Anweiler, ed., *Erziehungs- und Sozialisations-probleme in der Sowjetunion, der DDR und Polen* (Hannover: Hermann Schroedel Verlag, 1978), especially essays by Brämer, Busch, and Rüther.

instruments for advancing political ends. When one talks about education for democratic citizenship, one needs to temper the discussion by reflecting on the developmental needs of children, including their need for a culturally coherent life.[27]

We might well agree that it is legitimate and indeed commendable for schools to seek to arouse in their pupils convictions about the nature of the Good and to encourage the habit of acting virtuously in accordance with those convictions, yet question whether the state should be defining that Good for its citizens and prescribing such measures in schools that it controls and that pupils attend involuntarily. After all, the convictions permitted by liberalism

> must always be superficial and contingent. But the imperative and expectation of constantly changing one's deepest moral commitments stunts the development of one of the most necessary virtues for liberal regimes–that of self-control, which is developed by *commitment* to principles and persistence in them rather than their perpetual reconsideration and abandonment.[28]

Of course, there are norms of social and civic behavior about which broad agreement exists and that every school can be expected to promote through its expectations for student behavior and the instruction provided about the legal and political system. What is not legitimate is for schools that enroll their students involuntarily to presume to provide them with a distinctive worldview–or to communicate to them that, whatever their families may believe, there is no reality that "goes all the way down."

Surely it is profoundly inconsistent with a free society that "liberal education theory now virtually commands public schools to function as cultural counterpoints to parental teachings regarding the good and worthy life."[29] Of course, government is *not* in fact doing so, or at least in any effective way, in the United States. The "broken covenant" lamented by Robert Bellah[30] is nowhere more apparent than in the public schools, which–unless they have unusually strong leadership, as in some charter public schools–reflect the normlessness of a consumer

27 Rosemary C. Salomone, *Visions of Schooling: Conscience, Community, and Common Education* (New Haven: Yale University Press, 2000), 210.

28 Rita Koganzon, "Pork Eating Is *Not* a Reasonable Way of Life: Yeshiva Education vs. Liberal Educational Theory," in Bedrick, Greene, and Lee, *Religious Liberty and Education*, 36–37.

29 Shelley Burtt, "Comprehensive Education and the Liberal Understanding of Autonomy," in *Citizenship and Education in Liberal-Democratic Societies*, ed. Kevin McDonough and Walter Feinberg (New York: Oxford University Press, 2003), 187.

30 Robert N. Bellah, *The Broken Covenant: American Civil Religion in Time of Trial*, 2nd ed. (Chicago: University of Chicago Press, 1992).

society. It is unfortunately the case that, "while most high schools' formal statements of purpose identify 'ethical conduct' and 'citizenship' as goals for their schools, they shy away from specific programs toward these ends or even from carefully defining the words these statements employ."[31] Indeed, many in recent years have been using the umbrella of character education to cover a host of social-emotional "competencies" that have little or no moral significance. They include a range of social skills that can be used for either good or ill: for example, problem solving, awareness, social bonding, self-efficacy, and emotional literacy, any of which could readily promote antisocial goals unless they are guided by a clear moral compass.[32]

Government has tacitly acknowledged its inability to exercise leadership in this dimension; "promoting character was eliminated as a Department of Education priority in 2009."[33] The relentless focus on testing for instructional outcomes has forced teachers to direct their efforts elsewhere. In effect, "the emphasis on such areas as literacy and numeracy may mean there is little in the mainstream system that acknowledges alternative achievement which faith-based schools and communities value,"[34] such as loyalty, trust, helping others, and willingness to share ideas and to listen respectfully–qualities important to a healthy civic life. One survey "conducted by the U.S. Department of Education [found that] only 7 percent of public secondary school teachers ranked citizenship as a 'very important' goal for students."[35] This neglect is borne out by the persistently low scores of those students on assessments of their knowledge about civics.[36]

It has often been said that "tolerance" is the only virtue that public schools seek to teach, a tolerance that has little to do with genuine respect or understanding but is simply nonjudgmental relativism. Such an educational program has neither coherence nor the ability to equip citizens to work together productively despite their differences. This incoherence is not limited to schools, of course, though beyond question it is fostered by the fact that most American public schools dare not provide a coherent and persuasive account of the nature of a flourishing human life, lest that lead to controversy. This leaves youth vulnerable

31 Theodore R. Sizer, *Horace's Compromise: The Dilemma of the American High School* (Boston, MA: Houghton Mifflin, 1984), 122.

32 William Damon, *Failing Liberty 101* (Stanford, CA: Hoover Institution Press, 2011), 56.

33 Ibid., 6.

34 Marie Parker-Jenkins, Dimitra Hartas, and Barrie A. Irving, *In Good Faith: Schools, Religion, and Public Funding* (Aldershot, UK: Ashgate Publishing Limited, 2005), 127.

35 E. Louis Lankford, "Artistic Freedom: An Art World Paradox," in *Public Policy and the Aesthetic Interest*, ed. Ralph A. Smith and Ronald Berman (Urbana: University of Illinois Press, 1992), 248.

36 The Nation's Report Card, "See How Eighth-Grade Students Performed in Civics," https://www.nationsreportcard.gov/highlights/civics/2018/.

to the seductive vision of self-definition through impulse and unbridled consumption. Schools today love to talk about differences of color, of sexual identities and preferences, and of trivial customs, but not of convictions–these must remain unexpressed in the public-school context of "the bland leading the bland," and thus youth are often persuaded that deep-rooted beliefs play no part in defining a worthy life.

Avoidance of any discussion of deeply held convictions is based on a fear that this will introduce divisions among students or lead to teachers imposing their own beliefs; in fact, however, it leaves students unprepared, outside of the school setting, for fruitful encounters with peers whose convictions differ from their own, if indeed they have any convictions of their own. Rather than promoting civic peace, this incapacity to discuss "fundamentally different understandings of being and purpose"[37] contributes to the inability of Americans to listen to one another, so dangerously evident in 2020. After all, it is as a result of being "initiated into a particular home, a particular language, a particular culture, a particular set of beliefs" that children gain the security essential "before they can begin to expand their horizons beyond the present and the particular."[38] "Exposing them to plurality and a Babel of beliefs and values too soon," psychologist Elmer John Thiessen writes, "will in fact prevent the development of abilities which are a key to later functioning in a complex and pluralistic environment."[39]

The point, then, is not that American public schools are promoting a dominant and unifying ideology, a civil religion, but that the conviction that they *should* be doing so serves as an often-persuasive reason for opposing faith-based schools and other schools based on a coherent theory of how to form character and a clear understanding of the sort of character and loyalty essential for students to lead useful and fulfilling–flourishing–lives.

The myth of the common school, the insistence that government-operated schools are the unique source of social unity and civic virtue, has today, in consequence, only a negative function, as the leading political argument for opposing schools that promote alternative sources of meaning and loyalty. What was, or at least is nostalgically imagined to have been, the positive content of an educational program centered on developing patriotic commitment and citizen solidarity has long since been replaced by incoherence.

---

37 James Davison Hunter, *Culture Wars* (New York: Basic Books, 1991), 131.

38 Elmer John Thiessen, *Teaching for Commitment: Liberal Education, Indoctrination, and Christian Nurture* (Montreal: McGill-Queen's University Press, 1993), 222.

39 Elmer John Thiessen, *In Defense of Religious Schools and Colleges* (Montreal: McGill-Queen's University Press, 2001), 41.

How Should Civic Virtue Be Fostered?

There is an evident contradiction between a government's effort to use institutional schooling as an instrument for forming national loyalty and civic norms, and the reality that the qualities of character and the disposition to trust and cooperation essential to a flourishing society are formed primarily in family and community rather than in the anonymity of the wider society. Recent political developments in the United States (and, to some extent, in other countries) make the task of nurturing trust especially urgent, but its decline has been evident for decades. "From the late 1970 s to the early 2010 s the fraction of 12th graders from more educated homes (the top third) who say that most people can be trusted fell by roughly a third, whereas the fraction of trusters from the least educated third of homes fell by roughly one half."[40] The challenge for civic education is that distrust is directed even more strongly toward government: "trust in government was rising from 1958 to 1964. Thereafter, however, trust in government plummeted from 77 percent of Americans in 1964 to 29 percent in 1978,"[41] and it continues low, as exemplified by the Trump slogan attacking the national government: "Drain the swamp!"

As the diversity that has always characterized societies has become more assertive in recent decades, it has become increasingly difficult to find a common ground for talking about the requirements of life in society, resulting in the timidity characteristic of public schools. We should applaud the insistence of Horace Mann and John Dewey, that the only school that truly *educates* is one that goes beyond instruction in knowledge and skills to concern itself centrally with the formation of character. For each of them, though in very different ways, there was no question about the sort of character required by citizens. This was true, also, of Jules Ferry, Ferdinand Buisson, and others who shaped the French école de la République and did so more consistently than was possible under American conditions,[42] and it was true of their counterparts in a dozen and more other coun-

---

40 Robert D. Putnam, *Our Kids: The American Dream in Crisis* (New York: Simon & Schuster, 2015), 220.

41 Robert D. Putnam, *The Upswing: How America Came Together a Century Ago and How We Can Do It Again* (New York: Simon & Schuster, 2020), 103.

42 Jules Ferry, "Discours de M. le Ministre," in *Conférences pédagogiques de Paris en 1880: Rapports et procès verbaux* (Paris: Hachette, 1880); Mrs. Alfred-Jules-Emile Fouillée [G. Bruno], *L'instruction morale et leçons de choses civiques pour les petits enfants*, 41st ed. (Paris: Belin Frères, 1893); Gabriel Compayré, *Éléments d'instruction morale et civique*, 112th ed. (Paris: Delaplane, 1896); Ferdinand Buisson, *La foi laïque: Extraits de discours et d'écrits (1878–1911)* (Paris: Hachette, 1912).

tries. A similar consistency prevailed, indeed, under communist regimes that sought to shape some version of "the new Soviet man."[43]

But can anyone claim today, in Western cultures defined by consumerism and self-definition, that there is consensus about the sort of character required by citizens? All the evidence, whether from research or from the experience of recent decades, demonstrates that it is not. As we have seen:

> Government and public policy increasingly have come to be seen as lacking any legitimate concern with the formation of the character of the citizenry. Yet this development does not mean that law and legally sanctioned coercion have not been fostering conformity to a very specific and very narrow morality. Quite the contrary. Law, and public education sanctioned by law, has been instilling with intensifying moralism that specific and very narrow moral outlook that requires the liberation of the individual from all ties of solidarity, responsibility, tradition, and obligation that are not autonomously chosen. Rights have eclipsed responsibilities, freedom has obscured virtue, tolerance has rendered suspicious the passing of moral judgments, and concern for autonomous choice has come to outweigh concern for human fulfillment found in dedication and devotion.[44]

What is the answer? Should we seek, as Dewey did, to make the common public school the basis for moving humanity to a higher level of organization and of consciousness in response to the shattering of traditional community life? In "My Pedagogic Creed" (1897), one of his first and still most widely read statements about education, Dewey held out the promise that "through education society can formulate its own purposes, can organize its own means and resources, and thus shape itself with definiteness and economy in the direction in which it wishes to move."[45] The Great Depression provided an opportunity for Dewey and his allies to call for the abandonment of individualism, his code word for the free market and democratic politics based on competition and cooperation rather than guidance by experts. Dewey wrote in 1934 that there was "only one way out of the existing educational confusion and drift. That way is the definite substitution of a social purpose, controlling methods of teaching and discipline and materials of study, for the traditional individualistic aim." In another article the same year,

43 See Charles L. Glenn, *Educational Freedom in Eastern Europe*, 2nd ed. (Washington, DC: Cato Institute, 1995).

44 Lorraine Smith Pangle and Thomas L. Pangle, "What the American Founders Have to Teach Us about Schooling for Democratic Citizenship," in *Rediscovering the Democratic Purposes of Education*, ed. Lorraine M. McDonnell, P. Michael Timpane, and Roger Benjamin (Lawrence: University Press of Kansas, 2000), 23.

45 John Dewey, "My Pedagogic Creed" (1897), in *John Dewey on Education*, ed. Reginald D. Archambault (Chicago: University of Chicago Press, 1974), 438.

Dewey made explicit that public schools should be a force mobilized to transform society and its economic system, with every detail of its life and activity mobilized to serve a political agenda for which education was only an instrument.[46]

Is that the answer to our present cultural disarray? Should the beneficent authority of the state make use of compulsory schooling to foster common civic norms and thus overcome the loyalties and distinctive worldviews that characterize a pluralistic society, within which character has most reliably been shaped? Such a state agenda, while superficially appealing in our present distress, would be contrary to the democratic pluralism under which both voluntary communities and well-rooted individual character flourish. After all, as Anthony Appiah points out, we believe that children should be raised primarily in families and that those families should be able to shape their children into the culture, identity, and traditions that the adult members of the family take as their own. One liberal reason for believing this is that this is one way to guarantee the rich plurality of identities whose availability is, as I have said, one of the resources for self-construction.

This recognition should have implications for public policy around education; after all, we are bound to acknowledge that parental love includes the desire to shape children into identities the parents care about, and to teach them identity-related values, in particular, along with the other ethical truths that the child will need to live her life well. A state that actively undermined parental choices in this regard in the name of the child's future autonomy would be a state constantly at odds with the parents: and that would be unlikely to be good for the children.[47]

As we have seen, there is a long history in other countries of such conflicts, often resolved by the state stepping back from its effort to monopolize schooling and fostering structural pluralism in education. A notable example is the Netherlands, where, after seventy years of *schoolstrijd*, the political parties agreed in 1917 to a "pacification," resulting in the present situation in which most students attend publicly funded schools not operated by government.[48] Similarly, after bitter conflict, Belgium adopted and has maintained a "school peace" providing similar funding to government and nongovernment schools.[49] Both countries thus

---

46 John Dewey, "Education and the Social Order" (1934), in Boydston, *John Dewey: The Later Works, 1925–1953,* Vol. 9: *1933–1934,* 180; "Can Education Share in Social Reconstruction?" (1934), in ibid.

47 K. Anthony Appiah, "Liberal Education: The United States Example," in McDonough and Feinberg, *Education and Citizenship in Liberal-Democratic Societies,* 71 f.

48 Glenn, *Contrasting Models of State and School*; D. Langedijk, *De Schoolstrijd* (The Hague: Van Haeringen, 1935); Nan L. Dodde, *Geschiedenis van het nederlandse schoolwezen* (Purmerend: Muusses, 1981).

49 Glenn, *Contrasting Models of State and School*; Pierre Verhaegen, *La lutte scolaire en Belgique* (Ghent: A. Siffer, 1905); Jeffrey Tyssens, *Guerre et paix scolaires, 1950–1958* (Brussels: De Boeck & Larcier, 1997).

offer real educational choices without financial penalty to families. Schools are free, indeed under pressure, to express a distinctive identity, and researchers suggest that government-operated schools may be at a disadvantage in achieving such clarity and coherence of mission.[50]

Experience in the United States, as well, suggests that societal conflict over values forces the public "common school," serving all students drawn from a geographical district without parental choice, to become less and less clear about asserting any moral position other than a bland acceptance of differences–so long as they are not rooted in deep convictions.

Where Horace Mann and John Dewey went wrong (in their different ways) was in seeking to impose a single model of education for character and conviction; this agenda was based, in turn, upon a false assumption that society could not prosper unless its people shared common beliefs that overruled the partial beliefs of traditional religions. The public school was to be, in turn, the uniform and unifying crucible of national identity and shared convictions.

Common loyalties to the public good, yes, and common habits, respect for fellow citizens and for the law, but these civic behaviors need not be based on a shared understanding of the deeper purposes of life. More recent "comprehensive liberal" advocates for the liberating function of schooling, while they have little sympathy for the fostering of patriotism or of social coherence, have a similar goal of imposing, through universal popular schooling, a single form of character, and to do so by persuading students away from the attachments that they bring from their homes and communities.

In a sense, at the opposite extreme and more subtly pervasive than civic republicanism, but similarly hostile to the influence of families and religious communities, is the recent emphasis in "educationist" circles on using the common public school to promote the individual autonomy of its students in a manner that forswears any attempt to impose a moral code or a definition of the good life. We should note at once that parents should be free, under a regime of liberal pluralism, to choose such schooling for their children if it matches their own convictions; "Christian parents are often accused of indoctrinating, but this accusation is misguided because initiation is a necessary part of forming a self. Liberal parents, too, of necessity, initiate their children into a liberal tradition."[51] The conflict arises from imposition of liberal educational goals on families that do not share them.

Those who advocate for the educational mission of universal autonomy insist that policymakers should "avoid promoting a school system and civil society that purport to be neutral when they should in fact be partial to the value of autono-

50 J. F. A. Braster, *De identiteit van het openbaar onderwijs* (Groningen: Wolters-Noordhoff, 1996).

51 Thiessen, *Teaching for Commitment*, 128.

my." Like Rousseau's citizens "forced to be free," students should enjoy no autonomous choice about whether to cast off the restraints of tradition, since "nurturing the capacity for and exercise of autonomy must come *before* we respect it. The state should violate respect for autonomy in efforts to foster its exercise."[52]

Such advocates concede that "for the state to foster children's development of autonomy requires coercion–[that is], it requires measures that prima facie violate the principles of freedom and choice. The coercive nature of state promotion of the development of autonomy also means that children do not have the luxury of 'opting out' of public autonomy-advancing opportunities." This calls for something like a public-school monopoly, since "children can practice the civic virtues and establish them over time as habits of character only within a truly *public* school."[53]

This autonomy-oriented vision of the good life is of course by no means neutral; indeed, it rests, ironically enough, upon philosophical or religious premises that reject the right of the individual to choose his or her own concept of the good. Much of Levinson's book is given over to lamenting irreconcilable conflicts between certain Christians (especially "fundamentalists") and her own liberal "demands." Such religious folk would hold the free individual child responsible to an external moral authority; parental hopes of this sort could never satisfy the ideal of autonomy, hence are properly (could one say "morally"?) excluded from the liberal curriculum.[54]

Even a convinced spokesman for autonomy-oriented education concedes that "quiet obedience, deference, unquestioned devotion, and humility, could not be counted among the liberal virtues."[55] But does that mean that ways of life which value these qualities should be undermined by compulsory schooling that denigrates them? And is it in fact true that individuals who possess such qualities in a society that does not respect them are not authentically autonomous? Indeed, a good case can be made that

> the autonomous moral self required for liberal democratic citizenship is to be found not in Kant's universal rationality or in Rawlsian public reason, but in thick, dynamic ethical and religious traditions that offer concrete visions of what it means to be a good

52 Rob Reich, *Bridging Liberalism and Multiculturalism in American Education* (Chicago: University of Chicago Press, 2002), 7, 108.

53 Meira Levinson, *The Demands of Liberal Education* (New York: Oxford University Press, 1999), 38 f., 115.

54 John E. Coons, "Populism and Parental Choice," *First Things,* Nov. 2000, 16.

55 Stephen Macedo, *Liberal Virtues* (Oxford: Clarendon Press, 1990), 278.

> person and to live in a just society, acquired through subject-subject relations both among people–parents and children, teachers and students, children and their peers–and between students and the traditions into which they would be initiated.[56]

One result of an emphasis on the autonomous choice of a worldview will be, ironically enough, to make other choices impossible.

> Certain things of value may be lost in, or absent from, the forms of the good life that flourish in open, diverse, critical, experimental, uncertain, and ever-changing liberal societies. Stronger forms of community, deeper, unquestioning, untroubled forms of allegiance (to family, church, clan, or class) might embody genuine forms of the good life lost to societies that flourish in a liberal way. A lifelong, unquestioned devotion to a simple life in a small homogeneous community will hardly be available to one whose attitudes have been shaped by liberal individualism, social pluralism, tolerance, and critically reflective citizenship.[57]

This rueful concession does not weaken the author's determination, for the sake of a liberal regime, to "endorse and promote autonomy. But we still respect," he concedes, "the non-autonomous: people have the right to lead lazy, narrow-minded lives."[58]

There are two primary sources, in principle, of resistance to the ongoing extension of the role of government and its schools–even if with the most benevolent intentions–into ever-wider and deeper areas of social and personal life. The first is liberalism itself in its traditional meaning, the belief that government should be strictly limited in its interference with individual choice in order to protect rights of conscience as well as to permit the free deployment of personal and social energies. Recent history provides too many examples of the folly of relying on the self-restraint of even the best-intentioned government officials.

The other primary source of opposition to an overreaching government is theological–the belief of many Christians, Jews, and Muslims that the sovereignty of the state cannot be absolute because that would infringe upon that of God, the ultimate sovereign.

Whether motivated by theological considerations or by historical reflection, many would agree that it is essential to place limits on the reach of the state, es-

---

56 Hanan A. Alexander, "Competing Conceptions of Authenticity: Consequences for Religious Education in an Open Society," in *Commitment, Character, and Citizenship: Religious Education in Liberal Democracy*, ed. Hanan A. Alexander and Ayman K. Agbaria (New York: Routledge, 2012), 160.

57 Stephen Macedo, *Liberal Virtues: Citizenship, Virtue, and Community in Liberal Constitutionalism* (Oxford: Clarendon Press, 1990), 278 f.

58 Ibid., 253.

pecially limits that encourage institutions and associations in society whose independence is secured by both legal protections and their own vitality. In a society marked by deep disagreements about the nature of the Good (or whether in fact there is such a thing), and thus about the goals of education, it is offensive to both freedom and equality to impose any particular view upon all children, either by majority rule or by that of an elite clerisy. Of course, children are to be taught, by example as much as by instruction, the common norms of social life and civic participation, but it is not the role of the state to promote one of the competing beliefs about ultimate goods. And we need to maintain an understanding of the goals of education that reaches well beyond either civic knowledge and commitments (important as those are) or the ability to weigh choices and make decisions (essential as that is). After all,

> a truly successful comprehensive education creates adults with a sufficiently rich sense of a cultural or religious identity such that breaking away from that identity would seem to strike at the heart of who one is as a person. These individuals cannot, and will not, approach moral reflection on issues of identity and ultimate goals with the consumerist mentality generally taken by liberal theorists as evidence of autonomous capacity.[59]

The civic republican objection to faith-based schools was and continues to be based on the challenge that these pose to the unifying project of civic republicanism and its claim to shape the hearts as well as the minds of all the nation's children, even though public schools no longer effectively seek to shape hearts and all too often do not shape minds effectively either. The comprehensive liberal objection is that faith-based schools prevent the development of autonomous and thus authentic individuals. Surely it would be wiser to heed the advice of Jürgen Habermas, that "it is in the interest of the constitutional state to deal carefully with all the cultural sources that nourish its citizens' consciousness of norms and their solidarity."[60] And that brings us, as it brought Habermas, to considering the contribution of religion to civil society.

---

59 Burtt, "Comprehensive Education and the Liberal Understanding of Autonomy," in McDonough and Feinberg, *Citizenship and Education*, 182.

60 Jürgen Habermas, "Pre-political Foundations of the Democratic Constitutional State?," in Joseph Cardinal Ratzinger and Jürgen Habermas, *Dialectics of Secularization: On Reason and Religion*, ed. Brian McNeil (San Francisco: Ignatius Press, 2006), 46.

The Role of Religious Organizations

Strongly held religious convictions can in fact help powerfully to create the foundation upon which an ordered liberty must rest. Tocqueville famously concluded that "religion, which never intervenes directly in the government of American society, should ... be considered as the first of their political institutions, for although it does not give them the taste for liberty, it singularly facilitates their use thereof."[61] A recent author, seeking to answer the secularist charge that religion is dangerous, has made the point more universally: "it is fairly clear to any unbiased observer that in most societies, most of the time, religion is one of the forces making both for social stability and for morally serious debate and reform."[62]

It may seem strange to discuss "religion" in general, when of course the many actual religions are notorious for their disagreements, but in fact there is increasing evidence that the fault lines, at least in the West, do not lie between religions but between those who take some theistic religion seriously and those who do not. One major study found that "the extent of religious observance, our measure of religious commitment, divided our respondents more than their separate religious identities."[63]

One of the ways in which this difference is manifested is by tolerance, with the effects running contrary to what might have been expected on the basis of conventional assumptions about strongly held religious beliefs. Sound research suggests that, at least in the American context, weak religion that makes minimal claims on its adherents is associated with intolerance, strong religion with tolerance.[64] A number of empirical studies have similarly found that private schooling, most of which is religiously oriented, "has a positive effect on political tolerance."[65]

What do we mean by "strong religion"? We use this term not to distinguish among the usual denominational identifiers but to describe those individuals and groups who seek to live by the specific requirements of their religious tradition, and who do so in a manner which to some extent sets them at odds with the surrounding culture. The first thing to note about strong religions is that they tend to

---

61 Alexis de Tocqueville, *Democracy in America*, ed. J. P. Mayer, trans. George Lawrence (New York: Harper & Row, 1988), 292.

62 Keith Ward, *Is Religion Dangerous?* (Grand Rapids, MI: Wm. B. Eerdmans, 2006), 55.

63 James G. Gimpel, J. Celeste Lay, and Jason E. Schuknecht, *Cultivating Democracy: Civic Environments and Political Socialization in America* (Washington, DC: Brookings Institution Press, 2003), 142.

64 Ibid., 133.

65 Patrick J. Wolf, "School Choice and Civic Values," in *Getting Choice Right: Ensuring Equity and Efficiency in Education Policy*, ed. Julian R. Betts and Tom Loveless (Washington, DC: Brookings Institution Press, 2005), 216.

challenge the norms of the surrounding culture, often in ways that make others quite uncomfortable. This may indeed be part of their attraction for those who find the culture either hopelessly perverse or empty of transcendent meanings and assurances. Legal scholar Stephen Carter points out that, "at its best, religion in its subversive mode provides the believer with a transcendent reason to question the power of the state and the messages of the culture."[66]

Arguably, it is the strength and coherence of such convictions that make it possible for students who receive an education with a clear religious orientation to become authentically autonomous in the sense of being capable of making decisions, including about issues of public policy, on the basis of settled principles rather than simply through peer or media influence.

> Because public education generally shies away from controversial comprehensive values of any kind, its civic education is "thin." By contrast, religious groups bring their own stories and sacred histories to bear in support of democracy, endorsing civic virtues and democratic institutions from their own points of view, and thickening the grounds of commitment to democracy.[67]

Sometimes it is observers from another religious tradition who recognize, perhaps a little enviously, the power of such strong religion. Thus, Cardinal Ratzinger, later Pope Benedict, recognized the attractiveness of the evangelical churches, especially in Latin America, challenging the Catholicism that for centuries had been in a monopoly position. These churches, he wrote, are "able to attract thousands of people in search of a solid foundation for their lives. ... [T]he more churches adapt themselves to the standards of secularization, the more followers they lose. They become attractive, instead, when they indicate a solid point of reference and a clear orientation."[68]

Keith Ward makes the case that strong religion serves to keep raising issues that contemporary Western culture would rather forget, "questions of the significance of human life and of the right way to live. It keeps alive questions of whether there is a supreme human goal, and of how to attain it. And it keeps alive the question of whether there is an absolute standard of truth, beauty and goodness that underlies the ambiguities and conflicts of human life."[69]

---

66 Stephen L. Carter, *God's Name in Vain: The Wrongs and Rights of Religion in Politics* (New York: Basic Books, 2000), 30.

67 Nancy L. Rosenblum, introduction to *Obligations of Citizenship and Demands of Faith: Religious Accommodation in Pluralist Democracies*, ed. Nancy L. Rosenblum (Princeton, NJ: Princeton University Press, 2000), 19.

68 Joseph Ratzinger, "Letter to Marcello Pera," in *Without Roots: The West, Relativism, Christianity, Islam* (New York: Basic Books, 2006), 119.

69 Ward, *Is Religion Dangerous?*, 196.

For adherents to strong religion, living a moral life is not a matter of simply adhering to rules nor of consulting one's values, but of "a living relationship to a personal God of supreme goodness."[70] The believer's behavior is based in gratitude and in a desire to express it through concrete actions. By contrast, "if there really is no transcendent source of the good to which the will is naturally drawn, but only the power of the will to decide what ends it desires,"[71] then there is no reliable basis on which to overcome the selfishness of the consumerist culture that prevails in North America and Western Europe today.

Many, perhaps most, individuals living under conditions of secular modernity are not sustained by a community of shared moral commitments. "Secular morality is not inherently embedded in communal practices," Habermas points out. "Religious consciousness, by contrast, preserves an essential connection to the ongoing practice of life within a community."[72] In its absence, appeals to common purpose grow increasingly faint, and it is with a sense of nostalgic regret that many look back to the social movements or national crises of the past.

Societies cannot maintain shared norms for behavior or appeal to their members to make sacrifices for the common good unless those members recognize authority beyond their individual interests and impulses, as when "religion acts as a repository of human values and transcendental reference which can be activated in the realm of civil society."[73] Philip Rieff made the same point more starkly in *The Triumph of the Therapeutic:* "The question is no longer as Dostoevski put it: 'Can civilized man believe?' Rather: Can unbelieving man be civilized?"[74]

Stephen Macedo, no particular friend of religion, concedes that religions "often challenge the materialism, hedonism, and this-worldliness that is so dominant in our time. And religions provide sources of meaning outside of politics that should help keep alive the intellectual arguments by which truth is supposedly approached in a liberal polity."[75] Legal scholar Michael McConnell goes further, pointing out that "by most objective measures, religious Americans are more democratically engaged than most of their fellow citizens. Church attendance has

---

70 Ibid., 137.

71 David Bentley Hart, *Atheist Delusions: The Christian Revolution and Its Fashionable Enemies* (New Haven: Yale University Press, 2009), 227.

72 Jürgen Habermas, "A Reply," in *An Awareness of What Is Missing: Faith and Reason in a Post-Secular Age*, ed. Ciaran Cronin (Cambridge: Polity Press, 2010), 75.

73 David Martin, *On Secularization: Towards a Revised General Theory* (Farnham, Surrey: Ashgate, 2005), 24.

74 Philip Rieff, *The Triumph of the Therapeutic: Uses of Faith after Freud* (New York: Harper Torchbooks, 1968), 4.

75 Stephen Macedo, *Diversity and Distrust: Civic Education in a Multicultural Democracy* (Cambridge, MA: Harvard University Press, 2000), 220.

a high correlation to voter turnout–far higher than any other institutional affiliation." He adds that "education has less than half this effect, which may suggest–ironically–that churches, rather than schools, are our prime inculcators of democratic participation."[76] A massive study of the extent to which Americans volunteer for community building and other civic activities found that participation in churches–especially African American and white evangelical congregations–has a strong positive influence on involvement in the wider community as well.

Religious institutions are the source of significant civic skills which, in turn, foster political activity. The acquisition of such civic skills is not a function of socioeconomic status (SES) but depends on frequency of church attendance and the denomination of the church one attends. Individuals with low SES may acquire civic skills if they attend church–and if the church is the right denomination. Conversely, individuals who are otherwise well endowed with resources because of their high SES will be lower in civic skills if they do not attend church regularly–or if the church they attend is the wrong denomination.[77] And, again,

> [t]he domain of equal access to opportunities to learn civic skills is the church. Not only is religious affiliation not stratified by income, race or ethnicity, or gender, but churches apportion opportunities for skill development relatively equally among members. Among church members, the less well off are at less of a disadvantage, and African Americans are at an actual advantage, when it comes to opportunities to practice civic skills in church.[78]

This is consistent with the results of a study of adults nationwide who had graduated some years before from various types of high schools: those who attended "Christian" (that is, evangelical) schools were well integrated into their local communities, though rather less involved politically than graduates of other types of schools. The study found that

> in contrast to the popular stereotype of Protestant Christian schools producing socially fragmented, anti-intellectual, politically radical, and militantly right-wing graduates, our data reveal a very different picture of the Protestant Christian school graduate. ... [They] have been found to be uniquely compliant, generous individuals who stabilize their communities by their uncommon and distinctive commitment to their

76 Michael W. McConnell, "Education Disestablishment: Why Democratic Values Are Ill-Served by Democratic Control of Schooling," in *Moral and Political Education*, ed. Stephen Macedo and Yael Tamir (New York: New York University Press, 2002), 126.

77 Sidney Verba, Kay Lehman Schlozman, and Henry E. Brady, *Voice and Equality: Civic Voluntarism in American Politics* (Cambridge, MA: Harvard University Press, 1995), 282–83.

78 Ibid., 320.

> families, their churches, and their communities, and by their unique hope and optimism about their lives and the future ... committed to progress in their communities even while they feel outside the cultural mainstream.[79]

Summing up,

> religion matters to public life because it is an important teacher of moral virtues such as self-sacrifice and altruism. The transmission of religious beliefs to one's children can be thought of as instilling a valuable moral resource that contributes to participatory attitudes. On average, those growing up in homes with religious instruction and practice will be better socialized to contribute to society than those who do not, and a solid body of social science research can be mustered to support this contention.[80]

Sending one's children to a faith-based school is for many families an important aspect of nurturing for civic responsibility.

After all, "development of moral commitment among young people thrives on coherence in the social environment."[81] This is one reason why the incoherence of the typical public school works against the development of character, the settled disposition to practice civic and personal virtues. Paul Hill, a leader in research on American education reform, points out that a school which enrolls its students on the basis of parental choice rather than mandatory assignment "will be stabilized by its commitments and respond to the needs of a group of students and parents to whom it is committed rather than to the politically bargained preferences of society as a whole." This has the desirable effect that "social trust and community feeling are higher when schools are distinctive, and families have choices." In his research he has "found that students in schools based on a clear set of common premises are more likely than students in less well-defined schools to engage in vigorous discussion of values and social policy."[82]

In faith-based schools, as is clear from research on Islamic high schools,[83] "an ethos of trust opens space for teachers to feel comfortable introducing contentious

---

79 Ray Pennings et al., *Do the Motivations for Private Religious Catholic and Protestant Schooling in North America Align with Graduate Outcomes?* (Hamilton, Ont.: Cardus, 2011), 13.

80 Gimpel, Lay, and Schuknecht, *Cultivating Democracy*, 122–23.

81 William Damon, "To Not Fade Away: Restoring Civil Identity among the Young," in *Making Good Citizens: Education and Civil Society*, ed. Diane Ravitch and Joseph P. Viteritti (New Haven: Yale University Press, 2001), 131.

82 Paul Hill, "The Supply-Side of School Choice," in *School Choice and Social Controversy*, ed. Stephen D. Sugarman and Frank E. Kemerer (Washington, DC: Brookings Institution, 1999), 151.

83 Charles L. Glenn, *Muslim Educators in American Communities* (Charlotte, NC: Information Age, 2018).

issues into their lessons and allowing debate and discussion of those issues among the students."[84] Interviews with Muslim high school students and their parents across the country made it clear that they valued the Islamic school not least because it provided a secure vantage point from which to engage American society in a confident manner. Rather than serving, as some outsiders suspect, as bastions of resistance to participation in the wider community, "Muslim families, schools, mosques, and organizations in the United States ... have an important bridging function in that they give Muslim Americans the ability to connect and have conversations with outside institutions, religions, and governments."[85]

Religious identity, practices, and institutions may take on a heightened significance under those circumstances; they are no longer part of a taken-for-granted background, as may have been the case in the country of origin. There is nothing new or distinctively Muslim about such reactions. Michael Novak, in his influential book about the American descendants of European immigrants, pointed out that

> more than any other institution ... the [Catholic] church gave the immigrants cultural reinforcement and a sense of dignity; a feeling of belonging; support in the hours of being born, and dying; and comfort in the anxieties and disasters in between ... The church taught the immigrants to work hard, to obey the law, to respect their leaders, and to concentrate on private, familial relationships.[86]

A study of Polish immigrants in 1921 found that "when the parish is established in America, it has a much larger social function than it has in Poland. It assumes, to a degree, the character of a commune. Even Poles who are not religious are thus drawn into the parish institutions."[87] Similarly, David Martin compares the tight little communities of "store-front" Pentecostal churches to how

> people lash themselves together on rafts to survive in stormy seas. On that raft they adopt a regime of disciplined behaviour, shared learning and mutual assistance, otherwise they sink as rapidly as the millions floundering and foundering all around

84 David Campbell, "Civic Education in Traditional Public, Charter, and Private Schools," in *Making Civics Count: Citizenship Education for a New Generation*, ed. David E. Campbell, Meira Levinson, and Frederick M. Hess (Cambridge, MA: Harvard Education Press, 2012), 244.

85 Matthew Kaemingk, *Christian Hospitality and Muslim Immigration in an Age of Fear* (Grand Rapids, MI: Wm. B. Eerdmans, 2018), 289.

86 Michael Novak, *The Rise of Unmeltable Ethnics* (New York: Macmillan, 1973), 11.

87 Robert E. Park and Herbert A. Miller, *Old World Traits Transplanted* (New York: Harper and Brothers, 1921), 211, 213.

> them. Within the warm world of the Church Pentecostals assist each other, especially when in distress, and they acquire organizational skills and responsibilities that help them in the world outside.[88]

Immigrants participating in such small-scale and intense communities, typically drawn together by shared religious convictions, develop "social capital," based "less on the relative economic or occupational success of immigrants than on the *density* of ties among them. ... [M]odest but tightly-knit communities can be a valuable resource, as their ties support parental control and parents' aspirations for their young."[89] It may be an advantage in a large society to be raised within a particular community. People raised in a community are given values and a way of life that they can reject or revise when they are older. It may mean that a child has an idea of what it means to live a life guided by deep-seated values. As a teenager and adult, the person can look at other ways of life and compare them to his or her own. A child who is given many different options about how to live, however, will not experience any particular way of life deeply enough to have a basis for comparison.[90]

The importance of what Peter Berger and Richard John Neuhaus have called "mediating structures"[91]–including families and religious communities–to the health of society and of individuals has been affirmed from many different disciplinary angles. Legal scholar Mary Ann Glendon has given special emphasis to the way in which families, neighborhoods, religious associations, and other communities serve as the "seedbeds of civic virtue," the matrices within which "human character, competence, and capacity for citizenship are formed."[92]

Political philosopher Michael Sandel describes the burden of extreme individualism characteristic of modernity with its endless opportunities for self-definition. A person burdened by such individualism and self-definition would in fact be "morally disempowered" and rootless. Sandel comments on the irony that this

---

88 David Martin, *The Future of Christianity* (Farnham, Surrey: Ashgate, 2011), 71.

89 Alejandro Portes and Rubén Rumbaut, *Legacies: The Story of the Immigrant Second Generation* (Berkeley: University of California Press, 2001), 65.

90 Jeff Spinner-Haley, *Surviving Diversity: Religion and Democratic Citizenship* (Baltimore: Johns Hopkins University Press, 2000), 65.

91 Peter L. Berger and Richard John Neuhaus, "To Empower People" (1977), in *To Empower People: From State to Civil Society*, ed. Michael Novak (Washington, DC: American Enterprise Institute, 1996).

92 Mary Ann Glendon, *Rights Talk: The Impoverishment of Political Discourse* (New York: Free Press, 1991), 109.

could be the result of "a liberal ethic designed to establish the rights of the individual as inviolable."[93]

When I act out of more or less enduring qualities of character, by contrast, my choice of ends is not arbitrary in the same way. In consulting my preferences, I have not only to weigh their intensity but also to assess their suitability to the person I (already) am. I ask, as I deliberate, not only what I really want but who I really am, and this last question takes me beyond an attention to my desires alone to reflect on my identity.[94] In other words, we are more authentically autonomous if we act out of a stable sense of our own identity and the relationships and perhaps traditions that give it a stable character than if we simply choose based upon what we are feeling or experiencing at the moment. Political economist Francis Fukuyama stresses the importance of trust, and how that is best developed through associations based on shared beliefs rather than on any sort of social contract.[95]

The recent rise of an angry populism in Europe and North America reflects a measurable decline in trust among citizens. Concurrently, the decline in face-to-face sociability (the "bowling alone" phenomenon[96]) and its partial replacement by social media anonymity, further exacerbated by pandemic shut-downs, has made the social fabric seem unprecedentedly fragile. Fewer of us are raised in stable families, and "a weakened family is less able to produce children who have the character traits on which social virtue is based, children who are kind and considerate, trusting and trustworthy, responsible and hard working, honest and cooperative, and respectful of rules and authority."[97]

Hyperindividualism, reflected in the obsession with autonomy that we have noted in much current talk about the goals of education, is not real strength but an insidious vulnerability to fashion and impulse. More of us live alone; fewer of us have strong ties to community institutions. Millions of Americans, rejecting the institutional churches that have long organized much of local life, have become devotees of what one scholar calls "intuitional religions," which "place the locus of authority on people's experiential emotions, what you might call gut instinct. Society, institutions, credited authorities, experts, expectations, rules of conduct–

---

93 Michael J. Sandel, *Liberalism and the Limits of Justice* (Cambridge: Cambridge University Press, 1982), 139.

94 Ibid., 180.

95 Francis Fukuyama, "Trust: The Social Virtues and the Creation of Prosperity," in *The Essential Civil Society Reader: The Classic Essays*, ed. Done E. Eberly (Lanham, MD: Rowman & Littlefield, 2000).

96 Robert D. Putnam, *Bowling Alone: The Collapse and Revival of American Community* (New York: Simon & Schuster, 2000).

97 David Popenoe, "The Roots of Declining Social Virtue: Family, Community, and the Need for a 'Natural Communities Policy,'" in Glendon and Blankenthorn, *Seedbeds of Virtue*, 72.

all these are generally treated not just as irrelevant, but as sources of active evil."[98]

Nor is this weakening of the traditional structures of social life unrelated to the present crisis of American national culture. In David Brooks's bleak account,

> when a whole society is built around self-preoccupation, its members become separated from one another, divided and alienated. And that is what has happened to us. We are down in the valley. The rot we see in our politics is caused by a rot in our moral and cultural foundations–in the way we relate to one another, in the way we see ourselves as separable from one another, in the individualistic values that have become the water in which we swim.[99]

Under these conditions the continued vitality of faith-based institutions, including schools, where trust is based upon shared commitments, is a precious resource to society at large. After all, "religion seems to provide social bonds in a world in which so much conspires to produce alienation and anomie. There are remarkably few places nowadays where adults can meet and take a trusting relationship for granted."[100]

In Conclusion

Where are the virtues required for a healthy social order nurtured? We have seen that "only many small-scale civic bodies enable citizens to cultivate democratic civic virtues and to play an active role in civil life. Such participation turns on meaningful involvement in some decent form of community, by which is meant commitments and ties that locate the citizen in bonds of trust, reciprocity, and civic competence."[101]

Well-run faith-based schools and other schools united around shared convictions about the requirements of a flourishing life (including some exceptional public schools) are able to shape hearts and minds, not because they undervalue the demands of citizenship but because they foster a deeply rooted understanding of reality shared by staff and by those parents who enroll their children. In such

---

98 Tara Isabella Burton, *Strange Rites: New Religions for a Godless World* (New York: Public Affairs, 2020), 33.

99 David Brooks, *The Second Mountain: The Quest for a Moral Life* (New York: Random House, 2019), xxii.

100 John Micklethwait and Adrian Wooldridge, *God Is Back: How the Global Revival of Faith Is Changing the World* (New York: Penguin Press, 2009), 148.

101 Jean Bethke Elshtain, "Civil Society, Religion, and the Formation of Citizens," in Ravitch and Viteritti, *Making Good Citizens*, 264.

schools, young people grow to admire and emulate adults of virtuous character. Often such schools include, for older students, a requirement of community service, as we found in studying Islamic secondary schools. In these settings, often shared with students from other backgrounds, they form friendships and learn to accept differences because these are openly acknowledged and are not fundamentally threatening.[102]

The interests of national unity and social peace can best be served by such education, provided through a system of structural pluralism in schooling that shows respect for the diversity of deeply held convictions in society.

> Since modern liberal democracies are characterized by conflicting conceptions of the good, it is important that education for citizenship should not be seen as promoting any particular cultural conception of the good. Each cultural group must be free to pursue its own conception of the good within a framework of justice and equal respect. The freedom guaranteed to citizens by political liberalism includes the freedom to pursue non-liberal cultural goods within that basic framework.[103]

Effective structural pluralism in schooling requires that, as in the Netherlands, government provide equivalent funding to whatever schools parents may choose, leaving those schools free to offer a distinctive approach to education while holding them accountable for satisfactory outcomes of academic instruction.[104] Such an arrangement protects the interests of children, their families, and society by providing scope for the nurturing of the civic virtues appropriate in a liberal democracy.

---

102 Charles L. Glenn and Paul Zoontjens, "The Netherlands," in *Balancing Freedom, Autonomy, and Accountability in Education*, vol. 2, ed. Charles L. Glenn and Jan De Groof (Nijmegen, the Netherlands: Wolf Legal Publishing, 2018).

103 J. Mark Halstead, "Schooling and Cultural Maintenance for Religious Minorities in the Liberal State," in McDonough and Feinberg, *Citizenship and Education*, 289.

104 Glenn and Zoontjens, "The Netherlands."

Part Two:
National Contexts

Restoring the Value(s) of Religion in American Public Education

John Witte Jr.[1]

Introduction

This volume, along with others in this series, explores the role of sundry social systems, separately and together, in shaping individual character and collective values in late modern pluralistic societies. Here we focus on the shaping influence of schools and other forms of organized education. Like the family and the church, the school has long been viewed as a vital and perennial institution that incubates and inculcates morals and values in the next generation. The school's influence on character formation is more overt and visible than the more subtle but powerful influences of markets, laws, politics, the media, scientific research, health care, and the military that both cooperate with and often compete with the efforts of schools and, sometimes with churches and families, too.

Historically, and still today, *religious* schools–elementary, secondary, and higher educational institutions chartered and led by churches, synagogues, mosques, and other faith communities–have been overt in shaping the hearts, souls, and minds of their students. They teach students the values, norms, and habits of faithful living within specific denominations. They often prepare students for initiation into the life and leadership of the religious community. And they equip students with the methods and learning needed for an independent life of faith and work in the adult world.

Religious schools–or at least religious schooling–have been part of Western civilization from the very beginning. In modern societies, religious schools have been critical to the preservation and perpetuation of minority faiths like Jews and Muslims. But they are now often a refuge for once-majority Christian faiths as well; think of the many Catholic and Protestant schools now on offer in Western lands. To be sure, religious schools today face frequent criticism in late modern

1 This chapter draws on and updates John Witte Jr. and Joel A. Nichols, *Religion and the American Constitutional Experiment*, 4th ed. (Oxford: Oxford University Press, 2016), 154–203, hereafter RCE.

Western cultures. They are blamed for fostering countercultural beliefs and practices that harm democracy and balkanize society. They are charged with siphoning off the best students, teachers, and resources from public schools. And lately, religious schools have been castigated as bastions of economic privilege, cultural segregation, and racial discrimination. Even so, most Western constitutional democracies still protect the basic rights of private religious schools to exist, and states sometimes provide these schools with direct and indirect funding, so long as they meet the state's basic accreditation requirements.[2]

Until the later nineteenth century, *public* schools–K-12 institutions and public universities that are created, funded, and staffed by the state–had a comparable educational mission, albeit more religiously generic than overtly denominational schools. Many of the first public school systems in Europe and North America were established as parts and products of the sixteenth-century Reformation. Protestants emphasized that each citizen had to be literate enough to read the Bible in the vernacular at home, to understand Sunday sermons and catechisms, and to participate actively in church worship and liturgy. Each citizen had to prepare for the distinct vocation that matched their God-given talents. For Protestants, the clerical vocation was only one vocation to choose, and no better or more virtuous than any other purported secular vocation. The calling of the soldier, lawyer, housewife, or farmer was just as spiritual and conducive to salvation as the Christian vocation of the bishop, abbot, nun, or priest. The same devotion and disciplined learning and preparation that a cleric directed to spiritual and ecclesiastical ends could now be devoted to secular and material ends as well, with equal assurance of justification by faith.[3]

The Lutheran Reformation in Germany and Scandinavia established many of these premises and structures of Western state-run public education. In Lutheran lands, the magistrate was treated as the political "father of the community" (*paterpoliticus*) who created public schools that were built on state lands, funded by tax revenues, and regulated by detailed *Schulordnungen.* Education was mandatory for boys and girls alike and was to be fiscally and physically accessible to all. It was marked by both formal classroom instruction and civic education through community libraries, lectures, and other media. The curriculum was to combine biblical values and catechesis with humanistic and vocational training. Students were to be stratified into different classes according to age and ability, and were slowly selected for any number of vocations, with the

2 See American and European examples in John Witte Jr., *The Blessings of Liberty: Human Rights and Religious Freedom in the Western Tradition* (Cambridge: Cambridge University Press, 2021).

3 See, for example, Frederick Eby, *Early Protestant Educators: The Educational Writings of Martin Luther, John Calvin, and Other Leaders of Protestant Thought* (New York: AMS Press, 1971).

most precocious tapped for university training. The public school was to be, in reformer Philip Melanchthon's famous phrase, the "civic seminary" of the commonwealth designed to combine deep faith and deep learning at once. This educational system, born of the Reformation and of comparable humanist movements in Europe, eventually became a model for public schools in many parts of the Christian world, both in Europe and in its far-flung colonies.[4]

This ideal–if not idealized[5]–early modern picture of the public school as the civic seminary of the established Christian community stands in marked contrast to the typical picture of state schools in many late modern Western societies today. In the five centuries since the Reformation, the West has seen massive changes to the conditions and culture of education–growing religious pluralism and often disestablishment of religion; strong new antireligious political movements from the French Revolution to the rise of communism; modern pressures on states, the media, and the academy to foster religious neutrality and *laïcité*, if not overt secularization; the rise of scientific and technical specialization in lower schools and universities alike; and the gradual decline of the clergy and the church in shaping and guiding modern life, law, and lore. Important, too, was the powerful rise of the Western welfare state in the aftermath of the Great Depression, World Wars I and II, and the ensuing Cold War. The modern welfare state has taken over much of the education of late modern citizens. All of these movements and many more have changed dramatically the nature and object of public education in Western lands. Several fellow contributors to this volume–Charles Glenn and Ashley Berner, most notably–have documented these changes brilliantly in a long series of writings.

This chapter lifts up one small piece of this much bigger story of the interaction of religion, state, education, and character formation. My focus is on the prominent role of modern American state-run public schools in educating modern citizens and the deprecated role of religion in the delivery of this public education. This diminished role of religion was a product not only of some individual state constitutional initiatives from 1850 on, but also of a U.S. Supreme Court that zealously applied the First Amendment prohibitions on state establishments of religion. From the 1940 s to 1990 s, I show below, the Court systematically expelled religious teachers, prayers, texts, readings, symbols, and even private religious devotions from the public-school classroom. Since 1990, the Court has permitted voluntary religious activities outside of the classroom, but only if comparable secular activities are equally on offer, and even then, some limits on religion remain.

---

4 John Witte Jr., *Law and Protestantism: The Legal Teachings of the Lutheran Reformation* (Cambridge: Cambridge University Press, 2002), 277–92.

5 See critical comments in Gerald Strauss, *Luther's House of Learning: Indoctrination of the Young in the Lutheran Reformation* (Baltimore, MD: Johns Hopkins University Press, 1978).

The consequence of these constitutional policies and cases is that public school students are effectively taught that religion, much like alcohol, is a dangerous thing, to be indulged only in the privacy of one's home, and ideally postponed until a child has reached the age of majority and discernment.

This deprecation of religion in public school education has impoverished the values education and character formation of American students in primary and secondary public schools, and sometimes in public universities, too. It has deprived students of their ability to develop healthy democratic habits of engaging the religious other and understanding their own belief system in comparison with other beliefs and practices. It has fostered the false idea that religion and faith are only for the private and voluntary sphere, while reason and logic are the only valuable currency of public and political life. And it has hindered the ability of budding democratic citizens to engage responsibly the public and private roles of religion in modern life.

American Religion and Education in Cultural and Constitutional Context

American education is a massive social undertaking today. The United States has more than 130,000 lower schools (from kindergarten through twelfth grade), and more than 6,000 postsecondary schools. Nearly 100,000 lower schools are public or state-run institutions, with fifty-six million American children enrolled. Alongside these public schools are 33,000 private lower schools (two-thirds of them religious) with six million students. About 1.7 million American children are regularly homeschooled at least until high school–although that number temporarily approached forty million nationwide because of restrictions during the COVID-19 pandemic. The country is also home to some 1,650 state and 4,300 private colleges, universities, and academies enrolling nearly twenty million students. More than ten million employees work in these schools, and in 2019, education comprised 7.1 percent of America's GDP.[6]

American education is not only a massive industry but also a major battleground for constitutional struggles over religious freedom. While a complex scaffolding of federal, state, and local laws and regulations supports and governs

6 National Center for Education Statistics, 2019 Tables and Figures, Table 105.20, 105.50, https://nces.ed.gov/programs/digest/2019menu_tables.asp; and ibid., "Private Schools and Enrollment," https://nces.ed.gov/programs/schoolchoice/ind_03.asp. In addition, there are some 7,200 lower charter schools, which are public/private partnerships featuring state charters and funding but active private administration, including sometimes religious leadership. See https://nces.ed.gov/fastfacts/display.asp?id=30.

education,[7] all schools are subject to the same First Amendment guarantee that "Congress shall make no law respecting an establishment of religion or prohibiting the free exercise thereof." This constitutional guarantee of religious freedom has produced a substantial and shifting body of case law. Nearly one-third of the U.S. Supreme Court's cases on religious freedom–75 out of its nearly 250 cases issued through 2020[8]–have addressed issues of religion and education. All but six of these cases were decided after 1940, the year the Court first began to apply these guarantees to state and local governments as well as to Congress.[9] For each Supreme Court case, there are scores, sometimes hundreds of lower federal court cases and sometimes many state-court cases, too, adding further nuance and amplification.

The Court's cases on religious freedom and education address three main questions: (1) What role may religion play in public education? (2) What role may government play in private religious education? (3) What religious rights do parents and students have in public and private schools (and in home schools as well)? The Court has worked out a set of rough answers to these questions, albeit with ample vacillation over the past century. While government has the power to mandate basic education for all children, parents have the right to choose public, private, or homeschool education for their minor children, and government may now facilitate that choice through vouchers and tax relief for private-school students. While the First Amendment forbids most forms of religion in public schools, it protects most forms of religion in private schools. While the First Amendment forbids government from funding the core religious activities of private schools, it permits delivery of general governmental services, subsidies, scholarships, and tax breaks to public and private schools, teachers, and students alike. While the First Amendment forbids public-school teachers and outsiders from offering religious instruction and expression in public-school classes and at formal school functions, it permits public-school students to engage in private religious expression and protects these students from coerced religious activities. The amendment further requires that religious parties have equal access to public facilities, forums, and funds that are open to their nonreligious peers.

The Supreme Court has developed these holdings in distinct lines of First Amendment cases on the place of religion in public schools and on the role of government in private religious schools. These cases, however, have left blurrier

---

7 See Michael I. Levin, *United States School Laws and Rules*, 3 vols. (St. Paul, MN: Thomson Reuter, 2020).

8 See tabular summary of all these Supreme Court cases in RCE, appendix 3, pp. 303–38.

9 See *Cantwell v. Connecticut*, 310 U.S. 296 (1940) and *Everson v. Board of Education*, 330 U.S. 1 (1947), which incorporated the Free Exercise and Establishment Clauses of the First Amendment into the Due Process Clause of the Fourteenth Amendment and applied these guarantees for the first time against state and local governments.

distinctions between lower education and higher education in matters of religious freedom. Colleges and universities have thus often absorbed the Court's directives to primary and secondary schools, and vice versa. For example, many state universities adopted the Court's repeated mandating of strict separation of church and state in lower public schools, even though no Supreme Court case explicitly ordered the universities' application of the principle. In turn, the Court's more recent rulings about equal access and equal treatment were created for state universities but trickled down into public high schools and then public grade schools, and are now firmly rooted in the Free Speech and Free Exercise Clauses of the Constitution.

Telling this whole constitutional story could easily fill a five-foot shelf of books. Let me zero in on just the cases dealing with religion in public-school education, which affects the approximately seventy million students enrolled in these state-run lower and higher schools.

Separation of Church and State in Public Education

The Supreme Court's most famous First Amendment teaching is that the Constitution has "erected a wall of separation between church and state."[10] This teaching emerged most prominently in a series of cases from 1948 to 1987 that limited the place of religious teachers, prayers, texts, symbols, and teachings in public grade schools and high schools.

A common logic governed this forty-year run of cases. The public school is a government entity, often one of the most visible and well-known arms of the government in any community. The public school is furthermore a model of constitutional democracy and designed to communicate and facilitate core democratic norms and constitutional practices to students. The state mandates that all able students attend schools, at least until the age of sixteen. These students are young and impressionable. Given all these factors, the Court maintained, the public school must cling closely to core constitutional and democratic values, including the core value of separation of church and state. Some relaxation of constitutional values is possible in other public contexts, where adults can make informed assessments of the values being transmitted. But no such relaxation can occur in public schools, which youths are compelled to attend. In public schools, if nowhere else in public life, strict separation of church and state must be the norm.

The case that opened this series was *McCollum v. Board of Education* (1948). At issue was a release-time program adopted by a local public-school board for fourth- through ninth-grade students. Once a week, students were released from their regular classes to be able to participate in a religious class taught on the

10 *McCollum v. Board of Education*, 333 U.S. 203, 209–211 (1948).

school campus. Three religious classes were offered–Protestant, Catholic, and Jewish–reflecting the religious makeup of the local community. These classes were voluntarily taught by qualified outside teachers approved by the principal. Students whose parents did not consent continued their secular studies during this release time. The *McCollum* Court held that this program violated the First Amendment Establishment Clause, for it constituted the use of "tax-supported property for religious instruction and the close cooperation between school authorities and the religious council in promoting religious education."[11]

In *Engel v. Vitale* (1962), the Court outlawed a nondenominational prayer recited by public-school teachers and their students at the commencement of each school day: "Almighty God, we acknowledge our dependence upon Thee, and we beg Thy blessings upon us, our parents, our teachers, and our Country." Students who did not wish to pray could remain silent or be excused from the room during this recitation. The *Engel* Court found this practice to be unconstitutional:

> It is no part of the business of government to compose official prayers for any group of the American people to recite as part of a religious program carried on by government. ... When the power, prestige, and financial support of government [are] placed behind a particular religious belief, the indirect coercive pressure upon religious minorities to conform to the prevailing officially approved religion is plain.[12]

This prohibition on prayer in public schools was controversial in its day, but the Court has maintained and extended it. *Wallace v. Jaffree* (1985) struck down a state statute that authorized a moment of silence at the beginning of each school day for "meditation or voluntary prayer," because the legislature had betrayed its "intent to return prayer to the public schools."[13] *Lee v. Weisman* (1992) outlawed a local rabbi's prayer at a one-time public middle-school graduation ceremony on school premises, arguing that such prayers effectively coerced graduating students to participate in religion.[14] *Santa Fe Independent School District v. Doe* (2000) outlawed elected student invocations at public high-school football games, arguing that this policy not only coerced players, cheerleaders, and band members to participate in prayer but also constituted governmental endorsement of religion.[15]

Not only religious teachers and prayers but also "sectarian teachings" were forbidden in public schools. In *Abington Township School District v. Schempp* (1963), the Court outlawed the reading of ten Bible verses at the beginning of each

---

11 Ibid.

12 370 U.S. 421, 430–32 (1962).

13 472 U.S. 38, 57–60 (1985).

14 505 U.S. 577 (1992).

15 530 U.S. 290 (2000).

school day. Either a teacher or a volunteer student would read a biblical text of their choice, with no commentary or discussion allowed. Students whose parents did not consent could refuse to listen or leave the room. After *Engel,* the *Schempp* Court found this an easy case. "[I]t is no defense that the religious practices here may be relatively minor encroachments on the First Amendment," Justice Tom C. Clark wrote for the Court. "The breach of neutrality that is today a trickling stream may all too soon become a raging torrent." Responding to Justice Potter Stewart's sharply worded dissent that the Court's purported neutrality toward religion effectively established secularism as the religion of the public school, the Court offered a conciliatory word about the objective value and use of religion as a topic of public education:

> [I]t might well be said that one's education is not complete without a study of comparative religion or the history of religion and its relationship to the advancement of civilization. It certainly may be said that the Bible is worthy of study for its literary and historic qualities. Nothing we have said here indicates that such study of the Bible or of religion, when presented objectively as part of a secular program of education, may not be effected consistently with the First Amendment.[16]

While *Schempp* permitted objective instruction of religious topics in appropriate public-school classes, *Edwards v. Aguillard* (1987) struck down a state law that required equal time for "evolution-science" and "creation-science" in science classrooms. This statute, the Court held, betrayed a "discriminatory preference ... to advance the religious viewpoint that a supernatural being created humankind" and "to restructure the science curriculum to conform with a particular religious viewpoint." This was not a proper objective teaching of religion à la *Schempp.* Creation might be a good topic for a course in cosmology or ancient literature, but not for a science course. Separation of church and state also entailed separation of religion and science.[17] Lower courts have used this precedent to outlaw "intelligent design" teachings from public-school science curricula as well.

In *Stone v. Graham* (1980), the Court struck down a state statute that authorized the posting of a plaque bearing the Ten Commandments on the wall of each public-school classroom. The plaques were donated and hung by private groups in the community. There was no public reading of the commandments nor any evident mention or endorsement of them by teachers or school officials. Each plaque also bore a small inscription that sought to immunize it from charges of religious establishment: "The secular application of the Ten Commandments is clearly seen in its adoption as the fundamental legal code of Western Civilization and the Common Law of the United States." The Court struck down these displays

16 374 U.S. 203, 221, 226 (1963).

17 482 U.S. 578, 591–93 (1987).

as violations of the Establishment Clause. These displays were "plainly religious," in the Court's view. The Ten Commandments are sacred in Jewish and Christian circles, and they command "the religious duties of believers." It made no constitutional difference that they were passively displayed, rather than formally read aloud, or that they were privately donated rather than purchased with state money. The very display of the Decalogue in the public-school classroom served only a religious purpose and was thus inherently unconstitutional.[18]

These early Supreme Court separationist cases were focused on the place of religion in public grade schools and high schools. They were predicated on the reality that students were mandated to be in school until the age of sixteen and were young and impressionable. From the mid-1960 s forward, however, many state universities adopted comparable policies that limited the place of religion in the university campus, curriculum, and activities–even though their students were voluntary, more mature, and able to make their own choices about religion. Some of these new university policies about strict separation of church and state on campus were adopted as self-protective measures against expensive lawsuits brought under the First Amendment, especially as some lower courts began to order state universities to follow the religion policies of state high schools. Universities in some states were also subject to state constitutions that mandated the separation of religion and education, and these policies were more aggressively enforced by state regulators and courts.

But legal considerations were only part of the motivation for these reforms of higher education. Pushing religion to the edge of the college campus and curriculum also reflected the growing antireligious movements and countercultural sentiments of the American academy in the mid-twentieth century. Included were the "death of God" theology taught in some university religion departments and seminaries; Marxist and other critical and deconstructive attacks on traditional religion; and the strong rise of secularization theories of education and public life. It was significant, too, that many of the new cultural and educational leaders of the nation from the 1960 s forward had been reared in public schools that taught them that separation of church and state was the distinct and proper American way of engaging religion. Small wonder, then, that, upon reaching adulthood, this generation adopted separation as a guiding maxim of American higher education as well as lower education.

18 449 U.S. 39, 40–41 (1980) (per curiam).

The Rise of Equal-Access Cases

Criticisms of Separationist Cases

These Establishment Clause cases from 1948 to 1987 limiting religion in public-school classes and at official school events remain good law today.[19] But they have garnered significant criticism that has forced important limits on their logic and subsequent policy.[20] One set of critics has lamented the Court's removal of religion from public schools and has worked persistently to return prayer and other traditional religious activities to the classroom. These groups are often conservative Christians pressing the broader thesis that America was founded as a Christian nation and must democratically reflect this in its political institutions, including its state schools.

A second group of critics has charged the Court with establishing secularism in the public school under the guise of reason and neutrality. These critics argue that the purportedly secular and scientific instruction offered in the public school is just as laden with subjective moral values and ideological beliefs as traditional religious instruction. Drawing a secular/sectarian dividing line in these cases is too simplistic, these critics argue.

A third group of critics, including some specialists in education and child development, have charged that the policy of quarantining public-school students from instruction and experience in religion harms rather than helps them in cultivating the very democratic values and abilities the Court and country are trying to instill and protect in each new generation. Religion, they argue, is not like alcohol, to be avoided until adulthood. Religion is a powerful and perennial force in society, whether for good or ill, and every budding democratic citizen needs to learn from the start to deal with it responsibly. Such education groups have thus developed a range of ambitious curricular forums that seek to introduce religion judiciously into the public-school curriculum in appropriate courses.

Finally, some critics have charged that the Court has used the Establishment Clause to quash rights of free exercise and free speech. Why should students be muzzled in their religious expression as a condition for participating in a school

---

19 See the new summary of the law on religious expression in the public schools in Department of Justice, Civil Rights Division, https://www2.ed.gov/policy/gen/guid/religionandschools/prayer_guidance.html.

20 See analysis of the relevant literature and cases in Kent Greenawalt, *Does God Belong in Public Schools?* (Princeton, NJ: Princeton University Press, 2005); Michael D. Waggoner and Nathan C. Walker, eds., *The Oxford Handbook of Religion and American Education* (New York: Oxford University Press, 2016); Ashley Berner, *Pluralism and American Public Education: No One Way to School* (New York: Palgrave Macmillan, 2017); see also Ashley Berner's chapter in this volume.

that the state conscripts them to attend at least until the age of sixteen? Why should religious parents be compelled to expose their children to a pervasive learning environment that views their faith and identity as suspect and dangerous. Some critics add an economic argument: that the religious rights of the poor suffer disproportionately, since only students of more well-to-do families can afford to attend private schools, where their religious expression is not so muzzled.

Equal-Access Logic

These last two arguments in particular–the need to educate students about religion and to protect the students' rights to religious expression–have helped to drive the development of a new line of what are called equal-access cases. The principal logic of these cases is that religious students and other parties must be given equal access to facilities, forums, and even funds that the public school makes available to similarly situated nonreligious parties. These cases have not changed the longstanding rule that religion is not allowed in the public classroom during instructional time or at official school events. But they have allowed for private religious exercises on school grounds outside of formal instructional time, and they have allowed for extracurricular education on school premises, even if it is religiously motivated and inspired.

These cases were, at first, grounded variously in the Free Speech, Free Exercise, and Equal Protection Clauses, but they are now largely a staple of First Amendment free-speech jurisprudence alone. Equal-access cases first began in the public university and then worked their way into the public high school and eventually into the public grade school, though the most recent cases have imposed some limits on this equal-access logic in public schools.

Widmar v. Vincent (1981) was the opening case in this series. The University of Missouri at Kansas City, a state university, had a policy of opening its facilities for voluntary student groups to use outside of formal instructional time. More than a hundred student groups organized themselves in the year at issue, each paying a small registration fee each semester. One student group, called Cornerstone, met for private religious devotions and local charitable activities. They sought permission to use the university facilities but were denied access, given the university's written policy that the campus could not be used "for purposes of religious worship or religious teaching." Cornerstone appealed, arguing that this policy violated their First Amendment rights to free exercise and free speech as well as their Fourteenth Amendment rights to equal protection. The university countered that it had a compelling state interest to maintain a "strict separation of church and state," per the state constitution, especially in state schools.[21]

The *Widmar* Court found for the religious student group. When a state university creates a limited public forum open to voluntary student groups, the Court opined, religious groups must be given equal access to that forum. Here the university "has discriminated against student groups and speakers based on their desire to use a generally open forum to engage in religious worship and discussion." Religious speech and association are protected by the First Amendment and can be excluded only if the university can demonstrate that its prohibition serves a "compelling state interest and that it is narrowly drawn to achieve that end." But a general desire to keep a strict separation of church and state was not a sufficiently compelling state interest. The values of "equal treatment and access" outweighed the hypothetical dangers of a religious establishment.[22]

The *Widmar* Court explicitly limited its holding to the public university, arguing that university students, unlike public high-school and grade-school students, were more mature and discerning and, after the age of sixteen, were not required by school attendance laws to be there. The following week, the Court let stand a federal circuit court opinion that refused to extend the *Widmar* holding into public high schools.[23] In response, Congress passed the Equal Access Act of 1984, which extended *Widmar*'s principle to public high schools that received federal funding. The act provided that any such high school that opened its facilities to some students for voluntary after-school activities would have to give religious students equal access to these facilities. The religious students' activities, however, had to be completely voluntary and free from school endorsement or participation. In *Westside Community Schools v. Mergens* (1990), the Court upheld the Equal Access Act against an Establishment Clause challenge, holding that Congress had legitimately protected the rights of religious students to "equal treatment" and "equal protection."[24]

In subsequent cases involving lower schools, the Court rooted this equal access right more clearly in the First Amendment Free Speech Clause. *Lamb's Chapel v. Center Moriches Union Free School District* (1993) involved a public school that opened its facilities to various "social, civic, recreational, and political uses" organized by voluntary groups in the community and held after hours without stu-

21 454 U.S. 263, 270, 273 (1981). The Court later upheld the constitutionality of charging these flat fees, even to religious groups, finding no prior restraint on free exercise of religion. See *Board of Regents of University of Wisconsin System v. Southworth*, 529 U.S. 217 (2000).

22 Ibid.

23 *Brandon v. Bd. of Educ. of Guilderland Central School Dist.*, 635 F.2d 971 (2d Cir. 1980), *cert. denied*, 454 U.S. 1123 (1981).

24 496 U.S. 226, 248–50 (1990).

dent involvement. The school banned an otherwise qualified evangelical group because they wanted to show a film series on traditional family values. Citing *Widmar*, the *Lamb's Chapel* Court held that it was viewpoint discrimination to deny this group equal access to the facilities just because their film had a religious inspiration.[25] Similarly, *Good News Club v. Milford Central School* (2001) held that a public grade school that opened its facilities to licensed private groups to run after-school programs for students with parental permission could not exclude a group whose instruction came "from a religious viewpoint."[26]

In *Rosenberger v. Rector and Visitors of the University of Virginia* (1995), a sharply divided Court extended this equal-access principle to the distribution of state funds to religious students, one of the most controversial acts that two thirds of the individual state constitutions had overtly banned. The University of Virginia encouraged student groups to organize themselves for extracurricular activities and register with the university. Student groups were required to petition for the right to be recognized as such a registered group. Once registered, they could apply for monies from a general student activity fund to help defray costs of printing and activities. A Christian group sought reimbursement for the costs to print an overtly religious newspaper called *Wide Awake: A Christian Perspective at the University of Virginia*. The university denied their request since it violated the school's policy not to fund "any activity 'that primarily promotes or manifests a particular belief in or about a deity or an ultimate reality.'" The *Wide Awake* group appealed, claiming that this discriminatory treatment violated their free-speech rights.[27]

The *Rosenberger* Court held for the students. Writing for the Court, Justice Anthony Kennedy said that the state university policy improperly "selects for disfavored treatment those student journalistic efforts with religious editorial viewpoints." Denying funding to this otherwise qualified student group "is based upon viewpoint discrimination not unlike the discrimination the school district relied upon in *Lamb's Chapel* and that we found invalid." The constitutional principle of equal access applies as much to state university funding as to state university facilities, the Court held.

> Vital First Amendment speech principles are at stake here. The first danger to liberty lies in granting the State the power to examine publications to determine whether or not they are based on some ultimate idea and if so for the State to classify them [as religious]. The second, and corollary, danger is to speech from the chilling of individual thought and expression. That danger is especially real in the University setting, where the State acts against a background and tradition of thought and experiment

---

25 508 U.S. 384, 387, 394 (1993).

26 533 U.S. 98, 112–14 (2001).

27 515 U.S. 819 (1995).

> that is at the center of our intellectual and philosophic tradition. ... For the University, by regulation, to cast disapproval on particular viewpoints of its students risks the suppression of free speech and creative inquiry in one of the vital centers for the nation's intellectual life, its college and university campuses.[28]

New Limits on Equal-Access Rights for Religion

In its most recent cases, however, the Court made clear that this equal-access logic has limits in public schools and public university campuses alike. In *Morse v. Frederick* (2007), for example, the Court repeated its early 1980 s cases that said that "the constitutional rights of students in public school are not automatically coextensive with the rights of adults in other settings" and that the rights of public school students "must be applied in light of the special characteristics of the school environment."[29] In this case, a public high school in Alaska allowed students to watch the Olympic Torch Relay as it passed in front of the school. The event was televised and well attended. As the torchbearers came by, a group of students, led by Frederick, unfurled a fourteen-foot banner that read in large letters: "Bong Hits 4 Jesus." The principal confiscated the banner and suspended Frederick for promoting drug use in violation of school policy. Frederick sued, arguing that the school had violated his free speech rights and engaged in viewpoint discrimination against his offensive speech.

The *Morse* Court held for the school. The banner was perhaps a silly adolescent effort to gain attention and a spot on the evening news, Chief Justice John Roberts wrote for the Court. But the banner could not be reasonably read as anything but a pro-drug message–in direct violation of this school's clear, consistent, and "compelling" policy of deterring drug use by school children. School officials may suppress and sanction speech that will "materially and substantially disrupt the discipline of the school." Indeed, in an earlier case, the Court had allowed a public high school to sanction a student for using "lewd and indecent speech" at a school assembly, dismissing the student's free-speech claim. This case is of the same sort, the *Morse* Court concluded, notwithstanding the dissent's charge that the school had engaged in viewpoint discrimination against unpopular student speech with a religious reference.[30]

A few lower federal courts have used *Morse* to allow school officials to limit various forms of private religious expression in public schools, notably Christian

---

28 515 U.S. at 831–32, 836–37.

29 551 U.S. 393 (2007), quoting *Bethel School District No. 403 v. Fraser*, 478 U.S. 675, 682 (1986) and *Tinker v. Des Moines Independent Community School District*, 393 U.S. 503, 506 (1982).

30 551 U.S. 393, 394 (2007) (referring to *Tinker* as the earlier case).

messages, for fear of hostile reactions or eroding school policies.[31] It is easy to imagine how *Morse* could be used by a hostile or fearful public school official to prohibit the meetings or expressions of a religious student group–say, of devout Muslims, Jews, Catholics, evangelicals, or atheists–whose unpopular views are judged to "materially and substantially disrupt" the discipline or teaching of the school.

This scenario is what some observers have read into the Court's most recent case on point, *Christian Legal Society v. Martinez* (2010). This case involved Hastings College of Law, a state law school in California. The college officially recognizes all voluntary student groups through a formal registered student organization (RSO) program. Officially recognized student groups receive access to school funds and certain facilities and communication channels that are foreclosed to nonregistered groups. To qualify for RSO recognition, however, a group must comply with the school's nondiscrimination policy, based on state civil-rights laws, which bars discrimination on the basis of religion and sexual orientation, among other grounds. A group of law students sought to form a chapter of the Christian Legal Society (CLS) at the law school. Like all CLS groups in the country, this group required its members to sign a statement of faith and to live in accordance with prescribed principles; the group excluded anyone with religious beliefs contrary to the statement of faith and anyone who engaged in "unrepentant homosexual conduct." Hastings regarded this CLS policy as discrimination based on religion and sexual orientation and thus denied the group's application for official RSO status. CLS filed suit, claiming violations of their rights to free speech, expressive association, and the free exercise of religion.[32]

A 5–4 *Martinez* Court, led by Justice Ruth Bader Ginsburg, held for Hastings. The Court combined the CLS's claims to free speech and free association into one and subjected them to "a less restrictive limited-public-forum analysis" than the stricter scrutiny regime of *Widmar* and its progeny. Here, the Court said, the law school was only "dangling the carrot of subsidy, not wielding the stick of prohibition." Unlike the *Widmar* students, the CLS students could certainly meet on the Hastings campus and could use the school's chalk boards and bulletin boards, as well as their own social media to communicate. Unlike the *Rosenberger* students,

31 See, for example, *Jacobs v. Clark County School District*, 526 F.3d 419 (9th Cir. 2008) (upholding school dress code as a neutral and generally applicable law whose breach by religious apparel raised security and fairness concerns); *Corder v. Lewis Palmer School District*, 566 F.3d 1219 (10th Cir. 2009) (upheld school's disciplining one of fifteen valedictorians whose thirty-second speech included brief endorsement of religion); *Busch v. Marple Newtown School District*, 567 F.3d 89 (3d Cir., 2009) (upholding school decision to ban mother from reading from Psalms during her child's show-and-tell, while allowing another mother to recite Jewish religious stories in the same setting).

32 561 U.S. 661 (2010).

the CLS students were not singled out for special prohibitions because of their Christian perspective. They were denied RSO status, and its attendant special funds and other benefits, simply because they violated Hastings's general nondiscrimination policy. It is "hard to imagine a more viewpoint-neutral policy than one requiring *all* student groups to accept *all* comers."[33]

Summary and Conclusions

America operates with a basic three-tiered system of education: (1) public elementary schools, high schools, and state universities and other institutions of higher learning; (2) private (religious) lower schools, colleges, and universities; and (3) various forms of home schools. Cutting across these three tiers, a few states and cities have experimented with charter schools, magnet schools, and community schools that combine public and private funding and staffing to offer innovative forms of lower education. Some states offer vouchers and tax relief to enhance educational choice for parents and students in primary and secondary schools. Federal and state scholarship and loan programs are available to public and private university students.[34] But the three-tiered structure of American education has been largely constitutionally and culturally stable for the past two generations. The vast majority of government funds for education go to public schools and universities, and the vast majority of American students attend these public schools, even though students in private lower schools and some home schools do demonstrably better on various measures of academic performance and social well-being.

Before the twentieth century, individual states largely governed American schooling, taking a wide range of approaches to the place of religion in public schools and the role of government in religious schools. For the past century, however, the U.S. Supreme Court has been actively involved in shaping American education, devoting nearly a third of its First Amendment religious-freedom cases to issues of religion and education. These cases have not always followed clean logical lines, but one holding has been consistent: religious teachers, prayers, texts, and symbols are not permitted in the public-school classroom and curriculum, or even at one-time public-school events like graduation ceremonies. Voluntary private religious expressions and associations may be allowed when there are equivalent voluntary private secular counterparts, and so long as no faculty participate.

33 561 U.S. at 683, 692, 697.

34 See overview of current options in Stephen D. Sugarman, "Is It Unconstitutional to Prohibit Faith-Based Schools from Becoming Charter Schools," *Journal of Law and Religion* 32 (2017): 227–62.

But even then, schools may place limits on these religious activities to protect other students from religious harm or coercion.

This deprecation of religion in public school education has impoverished the moral values education and character formation of American students, and it has stunted some of the very democratic values and abilities that the country and Court are trying to instill and protect in each new generation. It has deprived students of their ability to develop healthy democratic habits of understanding and engaging a variety of forms of religious experience. It has fostered the false idea that religion and faith are only for the private and voluntary sphere, while value-free reason and morally neutral logic are the only valuable currency of public debate and political life. It has helped instill in students the secularist hypothesis that the spread of reason and science will slowly eclipse the sense of the sacred and restore the sensibilities of the superstitious.

The reality, however, is that religion–in both sectarian and secular forms–is a powerful and perennial force in society. Indeed, over the past three decades, another great awakening of religion has dawned–now global in its sweep, vast in its diversity, and sometimes frightening in its power. Even if North America and Western Europe now feature more "Nones" and "Neins" on organized religion than ever before, the Global Middle and Global South have seen powerful new upsurges of old and new religions. Globalized media, migration, marketing, and mission work have brought these religions, and their special needs and challenges, to the North and West, too. From kindergarten to graduate school, American students need to witness and study religions and the moral and value systems that they offer, for better or worse.

Not only democratic theory but the Court's own equality jurisprudence would seem to dictate this result. A democracy should represent, in its core institutions–including public schools–all beliefs and values, religious and secular alike. The logic of equal treatment should help decide not only which voluntary private groups may have access to public forums and funds, but also which subjects and activities should be allowed in the public-school classroom in the first place. To exclude religion and its attendant institutions and values from the classroom is not only to engage in bald viewpoint discrimination against religion, but also to defy the elementary demands of representative democracy. It is not only to undermine the classical religious foundations of morality and values, but also to also to enable secular prejudices and preferences to triumph under the guise of neutrality. Churches and states, schools and universities, students and teachers alike deserve better.

Stabilizing Continuity and Transforming Spirituality: Germany's Democratization after 1945 as an Example of the Impact of Education on Character Formation, the Communication of Values, and the Breakdown of Totalitarianism

Heike Springhart

Character formation and the communication of values are highly important for democratic and pluralistic societies. They are particularly challenging goals during times of transformation, such as during the ongoing process of shaping a pluralistic society not driven by various forms of populism after 1989–or 1945–in Germany. In these processes of transformation, education occurs in broad ways. It happens in families, schools, universities, churches, and through media, and it shapes the processes of character formation and the communication of values.

In postwar Germany, especially in the early years after 1945, education was considered the pathway to democracy. Democratization was "reeducation"–a program and process planned and driven after 1945 by the occupying American powers in Western Germany. Education in this context was much more than pedagogy, more than what was taught in schools, homes, or churches. Education was to be a process that would help shape people's maturity; education aimed at character formation.

This chapter presents aspects of Germany's democratization after 1945 as examples of the impact of education on character formation, the communication of values, and the overcoming of totalitarianism. In so doing, I am not primarily pursuing a historical interest, but offering a paradigmatic constellation that can help highlight the role of education in supporting character formation and the communication of values in a broader sense.

In research and publications on the American politics of democratization in postwar Germany, we see different approaches to an understanding of the impact of education on character formation, ethics, and the communication of values. At the time, just after the war, contemporary reports about American democratization politics, especially by those who themselves were protagonists of such politics, held the view that democracy had been imposed upon the Germans from outside–and was therefore doomed to failure.[1] Contrary to this estimation, papers from the 1960 s held the view that Germany turned toward democracy without any influence from the occupying powers.[2]

Since the 1990 s, thanks to research by the Munich Institute for Contemporary History (IfZ, *Institut für Zeitgeschichte*), it has become clear that "reeducation" was a central term used in American-German interactions and planning for the development of a democratic Germany after 1945.[3]

The first wave of publications that researched reeducation came in the 1970 s, when most of the United States Office of Military Government (OMGUS) documents were transferred to microfilm. Most of these works considered reeducation to be a process of education and training. Therefore, they focused their survey on the pedagogic sector.[4] Karl-Heinz Füssl draws a line from pedagogic considerations to the significance of the church in American reeducation politics. But he holds the view that it had not been possible to effect a real "restart" in connection with the churches.[5]

Sociological works in the 1990 s, especially those by the Heidelberg sociologist Uta Gerhardt, presented the reductionist view of reeducation as a mere pedagogic program; they focus on the dynamics of the transformation process charac-

---

1 Marshall M. Knappen, *And Call It Peace* (Chicago: University of Chicago Press, 1947); Harold Zink, *American Military Government in Germany* (New York: Macmillan, 1947); John D. Montgomery, *Forced to Be Free: The Artificial Revolution in Germany and Japan* (Chicago: University of Chicago Press, 1957); later also Richard L. Merritt, *Democracy Imposed: U.S. Occupation Policy and German Public 1945–1949* (New Haven: Yale University Press, 1995).

2 Ralf Dahrendorf, *Gesellschaft und Demokratie in Deutschland* (Munich: Piper, 1965).

3 Klaus-Dietmar Henke, *Die amerikanische Besetzung Deutschlands* (Munich: Oldenbourg, 1995); Christoph Weisz, ed., *OMGUS-Handbuch: Die amerikanische Militärregierung in Deutschland 1945–1949* (Munich: Oldenbourg, 1994); Beate Rosenzweig, *Erziehung zur Demokratie? Amerikanische Besatzungs- und Schulreformpolitik in Deutschland und Japan* (Stuttgart: Steiner, 1998); Felicitas Hentschke, *Demokratisierung als Ziel der amerikanischen Besatzungspolitik in Deutschland und Japan 1943–1947* (Münster: Lit, 2001).

4 Karl-Ernst Bungenstab, *Umerziehung zur Demokratie? Re-education-Politik im Bildungswesen der US-Zone 1945–1949* (Düsseldorf: Bertelsmann, 1970); Jutta Lange-Quassowski, *Neuordnung oder Restauration? Das Demokratiekonzept der amerikanischen Besatzungsmacht und die politische Sozialisation der Westdeutschen: Wirtschaftsordnung, Schulstruktur, Politische Bildung* (Opladen: Leske und Budrich, 1979); James F. Tent, *Mission on the Rhine: Reeducation and Denazification in American-Occupied Germany* (Chicago: University of Chicago Press, 1982); Birgit Braun, *Umerziehung in der amerikanischen Besatzungszone: Die Schul- und Bildungspolitik in Württemberg-Baden von 1945–1949* (Münster: Lit, 2003).

5 Karl-Heinz Füssl, *Die Umerziehung der Deutschen: Jugend und Schule unter den Siegermächten des Zweiten Weltkriegs 1945–1955* (Paderborn: Schöningh, 1994).

terized by reeducation and democratization. By analyzing the works of Harvard sociologist Talcott Parsons, Gerhardt came to an understanding of the post-1945 change as "controlled institutional change." She also analyzed psychiatric conceptions developed by Richard Brickner, who held that democratization in post-National Socialist Germany could happen by empowering the so-called clear areas of society–those social spheres that were not fully destroyed by National Socialism but remained "healthy" in the sense that democracy could flourish in them. Gerhardt's work offers an explanatory model that can help us deal with the question of religion and its role in reeducation.[6]

The survey of research to date in the field of reeducation and religion shows that the dynamics of the transformative process and of the impulses expected (and hoped for) from religion and the churches has been largely overlooked. Through an analysis and clarification of the spiritual and social changes after 1945, it is possible to reevaluate the significance that religion and the churches had in this process, to examine the potential which they were able to introduce into that process, and to analyze the specific notion of education in use.

Viewing the discourse of historical and sociological research from a systematic theological perspective widens the image of the church presented by current research. There are at least four perspectives and images of the church that can be observed in relation to our question. First, in terms of occupation politics, the church was considered by the military government to be a substitute for political institutions. Priests and pastors, for example, were often prioritized over mayors as the first persons of contact for military personnel.[7] Second, with respect to both the challenging postwar necessities and a reorientation of the church on the basis of its experiences with and in National Socialism, the image of the church as an *ecclesia reformanda* regained a high degree of relevance. Third, from a sociological perspective, the church was seen as an integral part of society, not existing opposite to society but within it. In other words: the church is part of the world, living out and toward God's revelation. Finally, one of the main goals of reeducation was to implement methods of free discourse. This aimed at shaping a climate of tolerance, enabling people to understand heterogeneity and pluralism as opportunities rather than threats. In this respect, the church was considered, fourth,

---

6 Uta Gerhardt, *Talcott Parsons on National Socialism* (New York: Aldine de Gruyter, 1993); Uta Gerhardt, "A Hidden Agenda of Recovery: The Psychiatric Conceptualization of Reeducation for Germany in the United States during World War II," *German History* 14, no. 3 (1996): 297–324.

7 See Beryl McClaskey, "The History of U.S. Policy and Program in the Field of Religious Affairs under the Office of the U.S. High Commissioner for Germany," Research Project No. 104, Historical Division, Office of the Executive Secretary Office of the U.S. High Commissioner for Germany (Feb. 1951), 16.

a space where one could communicate theological convictions and struggle with questions of truth and certainty.[8]

It is important to keep in mind that the term "reeducation" describes the process of democratization in total, and it leads us to a broader understanding of education when it comes to character formation.

In 1945, after the end of World War II, rapid and far-reaching changes occurred in Germany's churches as well as society. These changes were initiated by the reeducation program, promoted especially by the occupying American powers. A transformative process aimed at democracy began, and religion and the churches were expected to play a significant role in this democratization process. The process was fueled by the hope that religion and education would have an impact on character formation, ethics, and the communication of values in postwar Germany. This post-1945 process of democratization in Germany was largely experimental. The situation consisted of a complex conglomerate of trends and interdependencies, the dynamics of which were insightful, especially regarding the significance of religion in the role of social transformation.

In the early postwar period, reeducation was seen not only as a pedagogical program aimed at education but as an important part of the democratization process itself.[9] The concept of reeducation was based on the metaphor of a psychiatric therapy used to treat postwar Germany's illness. In the context of the mental health movement of the 1930 s, a method was developed that had its origins in a therapist-patient pact which sought to empower the healthy parts of the patient's personality. In 1943, the work of Richard Brickner titled "Is Germany Incurable?" made a connection between this new therapeutic method and the question of the treatment of Germany after the psychosis of National Socialism.[10] Crucially, Brickner compared German *social* structures with the paranoid structures of a person–rather than suggesting that every German person had a paranoid personality.[11]

---

8 The exploration is geographically limited to the north of Wuerttemberg-Baden, which was occupied by American forces. The main sources are documents from the Office of Military Government for Germany (OMGUS), especially record groups 260 (OMGUS/OMGWB), 226 (Office of Strategic Services, OSS), and 59 (State Department), housed at the U.S. National Archives, College Park, Maryland (hereafter, NA).

9 Tent, *Mission*, 5; Uta Gerhardt, "Das Reeducation-Programm der USA," in *"Gegen alle Vergeblichkeit". Jüdischer Widerstand gegen den Nationalsozialismus*, ed. Hans Erler (Frankfurt am Main: Campus-Verlag, 2003), 407.

10 Richard Brickner, "Is Germany Incurable?," *The Journal of Nervous and Mental Disease* 98 (1943): 680–82; see also Richard Brickner, "Germany after the War: Round Table 1945," *American Journal of Orthopsychiatry* 15 (1945): 381–441.

11 See Richard Brickner, "The German Cultural Paranoid Trend," *American Journal of Orthopsychiatry* 12 (1942): 611–32.

Within the socioscientific debates initiated and shaped by Brickner's proposals, the idea of clear areas as possible points of contact for democracy became a central pattern for Germany's postwar "treatment." Hence, the notion of reeducation became important, and aimed at transforming the basic patterns of behavior and conviction among Germany's people. Religion and the churches were thought to be centrally important to this process.

The Planning and Structure of Reeducation

The planning process began in the early 1940 s, and theological, sociological, and sociopsychiatric perspectives helped shape conceptual considerations. This was especially evident within the community of German émigrés to the United States, who raised the question of the existence of "the other Germany."[12] Paul Tillich, systematic theologian and immigrant from Frankfurt am Main to New York, became well known in these circles through his passionate discussions with Jewish author Emil Ludwig on this very question.[13] From March 31, 1942, to May 9, 1944, Tillich was the host of weekly radio broadcasts addressed to "my German friends."[14] These were broadcast by the Voice of America (VOA) network, which was the German service of the Office of War Information (OWI). In his broadcasts, Tillich had a twofold intention. The first was to support and inform his "German friends"–that is, the groups in Germany opposed to the Nazis. Second, as I wish to argue, Tillich's broadcasts had a performative character. In broadcasting and addressing his speeches to that "other Germany," he demonstrated to his American dialogue partners that oppositional circles did indeed exist. Of special interest is the fact that Tillich was chairman of the Council for a Democratic Germany.[15]

---

12 See Claus-Dieter Krohn, "'Let Us Be Prepared to Win the Peace: Nachkriegsplanungen emigrierter deutscher Sozialwissenschaftler an der New School for Social Research in New York," in *Deutschland nach Hitler. Zukunftspläne im Exil und aus der Besatzungszeit 1939*–1949, ed. Thomas Koebner (Opladen: Westdeutscher Verlag, 1987), 123–35, 123; Friedrich Baerwald, "Zur politischen Tätigkeit deutscher Emigranten im Council for a Democratic Germany," *Vierteljahreshefte für Zeitgeschichte* 28 (1980): 372–80.

13 See Paul Tillich, "Es geht um die Methode: Antwort Paul Tillichs an die Kritiker im 'Aufbau,'" in Paul Tillich, *Impressionen und Reflexionen: Ein Lebensbild in Aufsätzen, Reden und Stellungnahmen* (Stuttgart: Evangelisches Verlags-Werk, 1972), 281.

14 They are collected and published: Paul Tillich, *An meine deutschen Freunde: Die politischen Reden Paul Tillichs während des Zweiten Weltkriegs über die 'Stimme Amerikas'* (Stuttgart: Evangelisches Verlags-Werk 1973).

15 See Heike Springhart, *Aufbrüche zu neuen Ufern: Der Beitrag von Religion und Kirche für Demokratisierung und Reeducation im Westen Deutschlands nach 1945* (Leipzig: Evangeli-

It was the sociopsychiatric approach of Richard Brickner that brought the pattern of empowering and encouraging clear areas into the debate. This pattern essentially characterized the reeducation process.[16] Harvard sociologist Talcott Parsons considered controlled institutional change to be a means of social change. In the 1930 s, he analyzed the phenomenon of National Socialism from a sociological perspective in an effort to comprehend it–and to discover ways to overcome it. Three aspects of his analyses are relevant with regard to his suggestions for reeducation. First, Parsons considered the fundamental danger of National Socialism to be that it attacked the free institutions of a democratic society, especially academic liberty, liberal learning, and the Christian churches and their universalistic religion.[17] Second, Parsons considered it essential in a free society that a form of religion be present–a religion that shaped society and served as a critical counterpart. The third aspect addressed the challenges of rapid change that followed the age of industrialization. This period of rapid transformation was seen to have a destabilizing effect, offering fertile ground for the growth of authoritarian systems that communicated certainty by favoring structures of particularity.

In order to overcome National Socialism, Parsons suggested the need for controlled institutional change. He considered social institutions to be of central significance for the development of mentalities. As a consequence, a change and transformation of mentalities and character formation could be reached through controlled institutional change. Three approaches were thought to shape this change. *Regressive control* should avert a relapse into barbarism by punishment of war criminals and by the reinvention of the separation of powers. *Direct control* worked through the prohibition of National Socialist institutions and ideology in order to achieve democracy. In terms of religion, the third form of control was the most important: *permissive control.* It consisted of future-oriented, innovative politics that specifically promoted those social areas and institutions that could be considered clear areas in the sense of Brickner's definitions. In his differentiated approach to the functions of religion within the social system, Parsons considered religion to be a stabilizing factor. From a sociological point of view, religion was thought to play a significant role, particularly in tempering the alienating phases of social transformation.

---

sche Verlagsanstalt, 2008), 37–66; Petra Liebner, *Paul Tillich und der Council for a Democratic Germany (1933–1945)* (Frankfurt am Main: Lang, 2001).

16 See Uta Gerhardt, "Re-Education als Demokratisierung der Gesellschaft Deutschlands durch das amerikanische Besatzungsregime: Ein historischer Bericht," *Leviathan* 3 (2000): 355–85, 367 f.

17 Talcott Parsons, "Nazis Destroy Learning, Challenging Religion," in Gerhardt, *Talcott Parsons on National Socialism*, 81–83, 82. See also Uta Gerhardt, *Soziologie der Stunde Null: Zur Gesellschaftskonzeption des amerikanischen Besatzungsregimes in Deutschland 1944–1945/1946* (Frankfurt am Main: Suhrkamp, 2005).

Besides these conceptual considerations in socioscientific discourses, there was also an institutional and personal framework for reeducation. Political planning in the 1940 s entailed strategic and organizational plans. Centers were established to train occupying officers. On May 11, 1942, the School of Military Government at the University of Virginia was opened with the goal of training officers for military government and civil affairs service with the American armed forces in occupied territories abroad. The question of the possibility of soldiers taking over civilian tasks was broadly discussed.[18]

During the occupation phase, a special branch for Education and Religious Affairs (ERA) existed within the OMGUS in Germany.[19] The goals of that branch, and of reeducation in general, consisted of promoting freedom of religion, preventing National Socialism and militarism, and cooperating with the churches.[20] In its work, the ERA was based on a grassroots approach, starting with Brickner's clear areas. The underlying basic conviction consisted of the idea of democracy as a way of life rather than a government system. Democracy was regarded as the spirit of humanity–an almost civil-religious notion.[21]

The activities of the ERA were mostly focused on democratizing society by democratizing the structures of the church. These ERA activities were complemented by outside incentives, such as consultation programs with American experts, exchange programs to the United States for students and teachers, supplying curricula and teaching materials through textbook and teaching centers, the reintegration of the German churches into international organizations, and the establishment of interdenominational cooperation as a means of overcoming National Socialist isolation.

One of the main roles of the church, in the eyes of the occupying power, was to be a source of moral and spiritual guidance.[22] The church was expected to give ethical and moral orientation in order to help shape and stabilize society across

---

18 Hajo Holborn, *American Military Government: Its Organization and Policies* (Washington: Infantry Journal Press, 1947); "Die Ausbildung der amerikanischen Offiziere für die Militärregierungen nach 1945," in *Jahrbuch für Amerikastudien* 18 (1973), ed. Walther Fischer (Heidelberg: Winter 1973), 195–212.

19 See German Basic Handbook, NA, RG 260 OMGUS/OMGWB, Box 1298 (12/229-3/3).

20 See General Archive of the County of Baden-Wuerttemberg, Karlsruhe/Germany (Generallandesarchiv, hereafter GLA), RG 260 OMGUS, 12/93-2/91, General Policies for Religious Affairs, Functional Program. Section B.

21 Memorandum "Der gegenwärtige Stand der Erziehung in Deutschland," Archive of the Wuerttemberg Regional Church Stuttgart/Germany (Archiv der Evangelischen Landeskirche Württemberg, hereafter Wü), NL Wurm, D 1/205, 20 (NL is the abbreviation for *Nachlass* [estate]).

22 McClaskey, *History*, 17.

its different subsystems. There was the hope that church and religion would have a positive impact on democracy and on the communication of values in society.

The Americans considered it of central significance to differentiate between clerical and secular functions of the church.[23] To avoid violating the principle of separation of church and state, for example, the consulting work of experts from the United States was limited to the secular functions of the church, such as administration, questions concerning the church as an institution, and the pedagogical work of the church in schools and in youth work. In the realm of clerical functions, the churches were free and independent with regard to liturgy, confession, and theology. The best way to illustrate the process of social transformation after 1945 is to investigate the concrete actions of that time.

Reeducation and Democratization in Various Church Areas

A very important area of church work was schooling and youth work. Here reeducation was considered to be a process of education and training.[24] New methods, oriented toward free discourse, aimed at encouraging an individual sense of responsibility. A further goal in youth work and schools was to impart values that could instill certainty and provide ethical, cultural, and religious orientation. In the area of youth work, new structures were implemented which were oriented toward heterogeneity, pluralism, and differentiation–and toward empowering an individual sense of responsibility. In public schools, every child was to have the same right to education and training. The ERA officers held the view that a future German society required people who had strict morals and who lived a kind of "practical Christianity."[25] Hence, the church was responsible for the ecclesiastical fields of education and schools. A general principle of the work of the ERA was the so-called indirect rule.[26] As a consequence, teachers and pastors were trained in new education methods in order to serve as purveyors of democratic methods and spirit. An essential part of the ERA's activities in schools was the school food programs.

Similar goals can be observed in adult education institutions, especially the Protestant academies. The Protestant academies, which still exist today, are educational institutions separate from the universities. In these institutions, interest-

23 GLA, RG 260 OMGUS, 12/93-2/78, Memorandum Concerning Clarification of Status of Dr. Bodensieck and Bishop Muench.

24 General considerations can be found in Wü, NL Wurm, D1/205, Der gegenwärtige Stand der Erziehung in Deutschland, 42.

25 NA, RG 260 OMGUS/ OMGWB, Box 881, Folder 208.2 (12/86-1/24), John P. Steiner.

26 Handbook for Military Government in Germany (Dec. 1944), chap. 3, 74.

ed adults of different professions gather to discuss theological issues and ask questions concerning their role as Christians in their particular professions.[27] Since 1945, the work and role of the Protestant academies in German society have been considered a paradigm for the significance of religion in society. After their foundation in 1945, the basic concept of the Protestant academies was to provide the freedom for spiritual discussions within the different professional guilds, such as teachers, physicians, and lawyers.[28] Particularly through the work of the academies, the church became aware of its role as a space where democracy and democratic behavior could be studied and learned. The academies were places where the transformation process could be critiqued, and where students were trained to take individual responsibility in shaping this young democracy through discussions and debate. The Protestant academies–supported by financial and organizational aid from the United States–thus became geographically identifiable as sources of moral and spiritual support. Hence, the Protestant academies nurtured an increasing sense of public responsibility on the part of the church.

In addition to the educational institutions, other fields of ecclesiastical work were considered highly significant in society's democratic transformation. Ecclesiastical women's work was especially significant. As most of society's men were absent, being abroad as prisoners of war or having lost their lives on the battlefront,[29] women had to take over responsibilities not only in daily life at home but also in political life. Special courses provided leadership skills for responsible women.[30] It was intended that this new, democratic way of life would slowly clarify the different roles of men and women in private and public life and raise for discussion how these roles were to be justified or challenged.[31]

---

27 See Josef Olbrich, *Geschichte der Erwachsenenbildung in Deutschland* (Opladen: Leske und Budrich, 2001).

28 The descriptions and plans of the Protestant academies show similarities to the work of the National Christian Mission 1936/37 in the United States. There, the gathering of people for evangelization was also oriented to their professions. See Adolf Keller, *Amerikanisches Christentum–Heute* (Zollikon-Zürich: Evangelischer Verlag, 1943), 238; see also Rulf Jürgen Treidel, *Evangelische Akademien im Nachkriegsdeutschland: Gesellschaftspolitisches Engagement in kirchlicher Öffentlichkeitsverantwortung* (Stuttgart: Kohlhammer, 2001).

29 Institute for Contemporary History, Munich, Germany (Institut für Zeitgeschichte, herafter IfZ), RG 260 OMGUS, 5/341-1/11-12, 4/4, Article: Women's Organizations and Social Action, 1.

30 GLA, RG 260 OMGUS, 12/93-2/81, Interdivisional Reorientation Committee Form for Reporting Cultural Exchange Projects for 1950, Project No. 22 (Evangelical).

31 Wü, NL Wurm, D1/205, Der gegenwärtige Stand der Erziehung in Deutschland, 20.

The thinking was that the principle that all human beings are created equal could be adopted successfully in German society only if this conviction was also applied to the dynamics of the family unit. Of central importance for a successful democracy was the ability of individuals, especially women, to take on responsibility. This was new for German society, as up until 1945 the work of women was primarily focused on their private households. To empower them for public responsibility was a revolutionary change.[32]

Another field of high importance for reeducation politics was the diaconal work of Protestant relief organizations (*Evangelisches Hilfswerk*).[33] The success of democratization and reeducation was thought to depend on whether the daily necessities of life were satisfied. A central principle was that it is possible to win people over to new ideas and convictions only if they are given responsibility, instead of simply being recipients of material, spiritual, or educational help. For this reason, the German churches, especially their relief organizations, were given the task of distributing relief packages (such as CARE packages) to the populace.[34] At least two effects were thus reached: people were motivated to access the services provided by the church, and thus they made contact with the church to get help for their daily needs. The concept behind the CARE organization was that international and interpersonal relationships were the basis upon which to build reconciliation. Reeducation was an idea conceived by the occupying powers after the war, yet they considered it centrally important for the people not to know this. This hidden agenda was achieved by allowing German institutions to distribute the relief packages. Although the material goods came from abroad, relief was supposedly a project of self-help. Furthermore, one of the goals of reeducation was to ensure that the churches regained their public reputation and sense of public responsibility.[35]

The churches were expected to communicate their moral and spiritual values through the democratization process. Hence, broadcasting and print media were to become new fields of action for the church. The communication of religious values as basic principles of a successful and stable democracy had to be managed

---

32 See Marianne Zepp, *Redefining Germany: Reeducation, Staatsbürgerschaft und Frauenpolitik im US-amerikanisch besetzten Nachkriegsdeutschland* (Göttingen: Vandenhoeck & Ruprecht, 2007).

33 See Herbert Krimm, *Beistand: Die Tätigkeit des Hilfswerks der Evangelischen Kirchen in Deutschland für Vertriebene und Flüchtlinge nach 1945* (Stuttgart: Evangelisches Verlagswerk, 1974).

34 Springhart, *Aufbrüche*, 218.

35 See Godehard Weyerer, "Liebesgaben aus Übersee: Die CARE-Pakete," in *Die USA und Deutschland im Zeitalter des Kalten Krieges 1945–1990,* Vol. 1, *1945–1968,* ed. Detlef Junker (Munich: Deutsche Verlagsanstalt, 2001), 795–802, 798.

more effectively by a professional use of mass media.[36] To cope with this challenge, representatives of German churches were invited to take part in training programs. Ecclesiastical news agencies were initiated to guarantee that information would be independent from state agencies and to make it possible for the voice of the church to be heard in the secular media in a competent and informed way. The church as a clear area was not expected to stay protected in a hermetically sealed space away from public access. Due to the consequences of the war, many people were simply not able to reach a church, as there was no public transportation, and many church buildings had been destroyed by bombing.[37]

Instead, special attention was paid to the institutional points of contact between church and state that were considered important in the democratizing process. In the opinion of the American occupation authorities, the church's positive effect on a democracy could be fostered by entanglements—such as the state collecting taxes for the church, which is still the case in Germany today.[38] Religious education at school was also considered to be such a democracy-promoting entanglement.

In addition to democratizing factors from within Germany, incentives from abroad also supported democratization. Yet it is important to keep in mind that the guiding principle of these outside incentives was that successful democratization could be achieved only from within German society.

Special consultation programs by American experts supported the different areas of ecclesiastical and pedagogical work. Visiting experts from the United States came to Germany to discuss the new challenges,[39] and so-called liaison representatives from American denominations visited the German churches to discuss challenges and give support.[40] The hope was that through contact with the-

---

36 Wü, NL Wurm, D1/272, W. A. Maier, Bericht und Anregungen über Religiöse Rundfunkübertragungen in Deutschland (Amerikanische Zone), Oct. 14, 1947.

37 Allied Forces Supreme Headquarters, G-5 Division, Military Government Germany, "Technical Manual for Education and Religious Affairs," chap. 11, "The Religious Press"; see also Wolf-Dietrich Nahr, *Die befohlene Pressefreiheit* (Berlin: Wissenschaftlicher Verlag Spiess, 1981).

38 GLA, RG 260 OMGUS, 12/93-2/91, Report of the US Occupation of Germany, Religious Affairs Program, Sept. 23, 1947, 5: "The question of whether or not the traditional pattern of church-state-relations should continue to prevail in the future is a matter which has been left for the German people themselves to decide. US Military Government authorities have not considered it advisable to impose American ideas regarding separation of church and state upon the people of the US zone."

39 GLA, RG 260 OMGUS, 3/407-2/12, Quarterly Report, Jan.–Mar. 1947, Education & Religious Affairs Division, OMGWB, 3.

40 NA, RG 260 OMGUS/OMGWB, Box 942, Folder: Church-Liaison Representatives, (12/93-2/78). See also: Hermann-Josef Rupieper, *Die Wurzeln der westdeutschen Nachkriegs-*

ologians and church representatives from abroad, the German churches would have the opportunity to dialogue and to widen their perspectives.[41]

The Significance of Religion for Democratization: Conceptual Aspects

Historically, American planning institutions considered the churches as places of resistance against National Socialism. American occupation authorities knew of the churches' resistance to National Socialism between 1933 and 1945 and knew that they showed particular strength in the struggle against the Nazis.[42] Resistance against National Socialism was seen as having grown out of ecclesiastical roots; thus, the church became a recognizable place of resistance.[43] This was the main reason why the church was considered to be a clear area from Brickner's perspective.

Yet from a historical perspective, this interpretation that the churches (and especially the Protestant church) were places of resistance against National Socialism was not strictly correct. The American view was too optimistic. A close look at documents from the Office of Strategic Services (OSS) does reveal a more differentiated assessment of the failure of the church, either because the conflict between National Socialism and the church was not clearly evident or because it was (mis)interpreted as an interchurch conflict. Nonetheless, representatives of resistance groups expected the church to be a force in society that would eradicate

---

demokratie: Der amerikanische Beitrag 1945–1952 (Opladen: Westdeutscher Verlag, 1993), 353.

41 Henry J. Kellermann, *Cultural Relations as an Instrument of U.S. Foreign Policy: The Educational Exchange Program between the United States and Germany, 1945–1954*, Cultural Relations Programs of the U.S. Department of State, Historical Studies No. 3, (Washington, DC: Bureau of Educational and Cultural Affairs, U.S. Department of State, 1978), 109.
It was considered significant for the democratization process to overcome Germany's isolation by reintegrating the German churches into international organizations—for example, the World Council of Churches—and by fostering interconfessional cooperation. See Long-Range Policy Statement for German Re-education (05.06.1946), in *Germany 1947–1949, The Story in Documents* (Washington, DC: U.S. Govt. Printing Office, 1950), 542: "The Nazi heritage of Germany's spiritual isolation must be overcome by restoring as rapidly as possible those cultural contacts which will foster the assimilation of the German people into the society of peaceful nations."

42 See, for example, Franklin Hamlin Littell, *The German Phoenix: Men and Movements in the Church in Germany* (New York: Doubleday, 1960), 4.

43 Wü, NL Wurm, D1/208, E. E. Turner, Ein Abschiedswort an meine Freunde in der Bekennenden Kirche, Dec. 20, 1945.

Nazism from hearts and heads. Even though this was not the historical function of churches per se, the view still existed that there was a kind of spiritual substance within the church that enhanced resistant behavior. Religion was considered a critical force that could oppose state and society. The church's significance for the transformation process lay in that critical power. Religion and churches were considered areas that focus on the divine, which is radically differentiated from the world. At the same time, religion and churches were part of this world and were–following Karl Barth's theses in his Tambach speech–incorporated in God's activity within the movements of the world.[44]

There was also a political aspect to the planning institutions' interest in the church, which focused on the correlation between church and state. From a political and sociological perspective, the church was seen as an institution within the social system. In Talcott Parsons's theory, institutions are considered to be of central significance for transforming mentalities.[45] The individual person participates in different subsystems of society; consequently, transformation of the individual in one subsystem can lead to that individual helping to transform other subystems. Within this process, the political system is particularly significant. Religion was thought to be especially helpful in tempering the alienating process of transformation, offering specific proposals that could help answer the question of meaning. Religion could function as a strategy for coping with transformation.[46] Thus, religion played a twofold role within the democratization process. On one hand, religion was a system that both supported transformation and demanded it by widening peoples' perspectives, leading toward a special form of universalism that transcended national and ideological boundaries. On the other hand, religion had a stabilizing effect on the individual, offering comforting proposals of meaning within the tempest of social transformation. As a consequence, religion helped avoid those mechanisms that sought to escape processes of pluralization by pushing toward a tempting form of certainty offered by totalitarian concepts of unity.

Furthermore, there was an ecclesiological aspect to religion which formed its basis for reeducation. The military government had a special notion of the church, characterized by the differentiation between clerical and secular functions. In sociological terms, the church was characterized functionally, being described according to the functions that it fulfilled in and for society. The occupying powers considered the church to be the only social institution to survive National Social-

---

44 Karl Barth, "Der Christ in der Gesellschaft" (1919), in *Anfänge der Dialektischen Theologie*, vol. 1, 4th ed., ed. Jürgen Moltmann (Munich: Kaiser, 1977), 3–37.

45 Talcott Parsons, "The Problem of Controlled Institutional Change," in Gerhardt, *Talcott Parsons on National Socialism*, 291.

46 Frederic Spotts, *Kirchen und Politik in Deutschland* (Stuttgart: Deutsche Verlagsanstalt, 1976), 45.

ism. Based on the principle of the separation of church and state, the military government, especially the ERA branch, limited its cooperation and influence to the institutional aspects of the church and not the clerical functions, which were those areas related to the spiritual and religious functions of the church. Confessional questions, the ordination of pastors, sacraments, and preaching were independent from the military government.

In dealing with the question of the significance of religion in reeducation, one observes an illuminating tension between the ecclesiological concept and the general expectations regarding the possibilities of spiritual and moral reconstruction. The church was granted nearly unlimited freedom with regard to secular as well as clerical functions.[47] In order to adequately comprehend the significance of religion in reeducation, it is necessary to view these different functions as complementary. On one hand, the military government interacted with the church on the institutional or secular level. Yet, on the other hand, decisive democratizing impulses were expected to come from the clerical level.

These impulses are directly linked to education in ethics. In the light of ethics, it is clear that spirituality was a significant factor in the democratization process. The church was regarded as a source of moral and spiritual support.[48] The church was considered necessary for the success of democratization and, as an institution of continuity, served as a place of stability which could form the moral foundation of the developing democracy. Furthermore, the church was expected to represent and to communicate those spiritual and intellectual values that would help shape a democratic society. It can be said that the contribution of the church to the broad process of democratization called "reeducation" consisted of two pillars: "stabilizing continuity" on one hand, and "transforming spirituality" on the other.

Stabilizing continuity revolved around the quest for new and orienting answers to the meaning of life and around the longing for spiritual sustenance. It was expected that these issues would gain in importance after the collapse of the National Socialist regime. Values, based on the principles of Christian life and faith, were expected to help achieve social stability in the years after 1945. The

47 McClaskey, *History*, 17.

48 GLA, RG 260 OMGUS, 12/93-2/91, MGR, Revision of Title 8, Part 1. General. Section B. General Policies for Religious Affairs, Sept. 22, 1948, para. 8-110: "Religious institutions are recognized as a significant element in the social structure of Germany and shall be given commensurate consideration in the program of re-education and reorientation conducted for the building of a peaceful and democratic Germany. The values inherent in the moral and spiritual resources of the German people are recognized as essential to the realization of this program. The development of these resources will be stimulated and encouraged."

core notion was the need for "responsibility" in order to bring about a set of moral values.

Transforming spirituality was a matter of content. For example, it was considered a major advantage of the church's youth work that young people were able to identify with a matter that had a revolutionary ring to it. The church was seen as providing a challenge to the historical, cultural, and social reality, with its core message the radical challenge to the powers and forces of this world as viewed through the cross of Christ.

Religious pluralism was considered a challenge for the pluralism of democracy. In 1945, 96 percent of the German population belonged to either Catholic or Protestant churches. Yet a 1948 OMGUS document, titled "Basic Considerations,"[49] observed that religion was an ambiguous phenomenon in society, as it was both enriching as well as endangering. Being a moral and spiritual source, religion enriches the life of a society. However, as religion gives answers to questions of ultimate concern, religiocultural diversity can also endanger society. The Christian religion was considered to have the potential to shape pluralism, because it incorporated in itself the tension of unity and difference, which has its source in the triune God. The orientation on difference and plurality opens up spaces for shaping society, for promoting conversation, and for common truth seeking.

Thus, religion was seen as a means of coping with contingency in times of change. Following Parsons's analysis of the emergence of National Socialism, it was taken for granted that successful social transformation required a constructive exposure to the uncertainty and fear caused by rapid changes. By shaping transformation and offering an interpretation of transformation in Christian terms, the Christian religion helped bring about an attitude that could comprehend contingency not primarily as endangering, but as transforming challenges. Thus, religion could help people to cope with contingency.

As the process of reeducation aimed at transforming German society into a democracy, the relationship between Protestantism and democracy became highly important. This was evident in the learning process within the German church, which was paradigmatic for the learning process in society. However, there was no traditional connection between Protestantism and democracy in Germany. Therefore, the majority of Protestantism and Protestant theology before the war was oriented toward taking "orders" and was thus skeptical of democracy. But after 1945, every individual was able to participate in politics and influence every social subsystem. Thus, the Protestant religion gained a twofold role: it was constitutively related to the community and thus created a sense of solidarity and

49 GLA, RG 260 OMGUS, 12/93-2/91, Objectives Religious Affairs Branch (Jun. 25, 1948). Basic Considerations.

consciousness of responsibility;[50] and it was deeply rooted in the individual and strengthened the individual's position as a critically thinking and independently acting person.

Conclusion: The Impact of Education on Forming Democracy

It can be said that a stabilizing continuity (in the sense of a perpetuation of Christian traditions and values on one hand) and a transforming spirituality (in the sense of the Christian message revolving around critical and eschatological contexts on the other hand) were the two main points of importance regarding religion for reeducation and democratization in Germany after 1945.

Considering democracy today and the theological contributions that can be made to it, I suggest that "stabilizing continuity" and "transforming spirituality" are the two key points that proceed beyond the historical situation of postwar Germany. In dogmatic terms, that means that the church should not be considered primarily in opposition (and opposite) to culture and society, but as a part of culture. Both culture and the church are created out of the Word of God, and both are critiqued by the Word of God. Standing in the midst of culture and society, the church sustains the brunt of this critique, based on the message of the cross and based on the revelation of the self-endangerment of the world at the cross.

Furthermore, this critique is possible only because the church lives out of the power of the Resurrection and the realization of the victory over death in the Resurrection. Based on this deliverance, the church is sent into the world to shape society. In that sense, the church does have a function in society–without being functionalized.

If one considers religion to be a coping strategy during challenging phases for democracy, it has a transformational task by keeping and communicating the consciousness of a plurality that does not divide society. In other words, it promotes the ideal that individuals are different but still equal in dignity. Christian theology can offer concepts of universalism that stabilize continuity in the process of social transformation. However, it is important to differentiate between universalism and totalitarianism. Therefore, the second key point, which I call "transforming spirituality," is also important. It is based on the conviction that the foundations of church and society lie beyond both in God's creating power, and that this is God's story. It is a living story, and it becomes clear that the development of our societies is something that cannot be left apart from our theological thinking.

---

50 See Wolfgang Huber, "Protestantismus und Demokratie," in *Protestanten in der Demokratie. Positionen und Profile im Nachkriegsdeutschland*, ed. Wolfgang Huber (Munich: Kaiser, 1990), 11–36.

School Education in Australia: Building Character and Reforming the Nation

Jo-Anne Reid

> In Australia we are presented with a challenge to our nation, one that stems from history itself. The idea of Indigenous recognition seeks restoration in an exercise of reconciliation. But recognition walks a national fault line: history, race. These are things that can divide, yet cannot be ignored. Recognition itself challenges us to make good on the past, yet live free of its chains–to remember in order to forget. ... Recognition is the struggle for our moral conscience. It is also a test of how we are governed.[1]

I was in secondary school in 1967 when a national referendum granted Aboriginal people the right to be counted as Australian citizens. In my conservative working-class family, church, and state schooling, this was neither mentioned nor acknowledged. My ignorance was finally addressed, though not in the curriculum, when I entered university on a scholarship that would prepare me to later train as a secondary school teacher. For many of my peers gaining access to higher education at that time, reflection on the silences about this and other social injustices in our education fueled the rebellion of our generation–leading to student protests against the naturalized racial, gender, and class discrimination that surrounded us and was forming us as social subjects: fair and sun-freckled, emblematic Australians of exemplary "character." Thus "radicalized," we were committed to the value of education for social justice, and we entered the teaching profession determined to bring about change, and to educate our own students about social and political issues. But we were privileged–a "working-class elite" atypical among our schoolfellows, granted access to the rewards that would accrue to our upward social mobility in our famously "classless society": as the General Motors TV advertisement captured it, "football, meat pies, kangaroos, and Holden cars" are what identifies the *typical* Australian.

First among these is football. And when, in 2013, almost half a century after the referendum, a junior-high schoolgirl publicly shouted racial abuse at Adam Goodes, one of the all-time legends of Australian football, his reaction was widely

1 Stan Grant, *Australia Day* (Sydney: Harper Collins, 2019), 239.

reported. Goodes is a gifted and articulate sportsman, who the following year would become only the second Aboriginal person to be awarded the civic honor of Australian of the Year. He called out–and called time on–the naturalized racism that had characterized his childhood, education, and daily life as an Australian citizen. This was an important act of moral character, bringing out, at ground level, the importance and the implications of the 2008 National Apology to the Stolen Generations made five years earlier by then Prime Minister Kevin Rudd. In the Apology, Australia acknowledged the wrongs done to Aboriginal and Torres Strait Islander peoples by the race-based laws and policies of successive governments since colonization and the practices that have systematically attempted to destroy Indigenous culture over more than a century, particularly through the practice of forcible removal of children.

By the time Goodes called time on naturalized racism, half a decade after the Apology, a national conversation was underway among educated progressives, even though there was little real evidence of it on the ground. In 2017, a National Constitutional Convention held in central Australia agreed to begin a national process of *Makarrata*, a "coming together after a struggle," through the Uluru Statement from the Heart.[2] As yet, our federal government has provided only gestural response to this, and it has had little impact on public discourse. But in 2019, a documentary film telling the story of the last three years of Adam Goodes's celebrated career, *The Final Quarter*,[3] was broadcast nationally. It was made available to every Australian school as part of a comprehensive education package aligned to national curriculum in subject areas such as civics and citizenship, health and physical education, Aboriginal and Torres Strait Islander histories and cultures, English, and media arts. Later that year, the regular decadal review of the national Goals for the Education of Young Australians[4] was also held in central Australia and identified itself with the Aboriginal place name for Alice Springs–Mparntwe. The earlier documents are known as the Hobart (1989) and Adelaide (1998) Declarations, respectively, with the Melbourne Declaration of 2008 still in place at that time.

The naming of the Mparntwe Declaration can be seen as a significant symbolic turn toward the decolonialization of Australian education, indicating that the nation may finally be ready to acknowledge the full extent of the iniquities of its colonial past and move towards "Indigenous recognition." Commitment to improving outcomes of Aboriginal and Torres Strait Islander (ATSI) children in schools and ensuring that all Australians have knowledge of the history and cul-

---

2 "Uluru Statement from the Heart," https://ulurustatement.org/.

3 *The Final Quarter*, directed by Ian Darling (Melbourne: Shark Island Productions, 2019), video, https://www.imdb.com/title/tt7694570/.

4 Education Council, Alice Springs (Mparntwe) Education Declaration (Canberra: Australian Government, 2019).

ture of its first peoples have been two of the national goals since 1989. Yet in this thirty-year period, they seem to have had little impact on what happens in schools, and they have brought little real changes to the ongoing and widespread racism that characterizes this country. School students' knowledge, attitudes, and competencies related to these goals are tested in the National Assessment Program in Civics and Citizenship held every three years, using a sample of Year 6 and Year 10 students from all schools around Australia. The report on the 2019 assessment indicates that students who were performing above "the proficient standard" for civics and citizenship are more likely to "recognise the cultural significance of the land to Indigenous Australians and that cultural attitudes and values can change over time."[5]

However, the "proficient standard" is deemed to be level two on a five-band scale, and the percentage of Year 6 students achieving at or above level two in 2019 is only 53 percent. At Year 10 level, only 38 percent of students have demonstrated these capacities,[6] with only 8 per cent of Year 10 students reaching level four–and 1 per cent, level five.[7] This does not give cause for optimism. In spite of continuous critique and protest from the political left in relation to both Indigenous cultures and international humanitarian concerns about governmental restrictions on providing haven for displaced refugees seeking asylum on our shores, the 2019 assessment shows a significant decrease in the proportion of students who believe that citizenship includes learning about political issues from the media or learning about what is happening in other countries.[8] It seems that the everyday practice of schooling remains firmly framed by the value system adopted by the British settlers of the colonies who came to form this nation.

In taking up a hopeful position in this context, I must admit to employing a Gramscian "optimism of the will" that these recent events *can* mark a growing turn toward decolonializing social and educational practice–and that they *can* provide an opportunity for significant change in this country, and a chance to reform and reconstitute our national character. My optimism is bolstered particu-

5 Australian Curriculum, Assessment and Reporting Authority (ACARA), "NAP Sample Assessment Years 6 and 10 Civics and Citizenship Report" (2020), https://www.nap.edu.au/docs/default-source/default-document-library/nap-cc-report-2016-final-081217.pdf?sfvrsn=0, p. 22.

6 Ibid., 24.

7 Ibid., 51.

8 Australian Curriculum, Assessment and Reporting Authority (ACARA), "Students Are Engaged in the Community but Test Scores on Democracy Stall," Jan. 21, 2021, *https://www.acara.edu.au/docs/default-source/media-releases/20210121-media-release-nap-cc-2019-report.pdf.*

larly by increasing intellectual support from the fields of educational sociology,[9] curriculum theory and L1 ("mother tongue") education[10] (as well as broader historical and sociological writings[11] and the work of Indigenous intellectuals.[12] My aim here is to elaborate this position and the nature of such a reformative change.

Australia as a Modern, Pluralist Society

I begin with the observation that Australian society is noted as one of the most culturally and linguistically diverse in the world. It has a unique history in this regard, beginning from what was a widespread and already-diverse Indigenous population whose value system was tied to its spirituality and connection to country. Following invasive British colonization during the 1800 s, the first Australian government sought to create a single, uniformly white Australian culture a century later. The Indigenous population was decimated,[13] and the removal of "half-caste" children was begun to hasten the forced assimilation of those who had failed to "die out." Immigration was strictly controlled through an early piece of legislation, the Immigration Restriction Act of 1901, to ensure a "White Australia." Designed to limit "non-British" migration, it was highly successful, although from about 1950 the need for workers to support economic expansion led to a softening of the policy to allow migrants from postwar Europe. The aim of education for white Australian children was to advance this "Great British Nation in the South"[14]: Indigenous children were mostly schooled for service roles by Chris-

---

9 Amanda Keddie et al., "Is There a Need for Multi-Faith Education in All Australian Schools?," *EduResearch Matters*, Aug. 5, 2019, https://www.aare.edu.au/blog/?p=4284.

10 Lars Løvlie and Paul Standish, "Bildung and the Idea of a Liberal Education," *Journal of Philosophy of Education* 36, no. 3 (2002): 317–39; Bill Green and Per-Olof Erixon, eds., *Rethinking L1 Education in a Global Era: Understanding the (Post-)National L1 Subjects in New and Difficult Times* (Chalm, Switz.: Springer, 2020).

11 Bill Gammage, *The Biggest Estate on Earth: How Aborigines Made Australia* (Sydney: Allen & Unwin, 2011); Peter Cochrane, *Best We Forget: The War for White Australia 1914–18* (Melbourne: Text Publishing, 2018); Marilyn Lake, *The Bible in Australia: A Cultural History* (Sydney: NewSouth Publishing, 2018).

12 Stan Grant, "Reflection on the Importance of Language," *Charlie–Your Student Voice*, Charles Sturt University, July 6, 2017, http://charlie.student.csu.edu.au/2017/07/06/stan-grants-reflection-on-the-importance-of-language/; Bruce Pascoe, *Dark Emu* (Perth: Magabala Books Aboriginal Corporation, S. Griffin Press, 2014).

13 Pascoe, *Dark Emu.*

14 George S. Browne, introduction to George S. Browne, ed., *Education in Australia: A Comparative Study of the Educational Systems of the Six Australian States* (London: Macmillan, 1927), xvii–xxi.

tian missionaries. Postwar migration saw the provision of English language classes for adult migrants, although school children were expected to acquire English without additional instruction. Continued economic expansion gradually eroded the policy, and it was eliminated in the 1970 s and overturned by Gough Whitlam's Labor government in the Racial Discrimination Act of 1975. This prohibited racial and other forms of discrimination in accordance with international conventions on Human Rights, and it consolidated bipartisan support for multiculturalism as the basis for migrant settlement, welfare and social-cultural policy in Australia.

However, as Elsa Koleth[15] noted, the inclusion of Indigenous issues within multicultural policy was controversial: the assimilation process had not been successful, and including the diverse ATSI cultures as just one among many effectively silenced the calls of Indigenous Australians to be recognized as the first peoples. By the mid-1980 s, however, as "unacceptable" numbers of Asian migrants and refugees sought shelter after the Vietnam War and appeared to threaten to take Australian jobs, these inclusive values began to erode. A 1988 inquiry into Australia's immigration policies warned:

> Although settlement philosophy is much more welcoming today than it was 40 years ago, the community is still not convinced we have it right. The philosophy of multiculturalism is not widely understood, and the uninformed ensuing debate is damaging the cause it seeks to serve.[16]

In 1996, a more right-wing government won power, led by a vocal critic of multiculturalism. Support for migrants was reduced, and Labor's multicultural policy of supporting cultural identity, social justice, and productive diversity was itself overturned. The 1996 election also brought into public prominence, and Parliament, Independent member Pauline Hanson, "a controversial and provocative figure who garnered a great deal of public attention for, among other things, espousing views that were highly critical of what she perceived to be the special treatment afforded to Aboriginal Australians, and of multiculturalism."[17] Today –as in other countries–Australia is still struggling with the sociocultural integration of migrants and refugees, most recently those of Muslim background.

---

15 Elsa Koleth, "Multiculturalism: A Review of Australian Policy Statements and Recent Debates in Australia and Overseas," Research Paper no. 6 2010–1, Parliament of Australia: Social Policy Section, Oct. 8. 2010, https://www.aph.gov.au/About_Parliament/Parliamentary_Departments/Parliamentary_Library/pubs/rp/rp1011/11rp06#_ftn58.

16 Stephen FitzGerald, executive summary, "Immigration: A Commitment to Australia," sponsored by the Committee to Advise on Australia's Immigration Policies, 1988, http://www.multiculturalaustralia.edu.au/doc/fitzgerald_2.pdf, p. 3.

17 Koleth, "Multiculturalism," 13.

The challenge of shaping a population that will continue to uphold the values of a pluralist society is largely entrusted to the education system, through its national "civics and citizenship" curriculum. The problem the system faces can be demonstrated by the infamous Cronulla Riots of 2005, and the first response of the family of the schoolgirl in the Adam Goodes's incident: rather than regret, remorse, or even acknowledgement of the inappropriateness of the girl's action, her mother's first call was instead for Goodes to "man up" and apologize to her daughter for his actions in publicly identifying her. The debates that followed this incident, while taking a severe toll on Goodes himself, questioned the rights of all Australians to cultural safety and democratic freedom. Although Koleth reported that national studies showed an "overwhelmingly positive response to Australia's cultural diversity among a majority of the participants,"[18] Goodes forced the nation to consider the effects of the xenophobia promulgated by Hanson and others. The electoral power of conservative, fearful, less-educated, white, working-class voters that conservative leaders had termed the "little Aussie battlers" was strong. As in the United States and elsewhere, fear of sharing our "common wealth" seems to have turned many away from traditional Christian values and the more socialist, traditional working-class Labor sentiments of equality and social justice. But the strength of debate does indicate that this turn was objectionable to many.

A National Character in Need of Reform

As noted above, schools, particularly public schools, are charged with educating children from *all* these diverse cultural and social backgrounds: they are central to the success of a multicultural Australia.[19] In fact, the diversity of this pluralist society, with substantive differences among the familial values, cultures, and traditions into which children are born, means that the *schooling* may well be the *only* shared social institution that young people participate in prior to exercising their rights as citizens. Bill Lucas[20] reminds us that shared value systems are often "acquired in uniform," and that neither military nor sporting uniforms are worn by everyone. The role of compulsory schooling in building the nation and the national character is clear.

Yet I argue that Australian education is still reflecting what I see as the "moral emptiness" of the nation's underlying foundations as a Christian state–one that

---

18 Ibid., 34.

19 Keddie et al., "Is There a Need for Multi-Faith Education."

20 Bill Lucas, "Character Is a Meaningful Concept, Is Learned at Least as Much as It Is Taught and Can Be Woven into a School's Culture," TES, Sept. 23, 2016, https://www.tes.com/news/character-meaningful-concept-learned-least-much-it-taught-and-can-be-woven-schools-culture.

ignored its Christian values in the pursuit of wealth and status. Diane Reay[21] claims that "part of the problem is that educational systems are only as good as the societies they emerge out of." Has a national project founded on an "original sin"–the convenient lie of Australia as *terra nullius*–produced the discriminatory and undemocratic social outcomes that have come to characterize us? Can we survive the social unrest that must ultimately follow if Australia cannot achieve this sort of character reform through its education systems? As Indigenous commentator Stan Grant has noted, although the legal fiction of *terra nullius* "has been struck down by the High Court, … it is so deeply lodged in the Australian consciousness that it can still render us invisible. *Terra nullius* gave the British licence to write their own story here [because it] meant non-Indigenous peoples could imagine they were telling a story where no other story existed."[22]

At this point in time, when the "Statement from the Heart" names and challenges, in a civil and responsible manner, the ongoing colonialist presumptions of racial superiority in Australian society, the nation must respond accordingly if it is to progress in peace. As Grant says: "Recognition itself challenges us to make good on the past, yet live free of its chains–to remember in order to forget."[23] We need to build a strong moral character from the ground up, because the colonialist project of papering over the cracks and traces of the fatal flaw at the heart of the nation is no longer sustainable. The "Statement from the Heart" establishes that, as the Black Lives Matter protests remind us, the land we call Australia "is, was and always will be Aboriginal land." ***Aboriginal priority has never been ceded or extinguished, and coexists with the sovereignty of the Crown.***

As an exemplary "late modern pluralistic society," Australia faces an intellectual as well as a political challenge: it needs its schools to support and maintain a sense of itself through consciously engaging with a decolonializing curriculum for educating the next generation of young Australians. Its efforts will determine the society that our grandchildren will live in. Australians like to claim that, along with football and kangaroos, we value truth, care for others, equity, and the "fair go" of justice for everyone. The "Statement of Values for Australian Schooling"[24] certainly makes this claim, as does the succession of statements of our "National Goals for Schooling." Yet the "proud Australian values" I was taught are not (and never were) actually upheld or enacted by our nation. Because of the work of Indigenous leaders, scholars, and activists like Goodes and Grant, however, we have

21 Diane Reay, "Schooling for Democracy: A Common School and a Common University? A Response to 'Schooling for Democracy,'" *Democracy and Education* 19, no. 1 (2011): 2.

22 Grant, "Reflection on the Importance of Language," para 3.

23 Grant, *Australia Day*, 239.

24 Australian Government, Department of Employment, Education, and Workplace Relations, "National Framework: Nine Values for Australian Schooling," 2005, http://www.curriculum.edu.au/values/val_national_framework_nine_values,14515.html.

become more aware of and are actually beginning to *listen to* a larger, more diverse circle of voices in our national conversation. As we listen, we hear stories that unsettle and disrupt the assumptions about who we are as a nation, stories that have governed our education system for over a century.[25] They suggest, and argue convincingly, that rather than the values we espouse, the practices that characterize our education and social institutions, in fact, reflect more a legacy of *untruth*, *inequity*, and *injustice.*

This suggests the need to acknowledge the implications, for instance, of the fact that a major purpose of colonial settlement in Australia was for the British to manage their own population of criminals while laying claim to this new continent before other European countries could gain access to its resources. At that time, the idea of prisons aiming for rehabilitation and character reform was subordinated to the idea of deterrence through fear and hardship. It was not until the mid-nineteenth century that "prison reformers and administrators began to employ methods ... to convert or remould criminals which, by instilling habits of work and morality into prisoners, might return them to society as productive, 'well behaved' citizens." [26] The idea of reforming prisoners through "religious instruction, hard work, constant supervision and human contact" designed to "transform individuals, to reorganize or reform their character in order to re-assimilate them into society"[27] was still in the future. The expansion of empire was more important, and it was

> the combined aims of crime control and colony building [that] gave transported convicts a future. Having endured their sentence and served their time, convicts in Australia were given the unusual opportunity of re-entering the society they helped establish, hopefully free of stigma. In the process, cultures, attitudes and traditions transported along with convicts filtered into Australian life.[28]

This process could succeed only if the land that the convict (and, later, settler) population could aspire to own was available for the colony to give. The doctrine of *terra nullius* enabled this. The prison culture that was transported to this new land was understandably selfish—and inherently racist. In 1838, only fifty years after the first convicts and their jailers walked onto the land of the Eeora people,

---

25 Pascoe, *Dark Emu*; Grant, *Australia Day*; Lake, *The Bible in Australia.*

26 Louise Bavin, "Punishment, Prisons, and Reform: Incarceration in Western Australia in the Nineteenth Century," *Studies in Western Australian History* 14 (1993): 121–48, at 126, https://search.informit.org/doi/abs/10.3316/ielapa.940504846.

27 Ibid.

28 Gary Crockett, "Australian Convict Sites," Australian Government, Department of the Environment and Energy, 2020, https://sydneylivingmuseums.com.au/convict-sydney/australian-convict-sites-world-heritage, 1.

John Dunmore Lang preached a sermon in Sydney Cove arguing that "the colonists' mistreatment of their Aboriginal 'brethren' was nothing less than a 'national sin' for which the Lord was rightly punishing them with severe drought."[29] It was already clear that what the Australian settlers were being supported to "do unto others" was not at all what we would want to be "done unto us":

> "By their deeds shall you know them." Many white Australians are discovering this truth as they grapple with the legacy of how Indigenous Australians have been treated. The same is also true when our neighbours look towards us to consider what kind of people we are. If we are insular and self-absorbed, or our governments introduce policies that exacerbate inequality, it's a choice.[30]

Amid undeniable social division and disharmony, and the general decline of confidence in institutions and social norms, recent calls for constitutional reform do come "from the heart." There is increasing understanding that the economic progress we have made as a nation may have been at too great a cost to our environment to be sustainable. Australians face the need to rethink who and what we are, and what we believe in, as a nation. The role of school education in meeting this challenge is critical.

School Education in Australia

Schooling Australia has always been a challenge for government.[31] Although we are now a first-world, economically advantaged country, we are also geographically dispersed and socially diverse. Of nearly four million children (just under one-sixth of the total population) in primary and secondary schools in 2019, 65.7 percent were enrolled in government schools, 19.5 percent in Catholic schools, and 14.8 percent in private "independent" schools, most of which are faith-based.[32] As a legacy of the range of separate colonial settlements, public education is the responsibility of each state or territory. It is compulsory, free, and secular. States are supported by the federal government, which also provides sig-

---

29 Lake, *The Bible in Australia*, 95.

30 Tim Costello, "Australia's National Character Is Not Fixed. There Is Always Another Way," *The Guardian*, Jan. 26, 2015, https://www.theguardian.com/australia-news/commentisfree/2015/jan/26/australias-national-character-is-not-fixed-there-is-always-another-way.

31 Bill Green and Jo-Anne Reid, "Constructing the Teacher and Schooling the Nation," *History of Education Review* 31, no. 2 (2002): 30–44.

32 Australian Bureau of Statistics, "Schools, 2019," https://www.abs.gov.au/statistics/people/education/schools.

nificant funding for nongovernment schools, of which Catholic systemic schools form the largest group. According to the "Australian Good Schools Guide" for 2020:

> Parents in metropolitan areas can expect to pay approximately $4,455 per year for their child's secondary schooling in a government school, around $12,599 in a Catholic school and up to $22,450 if they choose the independent school route. Costs can rise significantly depending on school choice–some independent schools charge as much as $30,000 per year for tuition fees alone.[33]

While most students live and attend metropolitan schools, nearly 30 percent of Australian children live in regional or remote areas, where government schools predominate. Rural and remote schools, traditionally "hard to staff," have lower educational outcomes,[34] with significant variation in the educational achievement across equity groups. Indigenous students in remote government schools gain the least from their education, followed by rural/remote students generally, and those with language backgrounds other than English. Successful school outcomes are mainly achieved by students attending independent schools or government schools in prestigious metropolitan suburbs. The record of low equity in educational outcomes has been a policy concern for successive governments, particularly since the time of the National Apology, as international testing regimes have allowed unfavorable comparison with other countries (Melbourne Declaration of Goals of Australian Schooling 2008). But as the civics and citizenship assessments suggest, Australian schools face other problems too:

> Perhaps the culture of respect for others, in the classroom environment (for teachers and other peers who are in school to learn as best they can) might have disappeared from the minds of teenagers in Australian society. Overall, the latest PISA results point to students' lack of respect for others in Australian classrooms. [35]

What Wade Zaglas was measuring in his analysis of 2018 PISA data were disciplinary and disruptive issues of school climate, on which Australia was ranked a disappointing seventieth out of the seventy-seven PISA participants. The deterioration of social cohesion in schools has led to increasing disillusion with, and devaluing of, teaching as a profession.[36] Witnessing or participating in disrespect-

33 "The Good Schools Guide," https://www.goodschools.com.au/.

34 Philip Roberts and Bill Green, "Researching Rural Places: On Social Justice and Rural Education," *Qualitative Inquiry* 19, no. 10 (2013): 765–74.

35 Wade Zaglas, "Students Rude and Rowdy," *Education Review* (2020): 1, 15.

36 Gabbie Stroud, *Teacher* (Sydney: Allen & Unwin, 2018); Jo-Anne Reid, "What's Good Enough? Teacher Education and the Practice Challenge," *The Australian Educational Re-*

ful actions toward other people within the school system produces effects far beyond the school, and the general decline of confidence in institutions in Australia is increasingly acknowledged. Along with family, schools are the institutions on which *all other* social institutions rely to create our social norms, and education is seen as the single most important *policy* variable for effective social cohesion. As a senior state education bureaucrat has recently written, this "is why those countries where the teaching profession is highly regarded are also the ones celebrating their schooling outcomes and corollary benefits for their community."[37]

In Australia, where teaching is *not* highly regarded as a profession, the challenge for government is significant. If the proposition holds that the education system is the major, if not the only, way that Australia might attempt to reform its national character and build a citizenry democratic enough in character to steer us safely into a difficult future, this cannot be delayed. Australian teachers are not alone in facing tight curriculum control and instrumental, outcomes-driven accountability measures, of course. But the will to control and narrow teacher education in the interests of improving measurable academic outcomes has resulted in Australian teachers being effectively "deskilled": narrowly "trained," rather than more broadly "educated." There is no longer room to study educational philosophy, history, or theory in their professional training, and these disciplines are fast disappearing from the university curriculum.[38]

Teacher education is instead focused on a set of general "Standards for Australian Teachers,"[39] resulting in a technical view of both teaching and the project of education, concerned almost entirely with measurable outcomes in basic literacy, numeracy, and subject content knowledge. This focus works to deflect attention from more difficult-to-measure outcomes that might indicate development of character, social conscience and consciousness, and respect for others. As Basil Bernstein argued, while education cannot compensate for society, it still has the responsibility to try.[40] There is general consensus among scholars and policymak-

---

searcher 46, no. 5 (2019): 715–34; Amanda Heffernan et al., "Perceptions of Teachers and Teaching in Australia," Monash University Faculty of Education, Nov. 2019, https://www.monash.edu/thank-your-teacher/docs/Perceptions-of-Teachers-and-Teaching-in-Australia-report-Nov-2019.pdf.

37 Tom Alegounarias, "Opinion: Teachers Are Scrambling, Held to Account, and Ignored," *Sydney Morning Herald*, Feb. 10, 2020, https://www.smh.com.au/national/teachers-are-scrambling-held-to-account-and-ignored-20200207-p53ysp.html.

38 Craig Campbell and Geoffrey Sherington, "The History of Education: The Possibility of Survival," *Change* 5, no. 1 (2002): 46.

39 Australian Institute for Teaching and School Leadership (AITSL), "Australian Professional Standards for Teachers," 2011, https://www.aitsl.edu.au/teach/standards.

40 Basil Bernstein, Basil, "Class and Pedagogies: Visible and Invisible," *Educational Studies* 1, no. 1 (1975): 23–41.

ers in social studies, literature, and English ("mother tongue") education that the discursive construct of these subjects places history, intersubjectivity, social comment, "values education," and "character" at the center of their projects and directed toward the inculcation of the values that our society claims it wants a person of "good character" to enact.[41] Indeed, the civics and citizenship curriculum priority, like the materials related to the Goodes film, *Final Quarter*, is designed for such a range of curriculum areas.

Character Formation in Schools

If character is to be realized in the intersubjective and performative mode, rather than just as declarative knowledge, what can school education do in this regard? In some ways, this is a peculiarly educational–pedagogical–problem. Framing this in terms of discursive structures can help shed light on why the idea and practice of character formation in Australian schooling has become problematic. Svend Brinkman[42] argues that there are three different forms of social subjectivity currently threaded through educational thought and practice in Australia (and around the world).[43] First, we have–and still hold to–a premodern discourse of *character*, where people primarily interpret themselves according to a moral and religious perspective. For over a century now, this has operated alongside and interacted with a modern discourse of *personality*, a psychological perspective that stresses individuality and its development. And as digital technology has advanced economic and social globalization, Brinkman argues that a postmodern discourse of *identity* has produced more fluid self-interpretations within a consumerist, neoliberal perspective. Each of these discursive structures implies different things for public education, curriculum, and schooling. But they are *all* currently pervasive, overlapping in both teacher and public consciousness, and making it difficult for secular public schools and teachers to know exactly what they should be doing to help form character in the youth of the nation. This un-

---

41 Brian V. Hill, "Values Education in Schools: Issues and Challenges," keynote address, National Values Education Forum, 2004, http://www.curriculum.edu.au/verve/_resources/ve_acsa_paper.pdf; Department of Employment, Education and Workplace Relations (DEEWR); Bill Green and Philip Cormack, "Literacy, Nation, Schooling: Reading (in) Australia," in *Schooling and the Making of Citizens in the Long Nineteenth Century: Comparative Visions*, ed. Daniel Tröhler, Thomas S. Popkewitz, and David F. Labaree (New York: Routledge, 2011), 240–91; Keddie et al., "Is There a Need for Multi-Faith Education"; Alice Springs (Mparntwe) Education Declaration.

42 Svend Brinkmann, "Character, Personality, and Identity: On Historical Aspects of Human Subjectivity," *Nordic Psychology* 62 (2010): 65–85.

43 See also the discussion by Joachim Funke in this volume.

certainty is now claimed as an effect "of the never-ending educational tinkering by politicians and policymakers,"[44] and it has been argued that:

> the apparent difficulty of defining a consensus on common purposes at a high level, has left the door open for resolution at a more materialistic level, dominated by an economic rationalism which bases everything on market value under competitive conditions.[45]

Educators arguing for a democratic curriculum in the Australian context do so in response to ongoing Western traditions that put great emphasis on the individual and individual development, whether this is seen as a moral or an ideological project. When we think of "character development" in the traditional sense, the notion of individual *merit* or worthiness is called into play–and is fully entrenched in the education systems of almost all capitalist societies. The problem with this tradition is that we almost instinctively "regard virtues as personal possessions, hard-won through a gruelling process of character building."[46] Such a view makes the individual responsible for enhancing or acquiring the desirable attributes of good character, particularly if they have not inherited a capacity to display them from family, in a Bourdieuian sense. Part of the attraction of elite private school education in Australia is the idea that, along with superior academic outcomes, children will mix with "a better class" of peers and develop a "better" character as part of the identity they acquire in such schools:

> One particular argument for school choice in education stems from the perceived positive civic influence that religious schooling has for students and the positive role this plays in democratic society. The argument ... is that private religious schools often provide a stronger civic sense, better academic results and are more racially and socially integrated. The social capital presumably found in private religious schools is a significant argument for choice.[47]

---

44 Marco Cimino, "Our Poor Civic Literacy Is the Result of Endless Policy Tinkering," *Education HQ News*, Jan. 22, 2021, https://educationhq.com/news/our-poor-civic-literacy-is-the-result-of-endless-policy-tinkering-89258/#.

45 Hill, "Values Education in Schools," 3–4.

46 Nell Noddings, "Caring in Education," *The Encyclopedia of Informal Education*, 2005, http://infed.org/mobi/caring-in-education/.

47 James K. Campbell, "School Choice, Religion and the Public Good," refereed paper delivered at Australian Political Studies Association Conference, Jul. 6–9, 2008, https://www.researchgate.net/profile/James_Campbell19/publication/242287519_School_Choice_Religion_and_the_Public_Good/links/55dffcfe08aecb1a7cc1c437.pdf.

But in terms of identity construction, the school as an institution for the formation of character seems to be (like the family and church) less effective than social media in influencing the hearts and minds of the young. The neoliberal, consumerist, fast-capitalist values of Twitter and Tinder–of "edutainment" rather than education–increasingly structure our thinking about what needs to be done to engage children with learning. Our school system has not produced the confidence in too many school students to publicly denounce the racism of the "Australian character," as Adam Goodes did. And even when young people follow models like Sweden's Greta Thunberg, visibly and publicly demonstrating knowledge, values, and strength of character in calling for attention to the challenge of climate change for our nation's future, the system fails to support them. In 2019, schoolteachers in New South Wales (NSW) were publicly reminded that encouraging students to participate in this sort of democratic action may make *the teachers* subject to allegations of misconduct. At a private school in another state, students and parents were advised that students taking a public stand by attending a climate-change student rally would not be permitted "to complete any missed assessments."[48] In spite of data showing both Year 6 and Year 10 students' increasing interest and sense of responsibility in environmental issues,[49] it seems that schooling acts to control and limit such student agency.

Gert Biesta tells us that new and emerging democracies see education as a crucial factor in the development of a democratic culture,[50] and that established democracies call on education to counter political apathy among the young; this was, for instance, the rationale for the introduction of compulsory citizenship education in English secondary schools. Lars Løvlie and Paul Standish discuss the U.S. policy of using the school system to instill cultural solidarity within the "great melting pot" of that nation.[51] They highlight the way that the influential progressive curriculum work of John Dewey in the United States was built on the German tradition of *Bildung*, where the cultivation of self is seen as a profoundly moral and cultural education process. But this concept is largely unknown in Australian ed-

---

48 "NSW Teacher Loses Shifts after Raising Student Climate Strike," *The Guardian*, Mar. 12, 2019, https://www.theguardian.com/australia-news/2019/mar/13/nsw-teacher-loses-shifts-after-urging-students-to-join-climate-strike.

49 Australian Curriculum, Assessment, and Reporting Authority (ACARA), "Media Release: Civics and Citizenship Report: Students Are Engaged Citizens, but Test Performance Slips for Year 10," Dec. 13, 2017, https://www.acara.edu.au/docs/default-source/Media-Releases/20171213-nap-cc-media-release_final.pdf.

50 Gert Biesta, "Democracy: A Problem for Education or an Educational Problem?," in *Five Professors on Education and Democracy: Inaugural Lectures, 1999–2003*, ed. Thomas Englund (Örebro, Swed.: Örebro University, 2002), 89–109.

51 Løvlie and Standish, "*Bildung* and the Idea of a Liberal Education," 321. And see the chapters by Ashley Berner and Charles Glenn in this volume.

ucation theory, curriculum, or scholarship. Although influenced by the progressive education promulgated by Dewey and his followers, Australia's British colonial history has meant that we have never formally entertained the European educational philosophy of *Bildung*.

Why No *Bildung* in Australia?

While education in civics and citizenship is aimed at developing attitudes and capacities that will sustain democratic social governance in Australia, it has little to say about "character" or building the individual as a social and cultural subject. Outside the private school sector, the role of the school in character formation has remained implicit. As a nation, Australians vehemently require the secularity of all public schools, and although the internalization of social norms and preferred attitudes *is* promulgated, often incidentally, in school values statements and compulsory subject areas like those mentioned above, religious education is both non-compulsory and extracurricular in public schools. Ethics has been offered as an alternative to voluntary religious education since 2010–staffed by community volunteers who follow a series of scripted discussion starters addressing ethical questions on the basis of reason and logic rather than religious or cultural norms.

In contrast, *Bildung* arises from social agreement that the purpose of schooling is to "educate and form students who are able to rise above personal interests and take responsibility for the social whole."[52] As an educational philosophy, it aims to develop the self. "Character" is seen as an inner calling toward the honorable and the rational, rather than simply following rules that "religion has inscribed on them."[53] The enlightened subject is drawn toward the "good" of their own volition. The strong connections here with the Christian tradition are clear in Romans 12:2: "Do not be conformed to this world, but be transformed by the renewal of your mind, that by testing you may discern what is the will of God, what is good and acceptable and perfect."

Bernt Gustavsson[54] notes that although *Bildung* is normally "a concern of the elite classes in society, [in] Nordic countries this has extended to a much larger section of the population, where it has also had a democratising function." With *Bildung* informing practice, teaching and learning are more than the transmission and reception of knowledge, and the work of the teacher is clearly not instrumen-

52 Ellen Krogh, "*Bildung* and Literacy in Subject Danish: Changing L1 Education," in Green and Erixon, *Rethinking L1 Education in the Global Era*, 157–76, at 159.

53 Yotam Hotam, "Bildung: Liberal Education and Its Devout Origins," *Journal of Philosophy of Education* 53, no. 4 (2019): 619–32, at 627.

54 Bernt Gustavsson, "'Bildung' and Democracy: Mediating the Particular and the Universal," in Englund, *Five Professors on Education and Democracy*, 63–85, at 65.

tal. Knowledge as seen as a transformative tool to assist the self to unfold its individuality and sociability. As Løvlie and Standish put it: "The education of the self is undertaken with the transformation of contemporary culture in tandem."[55]

In Australia, the particular success of Finland in early PISA comparisons has led to it becoming an exemplary model of successful schooling. However, European philosophies and approaches to education are quite different from the Australian system, which, as described above, resembles the British school system. There, Reay argues, privilege is so entrenched that "the notion of 'character' remains a matter of class habitus."[56] David Hamilton explained this in terms of the highly segmented British class system,[57] which both determined the education provided for children and rendered what Louis Althusser calls "the silent music of the school"[58] an effective means of consolidating social stratification within the formation of the individual.

For Hamilton, "ideologies of human difference, predetermined mental capacity and social containment" not only "precluded the creation and dissemination of a developmental science of teaching"[59] within the British system, but it also led to the marginalization of a sense that the school curriculum is targeted toward building a different future for its citizenry. As in its mother country, Australia's strong colonial and postcolonial rendition of this ideological framework has meant that, while public education *espouses* a strong set of values in the Judeo-Christian tradition and claims to develop them though its Civics and Citizenship frameworks, it has ignored this fundamental purpose of education. Character education therefore happens both in the formal, mandated curriculum developing particular knowledge and capacities and via the silent, informal "hidden" curriculum that structures relational and social learning. As Michael Apple and Noel King argue, this strongly develops attitudes and practices of social inequality.[60]

---

55 Løvlie and Standish, "Bildung and the Idea of a Liberal Education," 320.

56 Reay, "Schooling for Democracy," 2.

57 David Hamilton, "The Pedagogic Paradox (or Why No Didactics in England?)," *Pedagogy, Culture, and Society* 7, no. 1 (1999): 135–52.

58 Louis Althusser, "Ideology and Ideological State Apparatuses (Notes towards an Investigation)," in *The Anthropology of the State: A Reader*, ed. Aradhana Sharma and Anil Gupta (Malden, MA: Blackwell, 2006): 86–111.

59 Hamilton, "The Pedagogic Paradox."

60 Michael Apple and Noel King, "What Do Schools Teach?," in *The Hidden Curriculum and Moral Education*, ed. Henry Giroux and David Purpel (Berkeley, CA: McCutchan Publishing Corporation, 1983), 82–99.

School Education – The Need for Reform?

Australia currently has two National Goals for Schooling:[61]

> Goal 1: The Australian education system promotes equity and excellence.
> Goal 2: All young Australians become
>
> - successful learners;
> - confident and creative individuals;
> - active and informed citizens.

In framing these goals, the Melbourne Declaration uses the premodern and modern discourses of character, outlined above, in its claims that: "As well as knowledge and skills, a school's legacy to young people should include national values of democracy, equity and justice, and personal values and attributes such as honesty, resilience and respect for others."[62] However, while these goals remain broadly constant, the revised Mparntwe Declaration of 2019 has removed explicit reference to "values" from its ambitions for its citizenry, perhaps acknowledging that these cannot be taken for granted. The discursive change is marked in its preamble:

> We recognise the more than 60,000 years of continual connection by Aboriginal and Torres Strait Islander peoples as a key part of the nation's history, present and future. Through education, we are committed to ensuring that all students learn about the diversity of Aboriginal and Torres Strait Islander cultures, and to seeing all young Aboriginal and Torres Strait Islander peoples thrive in their education and all facets of life.[63]

This is a declaration that refuses the colonialist assumption of the dominant white Australian. It maintains constancy in the less problematic discursive waters of "objective" academic knowledge in Goal 1, stressing that all Australian students will develop "strong literacy and numeracy skills in their earliest years of schooling" and will go on to develop "broad and deep knowledge across a range of curriculum areas." But the view of the student produced by schooling seems to have moved purposefully into the postmodern era in Goal 2, which now involves "[preparing] young people to thrive in a time of rapid social and technological change, and complex environmental, social and economic challenges."

---

61 Ministerial Council on Education, Employment, Training and Youth Affairs (MCEETYA), "Melbourne Declaration on Educational Goals for Young Australians" (Canberra: Australian Government, 2008).

62 Ibid., preamble.

63 Ibid.

Table 1, below, provides an elaboration of how the Melbourne Declaration (2008) defines "active and informed citizens," illustrating how the new Mparntwe Declaration (2019) replaces the term "citizens" with "members of the community." Mparntwe also refuses to overlook the diversity of Aboriginal and Torres Strait Islander peoples implicit in the use of "Indigenous." These are small discursive signals, but they mark a difference between colonial and Indigenist perspectives. It is these small forms of "remembering" that are significant for reconciliation and "moving forward together." In its outline of what might characterize "active and informed members of the community," the Mparntwe Declaration also adds the aspiration for "empathy for the circumstances of others" as a goal for Australian schooling. It adds words like "respect" for the rich social and cultural diversity of the nation, and "celebration" of Aboriginal and Torres Strait Islander histories and cultures. And it expands a goal to "value and celebrate cultural and linguistic differences, and engage in the global community, particularly with our neighbours in the Indo-Pacific regions," making clear reference to the multicultural policies of previous governments.

As noted above, the triennial assessment of civics and citizenship outcomes in Australian schools attempts to evaluate the extent to which the goal for the production of "active and informed citizens" is achieved. The report of the 2019 assessment noted government disappointment "that the results suggest our next generation isn't demonstrating a sufficient level of understanding of the significance and history of our democracy and shared values."[64]

Of more concern is that the data in this report underline the social divisions that produce these results. In 2017, ACARA reported figures showing that "Year 6 students with parents who were senior managers or professionals had scale scores that were 99 scale points higher than those with parents who were recorded as unskilled labourers, office, sales and service staff, and the difference among Year 10 students was 117 scale points."[65] In 2021, this difference is even more pronounced: "the average scale scores of students in these two groups were 115 and 133 scale points for Year 6 and Year 10, respectively."[66] The fracture lines between these divides are clearly indicating the failure of public education in this regard.

Although Australia seems to believe that schooling is highly significant in terms of character formation at both an individual and a national level, and although it vehemently requires the secularity of all public schools, its policies regarding teacher education leave much to be desired in relation to educational philosophy and theory. While citizenship education is aimed at shoring up the values that will sustain democratic social governance, it has little to say about "charac-

64 ACARA, "Civics and Citizenship Report," 2020, p. 2.

65 ACARA, "Media Release: Civics and Citizenship Report," 2017, p. 50.

66 ACARA, "Civics and Citizenship Report," 2020, p. 2.

ter," or "building" the individual as a social and cultural subject. The Mparntwe Declaration, looking to the future, is the first to explicitly name affective values such as empathy and respect as outcomes of schooling. This will require structural and curriculum change–curriculum decolonization–away from the rigid class/race-based educational frameworks imported from Britain. Reay cites Finland as an example of a more socially just education system, where "virtually all children enrol in identical comprehensive schools, regardless of class background or personal abilities and characteristics,"[67] and where, in 2006, the variance between schools was one-tenth of that found in British (and Australian) schools. In Britain, the notion of "character" remains a matter of class habitus, and "thick rich kids do better educationally than poor clever kids before they even get to school."[68]

As the effects of capitalist expansion and environmental pillage begin to be directly felt, and noted with alarm in Australia, and as the effects of the moral and ethical vacuum in our social character are exposed by people like Adam Goodes, the present does seem ripe for change. At the level of federal politics, for instance, echoing the turn to a more culturally inclusive approach in the Mparntwe Declaration, the Labor Party strongly opposes right-wing moves to weaken protections against hate speech, after a 2014 claim by the attorney general that all Australians "have the right to be bigots." Highlighting the increase in rise in race-based violence against Asian, Muslim, and Jewish people in recent years, Labor has called for "a national anti-racism campaign that promotes a zero-tolerance approach to racism."[69]

Building Character and Reforming the Nation?

However well a decolonized curriculum may fit with the espoused values of some faith-based independent schools, the work of character formation in Australian education must not continue to reproduce the social divisions that currently exist. While the national civics and citizenship assessment results suggest that the student population attending nongovernment schools has received a stronger, more successful moral education, the general privilege accruing to private education still reinforces the project of colonialism. The opportunity for change is real, but we need clarity about what such a change might look like in our schools. Indigenous cultural leaders are currently providing a vision to which education might

67 Reay, "Schooling for Democracy," 4.

68 Ibid., 2.

69 Andrew Giles, "Standing up to Racism Demands Strategy and New National Campaign," Apr. 28, 2020, https://www.andrewgiles.com.au/media-centre/media-releases/standing-up-to-racism-demands-strategy-and-new-national-campaign/.

aspire in this regard,[70] and which would assist in meeting the challenge of ensuring that this nation "remembers its past." Acknowledging that, as a nation, we are not yet able to deal with racism in particular is an important first step. Along with the potential for character formation and moral education that exists within vocational, literary, and environmental curricula,[71] there are ways that this can be seen to have begun and should be supported to continue in Australia. One is through the provision of a formal, democratic curriculum in ethics education, and another important step is through the refinement and strengthening of practices also already in place in early childhood education.

The Early Years Learning Framework

Here, the importance of recognizing the cultural diversity of the children entering the early childhood sector is a central tenet: "In Australian early childhood programs, cultural competence is first and foremost about recognising, respecting and responding to the histories and cultures of Aboriginal and Torres Strait Islander peoples. Cultural competence is a skill that is developed over time with continuous learning."[72] Explicitly framed around notions of young children "belonging, being, and becoming" in a pluralist society, the nationally endorsed Early Years Learning Framework (EYLF, 2009) traces its intellectual lineage to the Scandinavian "reconceptualist" movement in early childhood education. Turning away from the psychologistic, "developmentally staged" approach dominating U.S. and British education in the twentieth century,[73] the EYLF looks toward a more relational, *Bildung*-oriented conception of education.[74] Here, identity and belonging are core, with cultural competence and cultural and social inclusion closely allied to the project of building democratic society.

---

70 Tyson Yunkaporta, *Sand Talk: How Indigenous Thinking Can Save the World* (Melbourne: Text Publishing, 2019).

71 Besides this chapter, see the chapters by David S. Cunningham and Irene Pieper in this volume.

72 Early Childhood Australia, "Spend a Minute on Cultural Inclusion, 2020, http://www.earlychildhoodaustralia.org.au/wp-content/uploads/2020/03/Spend-a-Minute-on-cultural-inclusion.html.

73 Melinda Miller, "Reconceptualist Work in a Colonising Context: Challenges for Australian Early Childhood Education," in *Contemporary Issues and Challenge in Early Childhood Education in the Asia-Pacific Region*, ed. Minyi Li, Jillian Fox, and Susan Grieshaber (Singapore: Springer, 2017), 33–50.

74 Chris Peers and Marilyn Fleer, "The Theory of 'Belonging': Defining Concepts Used within Belonging, Being and Becoming–The Australian Early Years Learning Framework," *Educational Philosophy and Theory* 46, no. 8 (2014): 914–28.

Character formation in this context is seen to be achieved in and through regular practice of these values, in respectful daily interactions with culture and language. The ethical dimensions of such an approach are clear, although as a peak professional body, the Early Childhood Association of Australia understands that, until it is renewed through preservice teacher education, the work of teachers in character formation will be difficult. The association seeks to provide support for teachers in this sector to meet the aspirations in practice, acknowledging:

> A core principle of the ECA Code of Ethics is that children are citizens from birth with civil, cultural, linguistic, social and economic rights. Additionally, democratic, fair and inclusive practices promote equity and a strong sense of belonging. ... While educators may speak of inclusive practice, they may not have the skills to identify and reduce the impact of systemic racism, which is where additional professional learning and networks can help better these skills.[75]

The emphasis on social, moral, physical, and intellectual development within the early childhood sector is this nation's important first step in ensuring a decolonializing curriculum throughout schooling. But it cannot be left as a matter just for small children. And it cannot be left as an elective addition to a crowded curriculum, in the way that ethics education is currently provided.

Ethics Education

Apart from the social norms and preferred attitudes promulgated, often incidentally, in the crowded subject areas served by the civics and citizenship curriculum, and beyond voluntary participation in the denominational extracurricular religious education permitted in public schools, the formal teaching of values is not a priority, and the technical nature of Australian teacher education does not equip teachers to do this. In NSW, the most populous Australian state, ethics education classes have been offered as an alternative to religious education since 2010. As noted above, these are taught by community volunteers rather than teachers. Lessons are conversational rather than didactic, based on a series of increasingly complex ethical questions designed for children of different ages:

75 Early Childhood Australia, "Spend a Minute on Cultural Inclusion."

> Ethical questions are questions about what we ought to do and how we ought to live. Secular ethics explores these fundamental questions by means of reasoned argument about values and principles, rather than an appeal to religion or cultural norms. This secular approach has a long history, reaching back to Socrates and Aristotle, and is sometimes described as "philosophical ethics."[76]

With the emphasis in early childhood education on character formation resulting from regular practice, and the recognition that cultural competence is a skill developed over time with continuous learning, the need for this sort of democratic experience to become a part of the formal school curriculum more generally seems clear. But, as with the importance of ensuring that early childhood educators are well enough prepared and appropriately resourced to competently and confidently meet the ethical standards for practice in that sector, the need to prepare and resource primary and secondary teachers for a decolonized curriculum is real.

Conclusion

I have argued that the colonialist project of papering over the cracks and traces of the fatal flaw at the heart of the nation is no longer successful–that we need to consciously engage with a decolonializing curriculum in educating the next generation of young Australians. Key to this is recognizing the inherent rights of Aboriginal and Torres Strait Islanders to the land that we call home. As Grant argues: "The First Peoples do not have special rights, but inherent rights. It diminishes no one to acknowledge and protect that unique status, in keeping with the spirit and limits of our constitutional democracy. In this way we ensure allegiance. In this way we narrow our differences and strengthen our bonds. In this way we are all set free."[77] Grant claims that we need a new manifesto for Australia as a nation, "a Declaration of Country," that:

> does not speak only to Indigenous people, ...[or] to Britain or the homelands of those migrants who have made their way to these shores. It speaks first to this land, this place here before any human footprint, this place that is our home. A Declaration of our Country must speak to us all. It should speak to our sense of place: our home. It should be the work of poets. It should stand alone, apart from the constitution. Its words should be carved in monuments to fall from the lips of children not yet born.

[76] Primary Ethics, "Ethics Education for Children," https://primaryethics.com.au/about-ethics-classes/.

[77] Grant, *Australia Day*, 239–40.

While Grant sees these struggles as "strategic matters of social justice globally" now, "taking them seriously, and learning from them"[78] here in Australia is of crucial importance to all of us as teachers, as students, and as a nation.

Table 1. Elaboration of the Goal for Active and Informed citizenship* in Australia's national Goals for Schooling

Melbourne Declaration 2008	Mpartnwe Declaration 2019
- act with moral and ethical integrity	- act with moral and ethical integrity
- work for the common good, in particular sustaining and improving natural and social environments	- have empathy for the circumstances of others and work for the common good, in particular sustaining and improving natural and social environments
- appreciate Australia's social, cultural, linguistic and religious diversity, - have an understanding of Australia's system of government, history and culture	- appreciate and respect Australia's rich social, cultural, religious and linguistic diversity and embrace opportunities to communicate and share knowledge and experiences
	- have an understanding of Australia's system of government, its histories, religions and culture
- understand and acknowledge the value of Indigenous cultures - possess the knowledge, skills and understanding to contribute to, and benefit from, reconciliation between Indigenous and non-Indigenous Australians	- understand, acknowledge and celebrate the diversity and richness of Aboriginal and Torres Strait Islander histories and cultures - possess the knowledge, skills and understanding to contribute to, and benefit from, reconciliation between Aboriginal and Torres Strait Islander peoples and non-Indigenous Australians
- are committed to national values of democracy, equity and justice, and participate in Australia's civic life	- are committed to national values of democracy, equity and justice, and participate in Australia's civic life by connecting with their community and contributing to local and national conversations

78 Ibid., 209.

Table 1. Elaboration of the Goal for Active and Informed citizenship* in Australia's national Goals for Schooling *(continuation)*

Melbourne Declaration 2008	Mpartnwe Declaration 2019
- are able to relate to and communicate across cultures, especially the cultures and countries of Asia - are responsible global and local citizens.	- are informed and responsible global and local members of the community who value and celebrate cultural and linguistic differences, and engage in the global community, particularly with our neighbours in the Indo-Pacific regions.

* Goals in both Declarations have been reordered slightly to allow direct comparison.

An Analysis of the Impact of the Korean Education System on the Character, Ethics, and Values of Koreans and Its Implications for Late Modern Pluralistic Societies

Chung-Hyun Baik

Introduction

Former U.S. President Barack Obama often applauded South Korea's education for its educational performance, and especially for the role of Korean teachers.[1] However, disputes continue regarding the evaluation of Korean education.[2] According to the result of the 2018 Programme for International Student Assessment (PISA), Korean students on one hand showed higher scores than the other countries in their performance of reading, mathematics, and science.[3] Korean students ranked second to seventh in reading, first to fourth in mathematics, and third to fifth in science among the thirty-seven countries in the Organisation for Economic Cooperation and Development (OECD) and among the seventy-nine countries which participated in the assessment.[4] On the other hand, Andreas Schleicher, professor emeritus of Heidelberg University and director of education and skills of OECD, pointed out that Korean students routinely experience a great deal of schoolwork-related anxiety despite their high academic performance. In the Korea-OECD International Education Conference in October 2019, Schleicher delivered a keynote speech, arguing that Korea "has the lowest proportion of students who feel happy at school, just about 60 %."[5]

---

1 Pedro Noguera, "Obama Has a Long Way to Go on Education Reform," CNN, Jan. 17, 2011, http://edition.cnn.com/2011/opinion/01/27/noguera.obama.education/index.html.

2 Michael B. Horn, "What Koreans Wish Obama Understood about their Schools," *Forbes*, May 31, 2014, https://www.forbes.com/sites/michaelhorn/2014/03/31/what-koreans-wish-obama-understood-about-their-schools/#273982e0d5cc.

3 Programme for International Student Assessment (PISA), "Results from PISA 2018," Korea, https://www.oecd.org/pisa/publications/PISA2018_CN_KOR.pdf.

4 http://english.moe.go.kr/main.do?s=english.

5 *The Korea-OECD International Education Conference Program Book*, KINTEX, Ilsan, Korea, Oct. 23–25, 2019, https://www.researchgate.net/publication/338660293_Korea-OECD_

Such a discrepancy in evaluation of Korean education leads us to undertake a more detailed analysis of the Korean education system, especially in relation to its impact on Korean character, ethics, and values. In this chapter, "character" mainly refers to who we are as humans, "ethics" refers to how we live, and "values" refers to what we live for. With this in mind, the chapter examines the history of the Korean education system with reference to character formation, ethics, and communication of values in Korea. The chapter argues that Korean education has been strongly influenced by a highly competitive and exclusive meritocracy reinforced by egoistic familism. These features have caused both distortion and disorientation in character formation, ethics, and values for Korean culture and life. The chapter concludes with an attempt to draw some implications from such analysis for late modern pluralistic societies.

The Education System Throughout Korean History

Since the Gochoseon (Old Choseon) dynasty (2333 to 108 BC), Korea has passed through the Three Kingdoms period–consisting of Koguryeo, Baekje, and Shilla (the first century BC to 676 AD)–the United Shilla period (676 to ca. 935 AD), the Koryeo (Korea/Corea) dynasty (918-1392), the Choseon dynasty (1392-1897), the Korean Empire (1897-1910), Japanese colonization (1910-45), the U.S. military government (1945-48), and the Republic of Korea (1948 to the present).

The first state-established educational institution was Taehak, which was founded by Koguryeo in 372 to teach aristocratic children Confucian texts, literature, and martial arts, thereby training them to be government officials. The United Shilla also established Kukhak or Taehakgam in 682 to educate aristocratic children for governmental office. And Koryeo founded Kukjagam, also called Kukhak or Sungkyunkwan, in 992, to educate aristocratic children to be government officials. Likewise, Choseon from the outset continued and developed Sungkyunkwan, also known as Kukhak, for the purpose of educating children of the ruling class to be government officials.[6]

All these educational institutions had a specific purpose beyond education itself, that is, to educate children of the ruling class or aristocratic families to be government officials. This occurred through teaching and selecting of some children by examinations. As Confucianism–following the teachings of the Chinese philosopher Confucius (551-479 BC)–began to spread in Korea during the Three

International_Education_Conference_korea%27S_higher_education_system_through_california_eyes, p. 56.

6 Encyclopedia of Korean Culture (Korean language), https://encykorea.aks.ac.kr. Dae-Sik Kim, *The Historical Development of Education in Korea* (Korean language) (Seoul: Hakjisa, 2017), 77-82.

Kingdom period, all these educational institutions were considerably interlinked with politics, toward which Confucianism is oriented.[7]

Confucian texts were taught as a curriculum and provided the basis of civil service examinations through which successful students could progress to governmental office. One salient form of civil service examination was Gwageo. This examination was introduced in Koryeo in the year 958 and was finally repealed in the Gabo Reform of 1894–95. Passing such examinations was not only an honor for individuals but also a great glory to their whole family, both during the Koryeo dynasty and during the Choseon dynasty.[8]

After the 1880 s, and stimulated by several newly established mission schools (such as Paichai School in 1885, Kyungshin School in 1885, and Ewha School in 1886), the Korean government began a modern style of education through the Royal Edict of Education for the State in 1895. This edict was promulgated by King Kojong (who became Emperor Kojong in 1897) as one of the important measures undertaken in the Gabo Reform. The Gabo Reform abolished a social caste system between the ruling and the ruled classes and opened the door of education wider to include all common people. The Gabo Reform also repealed Gwageo, which had long been restricted mostly to the ruling class. In addition to the governmental education reform, several thousand private schools were established by the efforts of the Korean people to modernize education.[9]

However, such governmental reforms and civilian efforts for modern education were completely frustrated by the Japanese annexation of Korea from 1910 to 1945. The Japanese Government General of Korea controlled, oppressed, and distorted the Korean education system through the Choseon Education Law, which was originally legislated in 1911 and then revised in 1919, 1938, and 1943. This law aimed at making Korean people loyal to Japan, exploited their labor, and diminished their place in society.[10] In this way, the Korean education system became subjugated to the politics of Japanese imperialism.

Right after independence, in 1945, and during the U.S. military government of 1945–48, the Republic of Korea (ROK), often referred to as South Korea, was established in 1948. The Democratic People's Republic of Korea (DPRK), often referred to as North Korea, was established during this time north of the 38th parallel of the Korean Peninsula. Only after the Korean War (1950 to 1953), has Korea attempted to reform, restore, and improve its education system through seven reforms of education curriculum in 1954, 1963, 1973, 1982, 1987, 1992, and

---

7 Young-min Kim, Ha-Kyoung Lee, and Seongun Park, "The Confucian Tradition and Politics," *Oxford Research Encyclopedias*, https://oxfordre.com/politics/view/10.1093/acrefore/9780190228637.001.0001/acrefore-9780190228637-e-991.

8 Kim, *The Historical Development of Education in Korea*, 101–09.

9 Ibid., 149–58.

10 Ibid., 159–62.

1997, and through two revisions of the seventh education curriculum in 2009 and 2015. Through these changes, primary education and secondary education have become mandatory, and higher education has been popularized with a high college/university enrollment rate of around 70 percent.[11]

However, the major goals of Korean education in this period were closely connected with politics. This was accomplished by publicizing political agendas and/or informing students of political agendas–for example, an intensive anticommunist movement, an extensive range of economic development and industrialization, and a limited degree of democratization.

The Impact of the Korean Education System on the Character, Ethics, and Values of Koreans

As indicated above, one of the most remarkable characteristics of the Korean education system is its purpose. The purpose has not been education as such but something else. Specifically, it has been to teach and train students to be government officials in order to rule and manage Korea, or to publicize or inform people of some political agendas. In this way the Korean education system is closely related to politics and ruling elites. This characteristic has been more conspicuous in higher education but has also been prevalent in primary and secondary education as well.

The particular link between Korean education and political rule offers some clues to understanding the character, ethics, and values of Koreans–that is, who Koreans are as humans, how Koreans live, and what Koreans live for. This educational/political link means that the Korean education system is grounded in meritocracy, which is defined as "a social system, society, or organization in which people get success or power because of their abilities, not because of their money or social position."[12] Under this meritocracy, the top priority of education is for students to become government officials, an achievement that Koreans regard not only as individual success and honor in life but also as filial duty toward one's parents within the family. According to Hyokyeong–one of the representative thirteen Confucian texts which primarily give advice on filial duty–to rise in the world and gain fame is the completion of filiality.[13]

---

11 Ibid., 169–75. For more details, see the Korean language website https://ko.wikipedia.org/wiki/%EB%8C%80%ED%95%9C%EB%AF%BC%EA%B5%AD%EC%9D%98_%EA%B5%90%EC%9C%A1%EA%B3%BC%EC%A0%95.

12 "Meritocracy," *Cambridge Dictionary*, https://dictionary.cambridge.org/dictionary/english/meritocracy.

13 "Our body, skin, and hair are all received from our parents; we dare not injure them. This is the first priority in filial duty. To establish oneself in the world and practice the Way; to

In this way, the character, ethics, and values of Koreans are consciously, subconsciously, or unconsciously oriented toward advancing into governmental offices through education. Even though *Hogikingan*–literally, to broadly benefit humans–is the founding principle of the Gochoseon (Old Choseon) dynasty and also the ideal of education since 1945, the educational system has strongly emphasized social, political, and economic success more than character, ethics, and values. Even though the supreme principle of the Confucian view of humanity is *In*–which literally means that two humans are in a good relation with each other, namely, loving others–and even though the essential point of Confucianism is *Sukichiin*–literally, overcoming oneself and governing others well–excessive stress on success overturns such principles, ideals, and views in the education system.

In addition, such a tendency in the education system has been more severely reinforced by family centrism, which refers to egoistic familism, in which individuals strive to live not for themselves but for their own extended families. Under this family centrism, Koreans concentrate on education excessively, which incurs so-called parental education fervor only for children's success in society, but not for education itself. There are many stories about parents who sacrifice themselves for the education of children, even by selling cattle and farmland. And there are a lot of stories about children who devote themselves to studying only to support parents and other family members financially. Moreover, under this family centrism, Koreans share values within the family, communicating them between generations and extending them into society.

Furthermore, all these factors cause a hierarchical ranking system of colleges and universities in Korea, with the result that entrance examinations are excessively competitive. The most important criterion for deciding which college or university to apply to is neither the school's academic achievements nor the applicant's academic interests, but primarily the school's ranking, thereby giving rise to so-called SKY fever. Here SKY refers to the top three universities in Korea according to the ranking system based on Korean SAT scores. They are Seoul National University, Korea University, and Yonsei University, which might be compared to the Ivy League universities in the United States. This phenomenon is more intensified by the fact that the Korean education system is very exclusive, based on income available to afford university education. Those unable to afford college or university education are regarded as failures and losers. All students are supposed to strive to prepare themselves for entrance examinations in order

---

uphold one's good name for posterity and give glory to one's father and mother–this is the completion of filial duty. Thus, filiality begins with service to parents, continues in service to the ruler, and ends with establishing oneself in the world [and becoming an exemplary person]." "Selections from the Classic of Filiality," http://afe.easia.columbia.edu/ps/cup/classic_of_filiality.pdf.

to get into top schools. This expectation generates significant stress, anxiety, and fear, and also causes unhappiness at home, school, and society as a whole.

Some Implications for Late Modern Pluralistic Societies

The features of the Korean education system described above are so deeply rooted in the mindset of Koreans as to affect their character, ethics, and values. There is disagreement about how to distinguish between the modern and late modern periods in the history of Korea, no matter how those periods may be defined. Nevertheless, it is certain that Korea is now somewhere in the transition from a modern to a late modern period, or at least encompassing elements of both.

Under this social shift, new streams and trends can be observed in Korea. One outstanding example is an increasing awareness of diversity and plurality within Korea. This contrasts to the supposedly conventional view of Korean uniformity or homogeneity, which emphasizes one country, one nation, one culture, and one language. This difference is clear from the fact that contemporary Korea is now a multicultural society, defined as a society in which more than 5 percent of the whole population are foreigners. According to statistics compiled by the Korea Immigration Service within the Ministry of Justice, foreigners staying in Korea numbered 2.52 million at the end of 2019, nearly 5 percent of the entire population.[14] This increasing awareness of diversity and plurality is making extensive impacts on all areas of Korean life, such as family, school, culture, religion, society, economy, politics, law, and so on.

In addition, new streams and trends are also gradually emerging in the education system in various ways. In this respect, we might note the following. First, a centralizing, top-down, one-size-fits-all education system is gradually being weakened. Instead, the education system allows increasing freedom and autonomy to local educational governing bodies and agencies. Second, a conventional subject-centered curriculum is steadily being diminished. Instead, the education system places greater choice in the hands of students. Third, anticommunist education has been removed from the curriculum in order to foster peace education in preparation for the reunification of the two Koreas. Fourth, alternative teaching methods are being introduced and attempted in accordance with new educational situations, including digital education, online education, and cyber education.

All these streams and trends widen and broaden the potential and possibility of educating people in Korea with reference to character, ethics, and values. This means less impact on education by other factors, such as politics or political agen-

14 "Number of Foreign Residents in Korea Tops 2.5 Million," Yonhap News Agency, Feb. 17, 2020, https://en.yna.co.kr/view/AEN20200217003000315.

das. For example, like the United States, Korea since the 1990 s has witnessed the introduction and development of character education,[15] which is based on virtue ethics.[16] This enables the education system to focus on its own educational purpose, especially for character formation, ethics, and communication of values. Despite these new streams and trends, however, there continues to be the possible danger that education may be unduly impacted by the complicated and delicate pressures of politics or political agendas in each historical period.[17]

Conclusion

As the discussion above makes clear, education has not been an independent variable but a dependent variable throughout Korean history. For a long time, the education system has been heavily influenced and even determined by something other than education itself, that is, by politics or political agendas by which students are taught and trained to be government officials. This was the case with the premodern and modern periods of Korean history. However, with the transition to the late modern period, a new opportunity presents itself for education to become an agent for character formation, ethics, and communication of values. But all this possibility depends on how Korean society will deal with the complicated and delicate pressures of politics and political agendas.

15 Chang-Woo Jeong, *Theories and Practices of Character Education* (Korean language) (Paju: Kyoyookbook, 2017).

16 KAIST Future Strategy Research Center, *Korea National Future Education Strategy* (Seoul: Gimmyoungsa, 2017).

17 Gilsang Lee, *A History of Korean Education in the Twentieth Century* (Korean language) (Paju: Jipmoondang, 2007).

Public Education and Moral Formation in the United States: A View from the Early Twenty-First Century

Ashley Berner

Introduction

The purpose of this book series–Character Formation, Ethical Education, and the Communication of Values in Late Modern Pluralistic Societies–is "to identify the realities and potentials of ... core social systems to provide moral orientation and character formation in late modern societies."[1] This chapter explores this inquiry in light of the dominant educational model in the United States; examines this model's strengths and weaknesses with respect to moral formation; and concludes with a brief, and largely positive, comparative review of the pluralistic model that is in wide use among our democratic peers.

School systems are complex. They are always imperfect. The details of policy can make or break a system's capacity to accelerate, rather than to diminish, opportunity for all students. For the sake of argument, this chapter considers models from the United States and elsewhere in their ideal form, with the assumption that they have been put in place by democratic means.

The State-Control, or Uniform, Model in the United States

Since the late nineteenth century, public school systems in the United States have rested upon what scholar Charles L. Glenn calls the "state-control" model, in which the state funds, regulates, and exclusively delivers public education.[2] Most

---

1 See the preface to the series in this volume.

2 Charles L. Glenn, *Contrasting Models of State and School: A Comparative Historical Study of Parental Choice and State Control*, 1st ed. (New York: Continuum, 2011). Glenn uses the term "state-control model" throughout.

Americans[3] now identify the resulting schools with "public" or "district" education, because they are organized at the local level by a district central office. Currently, there are approximately 13,500 districts, which educate 82 percent of American students.[4] American public education is "uniform" because it is uniformly delivered by the state via the district–not because it is uniform in its effects.

From Plural to Uniform

It was not always thus; American public education was originally plural rather than unitary.[5] The early towns and cities of the United States levied taxes for schools that were Catholic, Protestant (in various forms), nonsectarian, and even de facto Jewish, as demography dictated. In locations with too few families to support entire schools based on (for example) Calvinist, Lutheran, and Episcopal tenets, so-called common schools developed that embodied a generalized Protestant Christianity.

In the 1830 s, a loose network of reformers pushed for uniform instead of plural school systems. Led by Horace Mann, who served as (the first) chairman of the Massachusetts Board of Education (1837–48), this group drew upon a civic republicanism that favored unity over difference and viewed sectarianism with suspicion.[6] Schools that provided a common, noncreedal experience for America's youth,[7] they argued, would promote civic harmony and democratic loyalty. This movement had little immediate influence on education, however; the major-

3 "Americans" generally indicates inhabitants of the United States and Canada. However, rather than constantly writing "citizens of the United States," I use "American" as shorthand for this denotation.

4 National Center for Education Statistics, "Table 98: Number of Public School Districts and Public and Private Elementary and Secondary Schools: Selected Years, 1869–70 through 2010–11" (Washington, DC: Institute of Education Sciences, 2012), https://nces.ed.gov/programs/digest/d12/tables/dt12_098.asp; National Center for Education Statistics, "School Choice in the United States: 2019" (Washington DC: Institute of Education Sciences, 2019), https://nces.ed.gov/programs/schoolchoice/summary.asp.

5 I refer throughout to two scholarly treatments of the early republic's pluralism and the eventual shift to the state-control (or uniform) model: Charles L. Glenn, *The Myth of the Common School* (Amherst: University of Massachusetts Press, 1988); Philip Hamburger, *Separation of Church and State* (Cambridge, MA: Harvard University Press, 2002).

6 Kathleen Knight Abowitz and Jason Harnish, "Contemporary Discourses of Citizenship," *Review of Educational Research* 76, no. 4 (Dec. 1, 2006): 653–90, at 657–59, https://journals.sagepub.com/doi/10.3102/00346543076004653.

7 We cannot forget that *enslaved* youth were not considered in this debate.

ity of Americans remained wedded to funding a variety of schools that reflected local demography and distinctive, usually religious, beliefs.[8]

This eclectic landscape changed in the mid-nineteenth century: a wave of immigration sparked a nativist movement that was pro-Anglo-Saxon, anti-immigrant, and, above all, anti-Catholic. Between 1845 and 1854, three million immigrants–many of them Catholic–were added to the fourteen million Whites and three million African Americans already in this country. By midcentury, the Catholic population had grown to 17.6 percent of the population. In some areas it was higher; in New Hampshire, the Catholic population grew from 1,370 to 85,000 (or 22 percent of the population) between 1844 and 1894.[9] By 1869, a full 20 percent of New York City's excise taxes were allocated to Catholic schools.[10] Other governmental agencies, such as the California legislature, funded Catholic education, while some cities allowed Catholic nuns and priests to teach in majority-Catholic public schools.[11]

The Anglo-Saxon Protestant majority felt besieged. What would the impact be on American identity of this wave of foreigners who (allegedly) answered to a foreign power, organized their worship in hierarchies, and spoke languages other than English? Protestant nativism, as a response, produced the midcentury American Party (the Know-Nothing Party) and supported the post-Civil War Republican Party. The nativist legislative agenda included outlawing foreign-language instruction and defunding "sectarian" schools–which was code for "Catholic." The ensuing culture war featured fearmongering in New England pulpits,[12] public marches in midsized cities, and Ku Klux Klan-led firebombing of Catholic neighborhoods–reflecting an animus that endured well into the twentieth century.[13]

In the wake of these and allied forces, some three-dozen states amended their constitutions to forbid funding for sectarian schools between 1870 and 1900, many of them explicitly requiring uniform systems in the process. These amendments are often called Blaine Amendments, after the failed attempt by U.S. Speaker of the House James Blaine to change the *federal* constitution.[14] They vary in

8 Glenn, *The Myth of the Common School*, 120–35.

9 Charles L. Glenn, "The Discriminatory Origins of New Hampshire's 'Blaine' Amendment, Unpublished Testimony," April 2013, 14.

10 Ibid., 10.

11 Ibid., 26, 33.

12 Hamburger, *Separation of Church and State*, 211–13.

13 Ibid., 216–17.

14 James G. Blaine of Maine was, in turn, speaker of the U.S. House of Representatives, U.S. senator, secretary of state, and serial presidential candidate. He represented the movement to "separate church and state." In 1875, Blaine proposed amending the U.S. Constitution to prohibit the states from funding religious schools. The so-called Blaine Amendment passed the House but narrowly failed in the Senate.

details. New York's Blaine Amendment allows some state funding for nonpublic schools in the form of transportation, technology, utilities, and security. Florida's Blaine Amendment is stricter. It forbids direct *and* indirect aid to religious schools and includes the term "uniform schooling" for emphasis.[15]

Note that the term "uniformity" indicates uniformity of *delivery* via the central school district. Schools in the United States are manifestly–and tragically–*not uniform* in terms of educational inputs (such as per-student funding or teachers' qualifications) or educational outcomes (such as students' academic achievement or attainment).[16]

From Protestant to Secular

Uniform delivery did not aspire to moral neutrality; on the contrary, the same legislatures that banned Catholic-school funding, reinforced Protestant hegemony. State after state passed laws requiring that the Protestant Bible be read in public schools: Pennsylvania in 1913, Delaware and Tennessee in 1916, Alabama in 1919, Georgia in 1921, Maine in 1923, Kentucky in 1924, Florida and Ohio in 1925, and Arkansas in 1930.[17] Cultural minorities responded by capitulating or forming their own networks of schools, sans state support (see below). In some states, these minorities had to litigate to be ensured the right even to exist.[18]

The Protestant atmosphere in district schools ended in the 1960 s, when the Supreme Court overturned many such laws and practices on the grounds that they violated the Establishment Clause of the U.S. Constitution, which prohibited state establishment of religion; the Court thus effectively secularized district schools.[19] For cultural minorities, this judgment was long overdue. For many Prot-

---

15 On this basis, in 2004, the Florida District Court of Appeals struck down a statewide voucher program: John Ellis "Jeb" Bush, etc., et al., v. Ruth D. Holmes, et al.; Charles J. Crist, Jr., etc., v. Ruth D. Holmes, et al.; Brenda McShane, etc., et al., v. Ruth D. Holmes, et al., No. SC04-2323 to SC-4-2325 (Supreme Court of Florida, Jan. 5, 2006).

16 Evidence for persistent achievement gaps between racial and socioeconomic subgroups is well documented. See, for instance, Sarah D. Sparks, "Nation's Report Card: Achievement Flattens as Gaps Widen between High and Low Performers," *Education Week*, Apr. 10, 2018, http://blogs.edweek.org/edweek/inside-school-research/2018/04/nations_report_card_2018_us_achievement.html?cmp=SOC-SHR-FB.

17 Glenn, "The Discriminatory Origins of New Hampshire's 'Blaine' Amendment," 29.

18 For example, Pierce v. Society of Sisters, 268 U.S. 510 (1925), 286 United States Reports 510 (Supreme Court of the United States 1925).

19 The Supreme Court rendered Bible reading for moral instruction, public prayers, and the teaching of creationism to be unconstitutional. See especially Engel v Vitale, 370 United States Reports 421 (Supreme Court of the United States 1962); Abington Township, Penn-

estants, the resulting secularism felt like as a profound loss, thus sparking a new round of culture wars–this time, in the late twentieth century.[20]

Whether tinged with Protestant or secular principles, however, public education in the United States has operated as a unitary system for more than a century, and most Americans continue to be educated by the district school. Americans' imaginations–and public debates–remain captive to this paradigm, in which only district schools are considered truly public. The past twenty-five years have brought diversified forms of delivery, via charter schools or state-supported private scholarship programs, but while these newer models are expanding in most states across the country,[21] their legitimacy remains contested. The cultural default is the uniform, common-school model.

Uniformity and Moral Formation

What are the effects of the U.S. uniform model upon schools' capacity to support the nonacademic correlates of education, such as character formation, social and emotional development, and civic preparation? The research literature on these three outcomes is extensive.[22] To align with the overarching theme of this volume, this chapter focuses on character education alone.

sylvania v Schemp, 374 United States Reports 203 (Supreme Court of the United States 1963); Chamberlin v Dade County Public Schools, 377 United States Reports 402 (Supreme Court of the United States 1964); Epperson v Arkansas, 393 United States Reports 97 (Supreme Court of the United States 1968). Note that the issue in *Engel v Vitale* was the attempt of New York's Board of Regents to allow a *voluntary* prayer that had been designed not to offend Jews, Catholics, or Protestants.

20 For example, Geoffrey R. Stone, "In Opposition to the School Prayer Amendment," *The University of Chicago Law Review* 50, no. 2 (1983): 823–48, https://doi.org/10.2307/1599511; Keith E. Durso, "The Voluntary School Prayer Debate: A Separationist Perspective," *Journal of Church and State* 36, no. 1 (1994): 79–96; Editorial Board, "Banning Prayer in Public Schools Has Led to America's Demise," *The Forerunner* (blog), May 1, 1988, http://www.forerunner.com/forerunner/X0098_Ban_on_school_prayer.html.

21 American Federation for Children Growth Fund, "2019 School Choice Guidebook" (Washington, DC: American Federation for Children, 2019), https://www.federationforchildren.org/wp-content/uploads/2019/10/2019-Guidebook-10.2.19.pdf.

22 There is a significant overlap between "character" and "social and emotional" development, although many contemporary scholars distinguish them from one another. Examples include A. Duckworth and D. S. Yeager, "Measurement Matters Assessing Personal Qualities Other than Cognitive Ability for Educational Purposes," *Educational Researcher* 44, no. 4 (2015): 237–51; Lex Borghans et al., "The Economics and Psychology of Personality Traits," *Journal of Human Resources* 43, no. 4 (2008): 972–1059; Greg J. Duncan et al., "School Readiness and Later Achievement," *Developmental Psychology* 43, no. 6

Moral Framework: From Protestant to Secular

The primary strength of a uniform model, and that upon which its case rests theoretically–as we saw from Horace Mann, above–is its potential to promote moral and civic cohesion across a heterogeneous population. The goal of uniformity, in this light, is to enable the next generation of citizens to join the majority culture. Canadian scholars Charles Taylor and Jocelyn Maclure call this approach "republican secularism,"[23] and Americans call it "civic republicanism."[24]

(2007): 1428–46, https://doi.org/10.1037/0012-1649.43.6.1428; Camille A. Farrington et al., *Teaching Adolescents to Become Learners the Role of Noncognitive Factors in Shaping School Performance: A Critical Literature Review* (Chicago: University of Chicago, Consortium on School Research, 2012), https://consortium.uchicago.edu/publications/teaching-adolescents-become-learners-role-noncognitive-factors-shaping-school; Jenny Nagaoka et al., "Foundations for Young Adult Success: A Developmental Framework," Concept Paper for Research and Practice (University of Chicago: University of Chicago Consortium on School Research, June 2015), https://consortium.uchicago.edu/publications/foundations-young-adult-success-developmental-framework. For a recent summary, see Alanna Bjorklund-Young, "What Do We Know about Developing Students' Non-Cognitive Skills?" (Baltimore, MD: Johns Hopkins Institute for Education Policy, June 2016), https://edpolicy.education.jhu.edu/what-do-we-know-about-developing-students-non-cognitive-skills/. For research on citizenship formation, see David Campbell, introduction to *Making Civics Count: Citizenship Education for a New Generation*, ed. David Campbell, Meira Levinson, and Frederick Hess (Cambridge, MA: Harvard University Press, 2012), 1–15; David Campbell, "The Civic Side of School Choice: An Empirical Analysis of Civic Education in Public and Private Schools," *Brigham Young University Law Review*, no. 2 (2008): 487–524; David E. Campbell, "The Civic Implications of Canada's Education System," in *Educating Citizens*, ed. Patrick Wolf et al. (Washington, DC: Brookings Institute, 2004), 186–220. For summaries, see Ashley Berner, "Education for the Common Good," *Education Next* (blog), Nov. 30, 2017, https://www.educationnext.org/education-for-the-common-good/, and Ashley Berner, *Pluralism and American Public Education: No One Way to School* (New York: Palgrave MacMillan, 2017), chap. 5.

23 Jocelyn Maclure and Charles Taylor, *Secularism and Freedom of Conscience*, trans. Jane Marie Todd (Cambridge, MA: Harvard University Press, 2011).

24 This is not to be confused with the civic republicanism (or civic humanism) described and debated by J. G. A. Pocock and Thomas Pangle. See J. G. A. Pocock, *Politics, Language, and Time: Essays on Political Thought and History* (Chicago: University of Chicago Press, 1989) and Thomas L. Pangle, *The Spirit of Modern Republicanism: The Moral Vision of the American Founders and the Philosophy of Locke* (Chicago: University of Chicago Press, 1988). It is, rather, the civic republicanism promoted by Benjamin Rush and George Washington–a common and nondenominational piety that sought public virtue, as described in John Witte Jr. and Joel A. Nichols, *Religion and the American Constitutional Experiment*, 4th ed. (Oxford: Oxford University Press, 2016), esp. 36–42.

The moral contours of American civic republicanism, and the intellectual resources upon which it draws, have changed over time. As legal scholar John Witte Jr. describes it, civic republicans in the early Republic propounded a moral foundation for social institutions, but one shorn of creedal particularism. Benjamin Rush, George Washington, and John Adams (to name a few) promoted a generic religion–one that held across the various Protestant sects and that could create a common moral culture.[25] Horace Mann's arguments for a uniform common school drew upon these currents, as did the late nineteenth-century Blaine Amendments and accompanying legislation that universalized noncreedal Protestantism.

As might be expected, contemporary theorists of uniformity eschew a religious framework, however anodyne, in favor of a secular one that prepares students for a secular public square. For instance, scholars Amy Gutmann and Meira Levinson hold that the state is uniquely qualified to inculcate a specific set of democratic values, such as individual autonomy, that comport with a secular constitution and nonreligious rationality.[26] Secularism has its own distinguished intellectual pedigree and contemporary resources.[27] An important role of district schools is to leverage these resources against religious and ethnic subcultures from which students may come, and towards a common culture that could mediate between domestic and public worlds.[28]

---

25 Abowitz and Jason Harnish, "Contemporary Discourses of Citizenship," 657–59.

26 Amy Gutmann, *Democratic Education* (Princeton, NJ: Princeton University Press, 1987); Amy Gutmann, *Democratic Education: With a New Preface and Epilogue*, 1st rev. pbk. ed. (Princeton: Princeton University Press, 1999); Amy Gutmann, *Democratic Education.* (Princeton: Princeton University Press, 2001); Meira Levinson, *The Demands of Liberal Education* (Oxford: Oxford University Press, 2002). I explore their work in depth, most recently in Ashley Berner, "Educational Pluralism: Distinctive Schools and Academic Accountability," in *Religious Liberty and Education: A Case Study of Yeshivas vs. New York*, ed. Jay Greene, Jason Bedrick, and Matthew Lee (Lanham, MD: Rowman & Littlefield, 2020).

27 For two different but striking accounts, see the description of Enlightenment rationalism in Alasdair C. MacIntyre, *Three Rival Versions of Moral Inquiry: Encyclopaedia, Genealogy, and Tradition: Being Gifford Lectures Delivered in the University of Edinburgh in 1988* (London: Duckworth, 1990), and the contrast between secularism and pluralism in a recent debate in the House of Parliament: Robert McNamara, "Debate on Denominational Schools" (House of Parliament, United Kingdom, Jul. 20, 2004).

28 Levinson in particular notes the importance of offering young people an alternative to the (possibly authoritarian) frameworks of their origins. See especially Levinson, *The Demands of Liberal Education*, 38–39, 139.

Challenges to Moral Cohesion

Whether they are tasked with reinforcing a nonsectarian Protestantism or an Enlightenment secularism, however, district schools face a challenge when it comes to moral formation: which intellectual resources and institutional practices could be broadly acceptable within a heterogeneous society, while also simultaneously countervailing the particularisms to which society's members belong?

First, creating educational conditions that could be acceptable to a heterogeneous–and free–society has always been problematic. Families who object to the majoritarian norms–the ideal "target market," as it were–often leave the system, if they can. For example, the defunding of Catholic schools sparked a national campaign to scale up Catholic education, a successful endeavor that reached its pinnacle with four million students enrolled annually by the 1960 s.[29] Jehovah's Witness families objected to the imposition of American values through the Pledge of Allegiance, a requirement they viewed as idolatrous and which they successfully litigated at the Supreme Court.[30] Another example: the Supreme Court's removal of Protestant norms from public schools alienated many evangelical families, who protested a secular approach to sex education and other required readings. These families often litigated and usually lost.[31] Widespread withdrawal from the district sphere resulted.[32] Finally, in recent years, homeschooling has flourished in every state, often because families find themselves culturally at odds with their district schools–whether on moral, pedagogical, or ethnic and racial grounds.[33]

---

29 United States Conference of Catholic Bishops, "History of the Catholic Church in the United States," http://www.usccb.org/about/public-affairs/backgrounders/history-catholic-church-united-states.cfm. For more extensive data on Catholic schools, see Margaret F. Brinig and Nicole Stelle Garnett, *Lost Classroom, Lost Community: Catholic Schools' Importance in Urban America*, repr. ed. (Chicago: University of Chicago Press, 2016).

30 West Virginia State Board of Education v. Barnette, 319 United States Reports 624 (Supreme Court of the United States 1943).

31 Eric A. DeGroff, "Parental Rights and Public School Curricula: Revisiting Mozert after 20 Years," *Journal of Law & Education.* 38, no. 1 (2009): 83.

32 Mary Ann Zehr, "Evangelical Christian Schools See Growth," *Education Week*, Dec. 4, 2004, https://www.edweek.org/ew/articles/2004/12/08/15private.h24.html.

33 The fastest-growing segment of the homeschooling population is African American. See, for instance, Institute of Education Sciences et al., "Homeschooling in the United States: 2012," NCES (Washington, DC: United States Department of Education, October 2016), http://nces.ed.gov/pubsearch/pubsinfo.asp?pubid=2016096; Aaron Hirsh, "The Changing Landscape of Homeschooling in the United States" (Bothell, WA: Center on Reinventing Public Education, 2019), https://www.crpe.org/sites/default/files/homeschooling_brief_final.pdf.

But there is a second, related concern. As a response to such controversies, district schools tend to attenuate moral messaging and even moral deliberation–thus forsaking, understandably and inevitably, the goal of providing an alternative approach to life from the domestic particularisms from which their students come. Indeed, research on classroom discussion shows that substantive debate about important issues is virtually absent.[34] One public school teacher described how he avoided a "potentially volatile" debate on human cloning:

> It was early in my high school teaching career, in the middle of a discussion about human cloning. Cheryl had been arguing for limits on scientific research, and her hand shot up again from the back of the classroom. "We shouldn't play God," she insisted.
>
> Maybe not, but can we talk about God? Or at least about the ways in which religious beliefs influence our lives in a diverse society? Cheryl made her comment in the midst of an eleventh-grade English class discussion of Aldous Huxley's *Brave New World.* The chilling images of the Hatchery, where embryos on conveyor belts were genetically modified, had struck a chord with my students.

The teacher, Robert Kunzman, "maneuvered around the comment" and refocused on Huxley. Kunzman noted, "If an administrator had been observing my class, she probably would have complimented my deft handling." For him, however, "it didn't feel like a fine pedagogical moment," because it indicated his unwillingness to grapple, with his students, with differing notions of the good–"and this grappling is the responsibility of informed, respectful citizenship."[35] Kunzman claims his experience is typical: "Versions of my English class 'pedagogical evasion' episode play out in classrooms throughout the country, and extend across the curriculum."[36]

Katherine Simon researched this and agrees: "Although moral and existential issues arise frequently, they are most often shut down immediately. If moral issues are not shut down completely, they are often relegated to assignments for individuals, rather than explored in public classroom discussion."[37] Simon studied literature, history, and biology classes in one public and two religious schools. She found that, despite the facts that "moral and existential questions are at the core of the disciplines" and "most people find moral and existential questions fas-

---

34 See, for instance, Robert Kunzman, *Grappling with the Good: Talking about Religion and Morality in Public Schools* (Albany: State University of New York Press, 2006); Katherine G. Simon, *Moral Questions in the Classroom: How to Get Kids to Think Deeply about Real Life and Their Schoolwork* (New Haven: Yale University Press, 2001).

35 Kunzman, *Grappling with the Good*, 1–2.

36 Ibid., 5.

37 Simon, *Moral Questions in the Classroom*, 53–54.

cinating," the classrooms she visited sidelined them. Fewer than 2 percent of the classes she visited engaged in any depth on matters of life, death, meaning, and purpose.[38]

As a final data source, the Johns Hopkins Institute for Education Policy, which I serve as director, designed a school culture survey to examine five core domains of school life. We conducted a pilot in Spring 2020 with twenty-six thousand participants across quite different school communities (district, Catholic, Protestant, and Islamic). While the survey was not yet nationally representative, we found widespread agreement, shared by teachers and students, that some of the most important issues–from politics to religion–are all but "taboo" in their classrooms.[39]

Note that the above examples are about *merely discussing* moral viewpoints–*not* promoting any particular one. If even discussing, and disagreeing about, contentious issues that are both universal to the human experience and particular to a society's current concerns, are off the table–can we expect schools to intentionally shape students' character? If so, on what basis?

Lack of philosophical depth is not a necessary outcome of our uniform public school system. District schools are allowed to teach *about* religion and philosophy, and many do. The observation to make, however, is that, *in the aggregate*, district schools have lost their mandate to articulate and enforce strong, normative claims and practices that could fulfill the aims expected by legislators and predicted by theorists. They might, however–as we shall see–do so unintentionally.

A Closer Look

What happens to moral formation in this context? The very question can confound, since the terms with which the field describes the nonacademic work of schooling change. While legislators in the nineteenth century wanted schools to impart a vague Protestantism, in the twentieth century, policymakers emphasized the role of schools in promoting "social efficiency," "social adjustment," and "individualism"–to name a few purposes.[40] The 1990 s called the nonacademic elements of schooling "character education;" today, many school systems, philan-

---

38 Ibid., 2.

39 An early report on this may be found in Ashley Berner, "In a Polarized America, What Can We Do about Civil Disagreement?," *Brookings* (blog), Apr. 10, 2020, https://www.brookings.edu/blog/brown-center-chalkboard/2020/04/10/in-a-polarized-america-what-can-we-do-about-civil-disagreement/.

40 Diane Ravitch, *Left Back: A Century of Battles over School Reform* (New York: Simon & Schuster, 2001).

thropic organizations, and think tanks use "noncognitives" or "social and emotional learning" instead.

Whatever we call these nonacademic capacities, however, schools cannot help but inculcate them–for better or for worse, intentionally or not. Schools are inherently meaning-making institutions; every component of a school's structure and content is educative for students. Even the omissions–what is unacceptable to discuss–are instructive. As Charles Glenn wrote in *The Myth of the Common School* (1988), "Formal education ... presents pictures or maps of reality that reflect, unavoidably, particular choices about what is certain and what in question, what is significant and what unworthy of notice."[41] It is thus impossible for schools *not* to promote values of some kind. But which values?

Observers often interpret the "hidden curriculum" of the classroom according to their own judgments about American culture writ large.[42] As for schools' *intentional* attempts to promote particular nonacademic qualities, there is no better analysis than James Davison Hunter's *The Death of Character: Moral Formation in an Age without Good and Evil* (2000). Hunter's award-winning book documents his study of the character-education programs that were put in place by all fifty states in the 1990 s to mediate what was perceived as the values-relativism of earlier decades. Hunter found that these programs eschewed the enduring "why" questions of human experience (for example, "why should we be good?" or "why should we eschew evil?").[43] They operated with strong claims, such as "tolerance," "kindness," and "respect," to be sure. But because they segregated such claims from the habitual practices of school life and from the intellectual or even religious sources that could make sense of them, these programs reinforced little more than individual self-interest and emotional well-being.[44] *They had no effect on students' conceptual or behavioral norms.*

---

41 Glenn, *The Myth of the Common School,* 11. I elaborate the inherent normativity of schooling in chapter 2 of Berner, *Pluralism and American Public Education.*

42 For Marxists, American classrooms promote consumerism and prepare students to be laborers or managers; see, for instance, Peter McLaren, *Life in Schools: An Introduction to Critical Pedagogy in the Foundations of Education,* 5th ed. (Washington, DC: Pearson, 2006). For others, they promote "the fast-paced, multiple task environments that many middle-class adults face in their jobs ... token economies, group projects, activity centers and rotations" implicitly "reinforced the market economy and personal choice," even though such concepts were not discussed nor necessarily desired. See Steven Brint, Mary F Contreras, and Michael T Matthews, "Socialization Messages in Primary Schools: An Organizational Analysis," *Sociology of Education* 74, no. 3 (2001): 157–80.

43 James Davison Hunter, *The Death of Character: Moral Education in an Age without Good or Evil* (New York: Basic Books, 2000), 212.

44 Ibid., 86–91.

This suggests that, in the modern age, the average American school simply reflects the majoritarian culture of what one sociologist calls "moral therapeutic deism" and "individual expressivism."[45] Schools are thus remarkably successful at imparting the individual autonomy called for by Gutmann and Levinson, albeit on terms that are devoid of depth, within classrooms that cannot articulate–much less debate–the merits of autonomy in the first place.

This should not surprise us. A uniform school system is designed to reflect the majority's view of what is good, for students and for democratic life. This is both the strength and the weakness of a uniform model.

A Pluralistic Model?

Most of the world's democracies design their school systems around a plural rather than a uniform structure. "Educational pluralism" refers to a system in which the state funds and regulates, but does not exclusively operate, a mosaic of schools. The Netherlands, for example, supports thirty-six different types of schools–including Catholic, Muslim, and Montessori–on an equal footing. England, Belgium, Sweden, Israel, Australia, and Hong Kong help students of all income levels attend philosophically and pedagogically diverse schools. So do most Canadian provinces. Funded schools in these pluralist systems are also subject to robust regulations and, in some cases, to a common academic curriculum. Importantly, educationally plural countries also provide for what the United States calls district schools; a third of Dutch students attend them. The difference is that, in educationally plural systems, *many types* of schools are considered to be part of the public education system.

Why does this matter for moral formation? It matters, because a plural design assumes that schools can and even should differentiate from the cultural majority in meaningful ways (within parameters, of course[46]). They can form distinctive cultures, whether Islamic, Jewish, Inuit, or secular. And one of the strongest research findings from studies of democratic education is that: "Schools with a distinctive identity ... offer educational advantages deriving from their clarity of focus."[47] Schools that operate out of an articulated and distinctive mission, one that is understood across constituents and that animates the institutional practi-

---

45 Christian Smith and Melina Lundquist Denton, *Soul Searching: The Religious and Spiritual Lives of American Teenagers*, repr. (Oxford: Oxford University Press, 2009), 162–70.

46 The limits of pluralism vary by country. I explore this and other issues in chapter 6 of Berner, *Pluralism and American Public Education.*

47 Charles Glenn, "What the United States Can Learn from Other Countries," in *What Americans Can Learn from School Choice in Other Countries*, ed. James Tooley and David Salisbury (Washington, DC: Cato Institute, 2005), 79–90, at 83.

ces within the school community, have a robust school culture. Of course, not every school has a strong culture, and the culture at some schools is hardly visible. But evidence from around the world–and within our own country–suggests that it matters tremendously for long-term beliefs and behaviors, from having friends of a different race or ethnicity, to volunteering at higher rates.[48] Educationally plural systems make these conditions more likely by, in some cases, requiring schools to publicize their distinctiveness and assessing them on their mission coherence.[49]

In the United States, because of the uniform structure, crafting normative school cultures happens more naturally in the private- and charter-school domains. Savvy districts are beginning to allow differentiation of schools through selective pedagogical, if not philosophical, focus. During the administration of Mayor Michael Bloomberg, for instance, New York City created 150 small high schools that are giving a leg up to disadvantaged students.[50] Under the leadership of Superintendent Pedro Martinez, the San Antonio, Texas, Independent School District is enabling schools to differentiate by aligning coursework with local industries, launching an International Baccalaureate program, or increasing socioeconomic diversity by design, among other means.[51] Miami-Dade, a large urban

---

48 Anthony S Bryk, Valerie E Lee, and Peter Blakeley Holland, *Catholic Schools and the Common Good* (Cambridge, MA: Harvard University Press, 1995); Karin Chenoweth, *It's Being Done: Academic Success in Unexpected Schools* (Cambridge, MA: Harvard Education Press, 2007); James S. Coleman, Thomas Hoffer, and Sally Kilgore, *High School Achievement: Public, Catholic, and Private Schools Compared* (New York: Basic Books, 1982); Scott Seider, *Character Compass: How Powerful School Culture Can Point Students toward Success* (Cambridge, MA: Harvard Education Press, 2012). Numerous specific studies suggest such connections, including Glenn, "What the United States Can Learn from Other Countries"; Ray Pennings, *Cardus Education Survey 2011* (Hamilton, Ont: Cardus, 2011); Ray Pennings, *Cardus Education Survey 2014* (Hamilton, Ont: Cardus, 2014); Marisa Casagrande, Ray Pennings, and David Sikkink, *Cardus Education Survey 2018: Rethinking Public Education,* Cardus, Oct. 2019, https://www.cardus.ca/research/education/reports/rethinking-public-education/; Martin West, "Education and Global Competitiveness," in *Rethinking Competitiveness*, ed. K. Hassett (Washington, DC: American Enterprise Institute Press, 2012), 68–94.

49 Department for Education, "What Maintained Schools Must Publish Online," Gov.UK, 2018, https://www.gov.uk/guidance/what-maintained-schools-must-publish-online; Ashley Berner, "Would School Inspections Work in the United States?," *Johns Hopkins Institute for Education Policy* (blog), Sept. 14, 2017, http://edpolicy.education.jhu.edu/would-school-inspections-work-in-the-united-states/.

50 Adriana Villavicencio and William Marinell, "Inside Success: Strategies of 25 Successful High Schools" (New York: Research Alliance for New York City Schools, Jul. 2014).

51 Robin Lake, "What Other Cities & School Districts Can Learn from San Antonio's Classroom Innovations," Oct. 2, 2018, https://www.the74million.org/article/san-antonio-isds-innovations-offer-national-lessons/.

school district with 345,000 students, also allows schools to attract families on the basis of their distinctive offerings. Miami, it must be noted, is located in Florida, which enables some 120,000 (low-income) students to attend private schools through various choice mechanisms, and more than 300,000 to attend public charter schools, which are funded by the state but delivered by independent organizations.[52] Of all the states, Florida and Indiana come closest to the pluralist norm in terms of options that are funded and academic accountability in place. As with all departures from the uniform model in the United States, however, diversification of delivery remains deeply contested.[53]

The structure of educational pluralism cannot *ensure* coherence of mission, of course. It merely makes it possible. A large-scale study on faith schools in the UK (2009), for instance, indicated that Anglican schools were not particularly Anglican: very few principals could articulate what made their schools different. School leaders failed to "engage with the Christian faith as a coherent rationale for life and learning." Heads of Catholic schools in the UK, by contrast, were much better grounded in the tenets and mission of the Catholic church and its educational imperatives.[54] A plural structure can, however, create space for schools to revive or reimagine their mission–as many Church of England schools have done in the wake of the 2009 report.[55]

Schools, like all human individuals and institutions, are located within concentric circles of cultural influence of which they, and we, are only partially cognizant. We take this as a given. However, when it comes to allowing, and even incentivizing, the conditions that maximize the odds of a "school effect" that is intentional–that either affirms or resists the cultural majority coherently and overtly–educational pluralism has an advantage over educational uniformity.

---

52 EdChoice, "Florida Choice Progams," *EdChoice*, Feb. 4, 2020, https://www.edchoice.org/school-choice/school-choice-in-america/; David Figlio and Cassandra Hart, "Competitive Effects of Means-Tested Vouchers," *American Economic Journal: Applied Economics* 6, no. 1 (Jan. 2014): 133–56, https://doi.org/10.1257/app.6.1.133; Matthew Chingos and Daniel Kuehn, "The Effects of Statewide Private School Choice on College Enrollment and Graduation" (Washington, DC: Urban Institute, Sept. 21, 2017), https://www.urban.org/research/publication/effects-statewide-private-school-choice-college-enrollment-and-graduation.

53 Patrik Jonnson, "In Florida, Vouchers Win Ground, but Courts May Have Ultimate Say," *Christian Science Monitor*, May 10, 2019, https://www.csmonitor.com/EqualEd/2019/0510/In-Florida-vouchers-win-ground-but-courts-may-have-ultimate-say.

54 Elizabeth Green and Trevor Cooling, *Mapping the Field: A Review of the Current Research Evidence on the Impact of Schools with a Christian Ethos* (London: Theos, 2009), 33–35.

55 Edward Malnick and Julie Henry, "Church of England Schools to Be 'Rebranded,'" *The Telegraph*, Mar. 17, 2012, http://www.telegraph.co.uk/education/educationnews/9150817/Church-of-England-schools-to-be-rebranded.html.

Whether school systems in the United States continue to pluralize, and to such an extent that pluralism replaces uniformity as the cultural default, remains to be seen.

Part Three:
Emerging Themes

Vocational Exploration as Character Formation: A New Direction for Higher Education

David S. Cunningham

Observers of North American higher education have begun to notice a subtle shift in the attitudes of some undergraduate students. In particular, many students seem to be pondering their future directions in life in rather different terms than would have been typical a generation or two ago. Particularly with respect to their future careers–but also with regard to where, how, and with whom they will live–a significant number of students are not thinking first and foremost about how much money they will make, or how they might most quickly climb the corporate ladder. These typical (and perhaps stereotypical) "American" traits do not have quite the hold on college students that one might expect. Students seem to be spending more time thinking about their personal strengths and weaknesses, pondering what will make for a meaningful or purposeful life, and sometimes even using the language of *vocation* or *calling* in their efforts to describe where their lives might be headed. Quantitatively speaking, this shift is very small; surveys indicate that a majority of university students are still interested in "getting a good job" above all else.[1] Nevertheless, by examining the increasing presence of words such as *meaning, purpose*, and *vocation* in the discourses of higher education in the United States, we can chart one very interesting path through which moral development and character formation is taking place. This language might have the potential to shape higher education in other national settings as well.

---

1 Good longitudinal data on the attitudes and interests of undergraduate students in the United States is available through the work of the Higher Education Research Institute (HERI), which provides data to institutions about the perspectives of their first-year and final-year students. Similarly, the National Survey of Student Engagement provides annual reports on the state of undergraduate education, with a particular focus on student attitudes and experiences. See *The American Freshman: National Norms Fall 2019* and *Findings from the 2019 Administration of the College Senior Survey* (Los Angeles: Higher Education Research Institute, 2020), as well as *Engagement Insights: Survey Findings on the Quality of Undergraduate Education–Annual Results 2019* (Bloomington: Indiana Center for Postsecondary Research, 2020).

In five sections, this essay explores the relationship between character formation and vocational reflection. The first offers a description of the context of higher education in the United States, explaining why the relationship between character and vocation has developed in some American institutions but not in others. The second section offers an account of the language of vocation, sketching its ancient theological roots, its historical sojourn, and its reintroduction as a term of art in twenty-first-century higher education. The remaining three sections explore the contours of educational programs that focus on vocational exploration and discernment, describing three features that make these programs especially conducive to the work of education in ethics and character formation in the late modern era.

The Context of Higher Education in the United States

North America (and particularly the United States) hosts two relatively differentiated systems of higher education. About fifteen million of the country's twenty-one million university students are enrolled in public institutions, which are funded in part by state governments and subject to the control (and sometimes the whims) of state legislatures. The remaining six million students are enrolled in private institutions of various kinds. These students are divided about evenly among for-profit, religiously affiliated nonprofit, and secular nonprofit institutions. Setting aside the for-profit institutions,[2] about four million students are enrolled in about sixteen hundred private institutions, roughly divided between those institutions that are religiously affiliated and those that are not.

The prohibition of any government-established religion in the United States means that public institutions tend to tread very carefully in any territory that is, or could be construed as, overtly religious. While departments of religious studies flourish at many public institutions, any activity related to moral formation, character development, and the communication of values must carefully sidestep any specifically religious content. As a result, any such programming at public institutions tends to be relatively vague and starkly subject to the vagaries of federal, state, and local politics.[3] Private institutions have a great deal more freedom to

2 These are highly controversial, and their numbers tend to rise and fall in different political environments. Most of them enroll students with the promise of a quick and direct path to employment, and very few offer the kinds of programs described in this essay.

3 To offer one example among many: educational institutions have been in a fight–previously with the Trump administration and now with a number of state legislatures–as to whether diversity and inclusion training activities may be allowed on campus. Most educational authorities see these activities as an important opportunity to form students in patterns of life that celebrate diversity and resist racism, whereas some politicians see

engage their students in various activities that form character and cultivate particular virtues, and to do so with regular reference to various theological traditions. Naturally, religiously affiliated institutions tend to draw on specific faith traditions in their efforts toward education in ethics. Yet even highly secular private institutions can bring religion into the conversation if they so choose, and without worry about lawsuits from those who seek to enforce the constitutional prohibition against governmentally established religion.

Private institutions, whether religious or secular, often use this "ethical freedom" as an advertisement for their curricular and cocurricular programs, as part of a broader strategy of recruiting students.[4] They can easily offer students full immersion into deep waters—waters into which public institutions can only wade. As a result, private institutions are often in search of concepts, language, and practices that can help them continue to build and renew their efforts at character development and moral formation. Depending on the institution's degree of religious affiliation, these languages, concepts, and practices may sometimes draw on theological insights. But given the increasingly diverse religious perspectives of their student populations, most private colleges and universities (even religiously affiliated ones) often limit their forays into theology—or at least, avoid making themselves narrowly beholden to any particular faith tradition or ecclesial perspective.

This combination of factors—the relative independence of private higher education, the desire to engage in ethics, and the country's increasing religious diversity—has made the United States into a very interesting laboratory for testing various approaches to character development and moral formation in the university setting. These factors also help to account for the means by which many educational institutions have chosen to carry out this work. They have done so by embracing some particular forms of an ancient, highly contested, and theologically weighted concept: namely, that of *vocation.*

---

them as indoctrinating students to cast blame on white people and to undermine "traditional" values. While the federal government cannot dictate educational policy, state governments can do so. In addition, American higher education is heavily dependent on government grants and other forms of funding, which can be withheld from noncompliant institutions. Even a threatened reduction in such funding can have a chilling effect on an institution's willingness to stand up to various forms of government intrusion.

4 Private institutions in the United States are typically more expensive than public ones; however, this gap has diminished somewhat in recent decades, due to decreases in state funding for public institutions and increases in financial aid budgets at private ones.

Tracing the History of Vocation[5]

The word *vocation* derives from the Latin *vocare*, to call. Hence, the words *calling* and *vocation* are etymologically similar, and both words came into English in the sixteenth century. The Latin noun *vocatio* was, in the medieval era, largely restricted to what we would today call "religious vocations" (priesthood and the monastic life). In the Reformation, the word's reference was extended well beyond its previous range; Martin Luther, in particular, helped to endow the German verb *rufen* (to call) with a range of reference involving all walks of life; hence, the closely related German noun *Beruf* has come to mean "occupation" or "profession." This helps to explain why we tend to associate the English word *calling* with a person's work or career; as Luther would put it, our work is one of the stations in life (*Stände*) that constitute the place to which God has called us.

This shift in the meaning of the word *vocatio* tended to accord a greater degree of dignity to a wider range of human occupations, marginally offsetting the more hierarchical structure of medieval life. But it could also tend to ratify the status quo; if one's stations in life, broadly defined, were seen as divinely appointed, then any self-motivated attempt to change one's status could be understood not only as politically revolutionary but also as rebellious against God. This tendency was mitigated somewhat by later strands of the Reformation; still, the language of vocation has often tempted people to use its resonances of divine sanction to encourage a certain kind of societal stability–and to discourage individuals from an ongoing consideration of shifts in their own vocational journey. More positively, however, it can also make people more open to the possibility that, as they consider the future course of their lives, a change in direction might sometimes be warranted.

I have tended to pair "one's work" with "one's stations in life" as a reminder that, although we may associate vocation and calling primarily with a person's occupation or profession, the semantic range of these words is considerably wider. Since most adults spend a significant amount of their time undertaking some form of employment (either for subsistence or for wages), a person's work certainly plays a significant role within the broader concept of vocation. And, indeed, the industrial revolution and the firm grip of late capitalism have only increased the general tendency of individuals to define their lives primarily by their employment. Clearly, though, one can be also be "called" to certain forms of life in the *polis*, the *ekklesia*, and the *oikos*. Moreover, one's various stations in life can also be affected by factors that we traditionally classify under the term *demographics:*

5 This section is derived in part from David S. Cunningham, "Time and Place: Why Vocation Is Crucial to Undergraduate Education Today," in *At This Time and In This Place: Vocation and Undergraduate Education*, ed. David S. Cunningham (New York: Oxford University Press, 2016), 1-19, at 7-12.

age, marital status, level of education, location of residence, socioeconomic class, religious alignment (or lack thereof), race, sex, gender identity, and sexual orientation. If we understand these categories to be not merely sociological statistics but deeply formative realities, we may come to recognize their importance for vocational reflection. These realities can prompt questions such as these: Where and with whom will I live? How will I engage with the economic and political systems that will shape my life? What sorts of civic, philanthropic, and religious institutions will garner my time and attention? How will I negotiate the larger global context that increasingly affects everything I do? How will I go about making the future decisions that I must inevitably face?

Precisely because the category of *calling* or *vocation* addresses not only the world of work but also a wider range of questions about one's stations in life, it can be particularly useful and effective language for helping university students think about the directions in which their lives might be heading. While students are often encouraged to think about their future careers, many colleges and universities are sensing a need to expand these conversations beyond matters of future employment to include every aspect of one's calling. This is why the title of a recently published book claims that academic institutions *must talk with their students about vocation.*[6]

In fact, many universities are already carrying out these expansive conversations with their students. A few institutions have been doing so since they were founded, while others have been making it a priority over the last several decades. Attention to the topic of vocation and calling has grown exponentially over the past twenty years, due to a large-scale initiative by a major American philanthropic foundation that focused on "the theological exploration of vocation," followed by the development of a growing network of colleges and universities that have recognized the potential of the concept and the language of vocation. As a result, more and more American institutions of higher education are providing professional development opportunities for faculty members and staff, and creating programs for students, that focus on vocational exploration and discernment as a means of addressing the aspirations and concerns of the college-age population.[7]

---

6 Tim Clydesdale, *The Purposeful Graduate: Why Colleges Must Talk to Students about Vocation* (Chicago: University of Chicago Press, 2015).

7 Beginning in 1999, the Indianapolis-based Lilly Endowment encouraged universities to develop Programs for the Theological Exploration of Vocation (PTEV), providing grants of up to two million dollars each to eighty-eight private institutions. Over the decade that followed, the colleges and universities that were developing these programs met in various settings to compare their work and to discuss best practices. In 2009, this group evolved into the Network for Vocation in Undergraduate Education (NetVUE)–a member-supported association that now includes over 250 private colleges and universities.

I want to suggest that students who participate in programs of vocational exploration and discernment also find themselves engaged, through these very programs, in a certain kind of moral education and character formation. If students are helped to reflect seriously on their various callings in life, they necessarily find themselves thinking not only about the coursework that they will need to undertake and the skills that they will need to develop but also about *the kinds of persons* that they will need to be, or to become, in order to live into their various stations in life. In fact, in a new book on the topic (aimed primarily at a student audience), the authors focus not so much on "having" or "finding" a calling but rather on "living vocationally." They use this terminology, they write, in order

> to emphasize that vocation pertains not just to certain areas of our lives, but is rather about all of life. Living vocationally creates a way of being in the world that shapes our lives as a whole. This is why we will continually stress that calling extends far beyond our jobs or our careers. ... The discovery of our callings must be guided by the discernment of the person we are meant to become. Who we are and what we are making of ourselves is a more crucial issue for vocational discernment than trying to determine the right career choice. ... Put differently, living vocationally reminds us that the most important question is not about *making a living*, but about *making a life.*[8]

In the remainder of this essay, I sketch out some of the ways that vocational exploration can operate as a program of moral formation and character development. I draw certain parallels among these practices, suggesting that vocational discernment has the capacity to help us see that certain elements of moral formation—elements that we tend to understand as dichotomies—actually have a dialectical structure, and that this dialectic becomes more obvious when *moral formation* and *character development* are understood through the lens of *vocational exploration and discernment.*

Individualized and Communitarian

The work of vocational discernment encourages students to focus on two elements at once: not only the very specific and individual contours of their own calling but also the way in which their vocations arise from, and will continue to shape, their relationships with others. Few things are more uniquely one's own than one's calling; and yet, only within a larger network of human relationships will that calling take on its full significance.

---

8 Paul J. Wadell and Charles R. Pinches, *Living Vocationally: The Journey of the Called Life* (Eugene, OR: Cascade Books, 2021), 2–3.

Stories in which people "hear a call" can often seem quite individualistic. A person is alone in a room, or in the desert, or in the woods, and suddenly hears (or feels, or sees) something that is understood as a request, or possibly a demand, from outside oneself. It may come from some element of nature (a tree, the sky, or animals), from an individual human being (a family member, a spiritual leader, or even a stranger), or from God. The story of a call often places the emphasis on the dyad of the caller and the called; the communication may be unidirectional or conversational, but it rarely involves more than two characters. These narratives tend to emphasize the specificity of the call; it is intended for one person, and only that person can fulfill its request, plea, or demand.[9]

And yet, these stories are never really limited to the two chief characters (the caller and the called). The one who is called is part of a larger community, and the call is often to serve that community in some way. Those who are called have been prepared to receive their calls–to discern their vocations–by the families, tribes, and other groups that have nurtured them and have given particular shape to their lives. Indeed, the fact that the call comes to this person, and to no other, suggests that the one who hears the call has been communally shaped to hear it, understand it, and (potentially) to respond to it. A few of these individuals may be called to genuinely monastic vocations; but for the overwhelming majority of people, a calling is an invitation to align oneself with a larger community (a neighborhood, a guild, a religious tradition), often as a way of serving an even larger community (a clientele, a city, or the entire world).

In this way, vocational exploration reflects one of the most important features of character formation, which is also focused simultaneously on the individual and the community. One's character is very much one's own; indeed, the various definitions of the English word *character* all focus on what makes something distinct and distinguishable from others–whether the word is defined as a personality trait, a specific feature, a letter of the alphabet, or a person portrayed in drama. And yet, in order for any of these forms of character to have meaning, we must make reference to the larger group of entities to which they belong and from which they can be distinguished. With respect to personality traits in particular (and the judging of them as positive or negative), we must refer to the communal setting within which they arise. What seems courageous in one context will seem foolhardy in another. The traits that mark Aristotle's description of magnanimity –a steady gait, a deep voice, and slow speech[10]–may strike us today as excessively reserved, slightly pompous, and very, very male. To reflect on one's vocation is to consider how one's individual traits (including strengths, talents, preferences, and ideals) fit into the contours of the communities of which one is a part–includ-

9 For more on narratives of calling, see Charles Pinches, "Stories of Call: From Dramatic Phenomena to Changed Lives," in Cunningham, *At This Time*, 122–42.

10 Aristotle, *Nicomachean Ethics*, IV.3.

ing those communities' needs, hungers, and hopes. As some etymologists have speculated, the Greek word for character (*ethos*) is not merely accidentally related to the word for tribe or people (*ethnos*).

Integrating and Differentiating

Closely related to the dialectic of individual and community is that of integration and differentiation. Both of these elements are essential for character development and moral formation, as encapsulated in Aristotle's observations concerning "the unity of the virtues."[11] Although the various excellences of character are different from one another, and although any given individual will embody certain virtues more successfully than others, this does not mean that some of them may be neglected altogether. If a person is deficient in one of the virtues, this fault cannot be compensated for by an extraordinary effort to maximize another virtue. Virtuous persons must seek to live in such a way that all of the virtues are integrated into their lives.

If this was a challenge in Aristotle's day, it is much more so in our own. Since the cultivation of a virtue is possible only through its repeated practice (such that it becomes a habit), a person must participate in a wide variety of activities in order to "practice" being courageous, moderate, just, and wise. Today, these activities need to be carried out in a variety of spheres, not all of which share the same assumptions about what counts as a good habit worth cultivating. As the editors of this volume note in the preface, the sources of normative coding and moral education today are rooted in a number of powerful social systems, including law, religion, politics, the family, education, the market, the media, the academy, health care, and defense. They go on to note that

> each of these social systems has internal value systems, institutionalized rationalities, and normative expectations that together help to shape each individual's morality and character. Each of these social spheres, moreover, has its own professionals and experts who shape and implement its internal structures and processes. The normative network created by the social spheres is harder to grasp today, since late modern pluralistic societies usually do not bring these different value systems to light under the dominance of just one organization, institution, and power. And this normative network has also become more shifting and fragile.

Hence, we face the challenge of attending simultaneously to all of these social systems and of cultivating habits that will develop into excellences of character

11 Ibid., IV.12–13.

that are proper to each one–while also finding ways for these disparate virtues to be integrated into a unified life.

This challenge is one to which the work of vocational exploration and discernment is able to respond quite appropriately. By asking students to think holistically about their callings in terms of various stations–career, family, civic life, leisure time–two goals can be achieved at a single stroke. First, students can come to see that the strengths, talents, and preferences that they will bring to one aspect of their future lives may not map perfectly onto other areas. For example, the precision demanded by the field of engineering might lead to something less than domestic tranquility if carried over directly into one's home life. Similarly, the open structure and multiple interpretations that are an essential part of the study of literature and drama may be less useful in constructing clear and precise legal descriptions. Hence, vocational reflection requires that we differentiate among the various life stations–and among the strengths and weaknesses that we bring to each. On the other hand, this process of contemplating one's many callings in life will also mitigate our tendency to isolate one element of these stations (say, paid employment) and to organize our entire lives around achieving that narrow goal, while ignoring how it might impact our lives as a whole. In the university setting, vocational exploration (understood in these broad terms) can help students to focus less on choosing a major field of study and preparing for a certain career, and more on pursuing a more comprehensive education that will prepare them for all walks of life.[12] This is vocation's virtue: it forces us to consider how these stations will be properly differentiated, while also providing a means of integrating them into a life marked by wholeness and unity.

Bound and Free

We can make use of Luther's account of the Christian life to describe a life lived with attention to one's calling: the life of a person who "lives vocationally." That person is "a perfectly free sovereign, subject to none, and a perfectly dutiful servant, subject to all."[13] In late modern pluralistic societies, individuals have a bewil-

[12] This point, of course, is specific to the United States, where many students enter college with a much spottier grasp of what one would call, in German, *allgemeine Bildung.* This is because, with a few exceptions, American high schools do not educate students to the level at which they might successfully complete the kinds of final examinations that are typical in European secondary schools (French *baccalauréat*, German *Abitur*, British A-levels). Entering American college students typically enroll in general education courses for the first one or two years and do not designate a specific field of study until the second year–a process often fraught with high anxiety.

[13] Martin Luther, *The Freedom of a Christian* (1520), 1.

dering array of choices as to how they will pursue their lives. Particularly with respect to paid employment, we tend to assume that, if we set our minds to the task and work very hard, we can achieve whatever goals we may set for ourselves. This notion is especially prevalent in the United States, where narratives of self-actualization and entrepreneurship are deeply embedded in the national ethos/ ethnos.

And yet, taken by itself, this narrative is a *myth* in the most pejorative sense. By the time they enter university, young people have either already received–or have failed to receive–the level of training that they will need to become, say, a classical pianist, a professional basketball player, or someone who speaks four languages with native fluency. Similarly, they likely will have already cultivated–or will have failed to cultivate–the habits of mind and body needed to complete the necessary coursework, score high enough on the tests, be endorsed by the best referees, and write the brilliant applications that will lead to admission into the best medical schools, law schools, or other highly competitive postgraduate programs of study. These strengths, talents, and habits are certainly not innate; but neither can they be summoned by mere fiat. To live vocationally is to recognize that while certain limitations are the work of oppressors (or merely a failure of the imagination and the will), others are real and quite concrete. Students should not be led to believe that they are bound to only one path in life, as may have been true for many of their premodern predecessors. But neither should they imagine that they can achieve absolutely anything to which they set their minds. We are free, but not infinitely so; indeed, our "finite freedom"[14] is actually one of the greatest gifts that we have been given. We are not condemned to the paralysis that results from an infinite variety of equally appealing choices.[15]

Once again, this aspect of vocational reflection provides an important form of support to pedagogical efforts toward moral formation and character development. It helps to explain why a quick and painless reversal of one's long-cultivated habits of character is unlikely to take hold, and even less likely to be retained over the long run. Pursuing one's vocation requires something similar to cultivating a particular moral perspective: it requires regular and consistent practices that will allow a person to develop the habits of mind, of body, and of spirit that will make one's calling (or one's character) an integrated part of one's essential personhood. Vocational reflection may lead a person to say, for example, that "I believe that I am called to be a theologian, an administrator, a good father, and a

---

14 See Hans Urs von Balthasar's discussion of "finite freedom" in *Theo-Drama: Theological Dramatic Theory*, trans. Graham Harrison (San Francisco: Ignatius Press, 1990), II:189–284.

15 For a thoughtful application of this point to vocational exploration in particular, see William T. Cavanaugh, "Actually, You *Can't* Be Anything You Want (And It's a Good Thing, Too)," in Cunningham, *At This Time*, 25–46.

persuasive voice for better public policy." But it is not enough to declare this as an intention and a goal; the next step is to consider the kind of person that I will need to be, or to become, in order to live into this calling. And in order to become the kind of person that I hope to be, I will need to subject myself to a certain kind of *askesis*–not in the common use of "ascetic" as severe (usually religious) self-discipline, but in the original Greek meaning of "training" or "practice." If I am to become the person that I believe I am called to be, I will need training that will build up the habits necessary to carry out this work, such that it will become almost second nature to me. The discernment of my vocation goes hand in hand with the formation and development of my character.

As an added bonus, this element of vocational reflection also provides a means of bridging the gap between religious and secular approaches to its execution. Recalling the roots of the word *religion* (Latin *religio*, to bind), exploring our callings requires us to examine those beliefs, practices, and convictions to which we consider ourselves bound (whether or not this binding takes the form of a particular faith tradition). In fact, to avoid the confusion created by the contemporary tendency to merge the word *religion* with the phrase *faith tradition*, it may be best to adopt a new word altogether; I propose *lifestance.* The process of vocational reflection asks us to reflect on our *lifestance*–that is, "the style and content of an individual's or a community's relationship with that which is of ultimate importance; the presuppositions and commitments of this, and the consequences for living which flow from it."[16] To which elements of our lives are we most committed? Which beliefs and practices are so integral to our lives that we could not dispense with them and retain our identity? These are the ways that we are "bound," whether or not we use variations on the word *religio* to describe them. The difference between religious and secular is not the difference between bound and free; we are all both bound and free in particular ways, whether we see ourselves as secular or religious persons. The nature and degree of our various "bindings" is part of what constitutes our lifestance; and although we are free to deviate from it, our character comes to be aligned with it and perceived through the beliefs and practices that it comprises. Similarly, one's lifestance affects one's efforts at vocational exploration and discernment, and those efforts will also tend to shape and reshape the contours of one's lifestance.

---

16 Harry Stopes-Roe, "Humanism as a Life Stance," *New Humanist* 103, no. 2 (Oct. 1988): 21, cited (with additional reflections on the usefulness of the term) in Rachel S. Mikva, "The Change a Difference Makes: Formation of the Self in the Encounter with Diversity," in *Hearing Vocation Differently: Meaning, Purpose, and Identity in the Multi-Faith Academy*, ed. David S. Cunningham (New York: Oxford University Press, 2019), 23–41.

Envoi

This essay has argued that the exploration and discernment of one's callings in life can function as a form of moral development. The two enterprises share certain characteristics, including their individual and communal nature, their integrative and differentiating elements, and their usefulness as a reminder that we are simultaneously bound and free. By asking students to reflect on their vocations–not only in matters of employment, nor only in the economic sphere more generally, but also in the realms of domestic and civic life, voluntary associations, and leisure pursuits–we are also asking them to consider the kinds of persons that they hope to become. When programs of vocational reflection are designed and carried out with thoughtfulness and care, they can align with the work of character development and moral formation that has become an essential element of higher education in the late modern era.

This particular American experiment is ready to be exported to other educational systems. Higher education in the United Kingdom, the British Commonwealth, and the European Union is structured in a way that would make these environments fertile ground for various forms of professional development and student-focused programming on vocation and calling. Admittedly, in most of these educational systems, students enter university life with a deeper focus on a particular area of study than is the case for American students. This fact might, at first glance, seem to make vocational exploration less important at the baccalaureate level in these educational systems. But in fact, the opposite is the case: while students may have chosen a particular direction for study, they may be less aware of how much discernment they still have to do–not only about the particular kinds of work they will undertake but also about how they will live their lives in the domestic, civic, and leisure spheres. In addition, baccalaureate students in many European and Commonwealth university settings face even more neuralgic circumstances if they sense that they may not have chosen a field of study that aligns with their callings. Given the strictures of these educational systems, students who might want to change direction need a great deal more support and encouragement in order to overcome the obstacles to undertaking such a change.

I would therefore propose a greater level of conversation among American, Commonwealth, and European universities on the topic of vocational exploration and discernment. Not only would this conversation create more opportunities to consider the implications described in this essay (with respect to moral formation and character development); it could also improve outcomes for undergraduate students in all of these educational systems. Perhaps the time has come for those of us who work in higher education–across all borders–to do a bit of vocational discernment of our own. To what new ventures are we being called, in order that our students might prosper? How will we explore these paths, in conversation with one another? What obstacles need to be overcome in order to implement professional development opportunities and student-centered programming in these areas? If we take these questions seriously, we, too, may discern new callings as educators–and thereby experience the same kinds of moral formation and character development that we would wish for our students. May we, as educators, become the change that we wish to see in the world.

Character Formation and *Literarische Bildung:* Aims and Potentials in Literature Education

Irene Pieper

How does literature education relate to the challenges of preparing for and shaping of contemporary societies? How should literature education contribute to character formation and the ethical development of students nowadays? Or should one rather leave these questions aside, given the manifold urgent tasks of formal schooling and the language arts with regard to basic literacy education for all students, and given the ambivalent history of moral education via literature in so many countries and in Germany in particular? Of course, the last question is strongly rhetorical, but if I had asked *would* one rather leave these questions aside, I am afraid the answer would be less clear for a considerable part of current discourse around the subject.

Yes, it is commonly accepted that literature education should be considered in the frame of personal development, of *Bildung* in its strong sense, and yes, this process of maturation is seen as a complex interaction of individualization, socialization, and enculturation. But when it comes to more focused questions about aims or practices in literature education, the normative issue of personal development brought about via encounters with literature may become a rather vague and distant construct, perhaps even losing its potential to orient professionals in the educational process. My assumption is that this is at least partly due to the fluidity that characterizes the concepts of "person," "self," "subject," "literature"—and, of course, *Bildung.* This openness may help in fostering and accepting diversity in our social and cultural environments. At the same time, however, it creates a demand to (re-)consider how a person may develop in the educational process and how the potential of literature as a source and mediator of this process may be grasped.

Given my disciplinary background in languages and literature, my observations will focus on literature in education and develop the notion of character formation from there, taking up the current discourse on subjectivation in German educational research. Subjectivation is considered as a relational process in a sociocultural environment. Education plays an important role in this process. In situations of teaching and learning, positions are assigned to the various actors, and the way human beings address each other contributes to subjectivation.[1] This nonessentialist approach fits theories of cognitive development in the line of Lev Vygotskij which hold that co-construction is constitutive for all learning.[2] Such processes also shape or even determine encounters with literature, particularly with learners. While both hermeneutics and cognitive psychology hold that the reading process is to be considered as a construction shaped by interaction between the reader and the text, lifting the potential of literature to stimulate personal development is a task that again needs an environment allowing for co-construction, particularly via communication. Such an environment may be provided by family; it certainly should be provided by formal education at school.

In this dynamic frame, literature can never be mere content. It is the way in which literature is perceived, discussed, and enjoyed that assigns relevance to literature in the process of development. And despite the fact that the concept "literature" is debatable, and the line between literature and nonliterature permeable rather than strict, we may hold that literature has a contribution to make in understanding the world and surpassing what "is" for an imaginary "could" or a challenging "should." Particularly from the perspective of development, literature has a lot to offer since it may take up any theme that might be interesting and thought provoking for an audience that is generally busy with finding its way through the world. Much of the literary canon and contemporary literature alike shows a critical stance toward how we live, how societies are shaped or justice questioned, and how the environment is degraded. My assumption is that the strength of literature needs not only the enthusiasm but also the informed support of professionals in the classroom in order to be unfolded.

My perspective is situated in a German-speaking environment. However, international discussions on education in the language arts show that the general tendencies are largely shared in Western and now even in global contexts.[3]

---

1 See Norbert Ricken, *Die Ordnung der Bildung: Beiträge zu einer Genealogie der Bildung* (Wiesbaden: Verlag für Sozialwissenschaften, 2006). Rickens's approach within a theory of practice follows Michel Foucault and Judith Butler and develops a relational concept of "subjectivation" that sets processes between subjects as constitutive for the self, a notion that is familiar to both theology and philosophy.

2 Lev S. Vygotskij, *Problems of General Psychology, Including Thinking and Speech*, vol. 1 of *Collected Works I/R*, ed. Robert W. Rieber (New York: Plenum, 1987).

3 See Bill Green and Per Olof Erixon, eds., *Rethinking L1 Education in the Global Era: Understanding the (Post-)National L1 Subjects in New and Difficult Times*, vol. 48 of *Educational Linguistics* (Dordrecht: Springer, 2020). For developments in literature education and current challenges in a broader perspective, see Irene Pieper, "L1 Education and the Place of Literature," in Green and Erixon, *Rethinking L1 Education*, 115–32. It is very common in education that literature is not a subject of its own but forms part of the lan-

I start with a brief consideration of literature education in a diachronic perspective in order to develop my perception of today's situation. In the second section, I consider aims and practices evident in recent empirical studies from my own research environment. Against this background, I ask once more about the potential of literature in education to shape the process of personal development at the beginning of the twenty-first century. I argue that there is a need for a differentiated concept of literature in relation to experiences we have in everyday life and expectations we might develop toward society. Abstract agreement on such a concept needs to be transferred into thorough encounters with literature as subject matter by teachers.

Literature as "The Good Seed"?

One could ask far more modest questions about the potential and even responsibility of the language arts in education than the one about its contribution to character formation–and there were times when routes to clear-cut answers were more easily taken. In the 1950 s, a widely used textbook in German compulsory schooling was called *Die gute Saat*–"The Good Seed"–thus indicating that literature was to serve as the good seed that will lead the good (Christian) child to a rich harvest. The volume for grade two, designed for students at the age of seven, started with a morning prayer and ended with an evening prayer. Metaphors around fruit and grain were common at the time as textbook titles or mottoes–continuing the assumptions of the early twentieth century, and even the Nazi period,[4] that the right literary texts, poems, stories, and fables should and would help the formation of a moral self and were indispensable for formal schooling.

This instrumental concept of literature in a rather rigid frame of moral–and often nationalist–education is no longer acceptable, particularly after the late 1960 s in Western modern societies. At the same time, another trait of literature education that was particularly present in pre-university education and that

guage arts–for example, as part of the study of German in Germany or English in the UK or the U.S. ("first language education" or "L1").

4 *Die gute Saat* was published by Westermann (Braunschweig) from 1955 on. Another example is *Die Sieben Ähren* (The seven ears) by Schwann (Düsseldorf), starting in 1950, or *Lebensgut* (The good of/for life) by Diesterweg (Frankfurt) from 1955 on. See Ulf Abraham and Matthis Kepser, *Literaturdidaktik Deutsch: Eine Einführung*, 3rd rev. ed. (Berlin: Erich Schmidt, 2009), 187, also for an indication that the German situation of the 1950 s differed from the French. However, the general development as sketched in this paragraph is comparable for much of Western Europe; see Wayne Sawyer and Piet-Hein van de Ven, eds., "Paradigms of Mother Tongue Education," Special Issue, *L1–Educational Studies in Language and Literature*, 7, no. 1 (2007).

aimed at forming a cultural elite via encounters with the literary canon also came under pressure. Now, emancipatory concerns started to shape the view of education as well as of literature to a large extent. Literary studies with their focus on linguistic features and aesthetic structures of literature became more influential in the curriculum. Conceiving of literature as providing straightforward moral insights did not fit these changes, nor did the notion of highly valued literary texts, which were often considered to exert a self-evident aesthetic authority. The concept of literature in school was broadened. Canonical texts were now complemented by and distinguished from other texts and media that might be more present in the social environments of the time. Students were to reflect on the sociocultural contexts of literature and should be enabled to emancipate themselves from any form of manipulation–for example, the emotional manipulation of potentially confirmative light fiction.

Three more shifts in the conception of learners and of subject matter since then need to be mentioned in order to grasp today's situation. First, more clearly than before, the learner has by now gained the anchor position from which the literature curriculum is designed, not only with regard to processes of learning but also with regard to his or her experiences of and motivations for reading. This shift again reflects changes in society and research, particularly the impact of reader response theory and approaches by cognitive psychology to the reading process since the 1970 s that stress the active role of the reader in both constructing meaning and bringing about multitudes of interpretation. This change has had a strong influence on the choice of texts to be taught, with youth literature gaining ground and an increasing readiness to meet students' interests. In conceptual work on literature education, this shift is linked to explorations of the potential of literature (education) for the development of "identity."[5] Despite an increased openness to include literature of all kinds and qualities, leading voices in German discourse, such as Jürgen Kreft, stress that it is the aesthetic potential of literature that contributes to development, and only afterward can society tolerate any instrumental approach that asks for messages or functions.

Second, the turn toward the outcome of formal schooling in a competence-based framework since 2000 has put much emphasis on linguistic abilities in general and the reading performance of students in particular–not literature.

Third, connected to these changes is the stress on differences among learners. Though diversity regarding the socioeconomic and cultural background had already been considered, particularly since the 1970 s, more attention is now given to differences in the linguistic backgrounds of students. The central role of liter-

5 In the German context, Jürgen Kreft's founding work is indicative of this shift, using the key notions of social and individual development in context: Jürgen Kreft, *Grundprobleme der Literaturdidaktik: Eine Fachdidaktik im Konzept sozialer und individueller Entwicklung und Geschichte* (Heidelberg: Quelle und Meyer, 1977).

acy in schooling and its importance for learning is acknowledged. Reflections on curriculum design for the language arts have stressed that this turn toward all students' competences in reading, writing, language, and media should not lead to a narrow literacy approach. Such a focus on basic literacy does not meet the students' entitlement to rich educational experiences as the basis for participation in social, cultural, and professional life in its full sense, but reduces education to a primarily functional concept.

Thus, the Council of Europe's guides on the languages of schooling develop the notion of educational values in a plurilingual and intercultural environment, aiming at informing international curriculum development in the field of languages.[6] Current formal curricula for literature within the language arts often also stress the broader notion of personal development via encounters with literature. In an international study on curriculum, a major finding concerns the prominence of the "personal growth paradigm" from primary through upper secondary education.[7] In Germany, preamble-like parts of the curricula set such a normative frame, stressing the importance of developing aesthetic judgement and appreciation via encounters with a multitude of literary works, the potential of experiencing the other via literature in various formats, and the value of literature in contributing to cultural continuity and identity formation in complex social and cultural environments.[8] This certainly sets a demanding agenda for the literature classroom, moving far beyond a technical treatment of literary texts. It links engagement with literature to students' personal development and surpasses potentially narrow individualistic concepts. However, the most frequently mentioned basic and general aim for primary and lower secondary education appears far less ambitious: to support pleasure and interest in reading, thus insisting on joyful experiences of the students in a highly general way–neutral toward the character and quality of subject matter (namely, the texts read) and toward the notion of development and learning.

---

6 See the website of the Language Policy Unit of the Council of Europe, "Platform of Resources and References for Plurilingual and Intercultural Education," https://www.coe.int/en/web/platform-plurilingual-intercultural-language-education/home.

7 Theo Witte and Florentina Sâmihăian, "Is Europe Open to a Student-Oriented Framework for Literature? A Comparative Analysis of the Formal Literature Curriculum in Six European Countries," *L1–Educational Studies in Language and Literature* 13 (2013): 1–22.

8 The sixteen German *Länder* set up their own curricula within the frame of the so-called educational standards that also show the structure I describe above; for the most elaborate version, see the standards for the final examinations at the end of upper secondary (*Abitur*): "Bildungsstandards im Fach Deutsch für die Allgemeine Hochschulreife: Beschluss der Kultusministerkonferenz vom 18. 10. 2012," kmk.org, http://www.kmk.org/fileadmin/Dateien/veroeffentlichungen_beschluesse/2012/2012_10_18-Bildungsstandards-Deutsch-Abi.pdf, Fachpräambel, p. 13.

It needs to be stressed that the main part of current curricula spells out rather precise performative aspects of competences, setting so-called standards that would include a certain knowledge of genres and stylistic features and a repertoire of tools for textual analysis, with older students often including contextual knowledge (literary history and theory). In general, the new curricula take up traditional disciplinary traits of literature education that are adapted so as to fit the competence-based approach.

What has become of the textbooks in the meantime? The anthology format seems rather outdated, and titles are reticent about any messages the books convey. *Die Bücherkiste* (Book box) and *Magazin* are two examples in Germany that indicate an ample number of literary texts, but do not qualify them further. Textbooks nowadays cover the whole agenda of the language arts. One is simply called *Deutschbuch* (German book), and another one–dating to 1979 and constantly updated in new editions–*Praxis Sprache* (Praxis of language).[9] The rather straightforward (or pragmatic) titles focus on language or language performance and presumably indicate a consensus on what the subject is about.

All in all, the present focus is on more observable, precisely defined learning outcomes. These are monitored regularly and feature in tests or exams. National and international surveys in language education gain a lot of attention. Much effort in research and administration, including financial resources, goes into developing formats for assessing outcomes. For literature education, the shift toward reading competence has brought about changes in priorities on the level of public discourse, changes of the formal curriculum, and changes in the agenda of institutions responsible for education. The aim is to measure reading competence as a capability that students can rely on in various situations. The design of tasks for learning and assessing competencies has changed, and progress has been achieved in specifying the requirement for texts to be understood, including those from the literary spectrum. Awareness of the linguistic challenges of learning has risen. Thus, a simplistic critique of the much-debated changes in education misses out on the potential for meeting demands in subject matter that may well have been overlooked in the past, namely, the text-based challenges students face given their different linguistic backgrounds and learning conditions.

However, the question about what particular literary texts have to teach about our various worlds and how they stimulate our imagination and thinking may become decoupled from the construction of meaning–which is what students should be enabled to do via a competence-based approach. One may ask how the more challenging expectations of literature that have been spelled out in the frame of personal growth may be present in the literature classroom, as well as

9 *Die Bücherkiste* was published by Volk und Wissen (Berlin) between 1991 and 1998, *Magazin* by Cornelsen (Berlin) between 2000 and 2004. *Deutschbuch* also has been with Cornelsen since 1997, and *Praxis Sprache* with Westermann (Braunschweig) since 1979.

in the teachers' professional beliefs and the orientations that guide their practices.

Teachers' Aims in Secondary Education and Classroom Practices

In a recent study that my colleagues and I carried out in parts of Germany and German-speaking Switzerland, we tried to follow up the dynamics sketched above. In TAMoLi–Texts, Activities, and Motivations in Literature Education–we wanted to know whether literature education would still be a priority with teachers of German, what aims the teachers would pursue, and what current practices in the classroom were like. We also asked students about their experiences with literature education and their motivations. Our focus was on lower secondary education–namely, grades eight and nine, the age group that is regularly assessed in the Programme for International Student Assessment of the OECD (PISA) – when the literature curriculum becomes increasingly demanding regarding disciplinary aspects of treating literary texts. In a mixed-methods design, we followed up students' and teachers' perspectives via a survey and carried out interviews and a video study with some classrooms to get insights into actual teaching. The survey was carried out in 126 classrooms, 2,173 students took part, and 116 teachers filled in the questionnaire. All prominent forms of secondary schooling were included. This chapter is not the place to go into details regarding methodology and all the results.[10] Rather, I concentrate here on the teachers' priorities and the challenges that surface regarding an approach to character formation in our current cultural and sociopolitical context.

The majority of the teachers in our study gave some priority to reading and dealing with literature. Next to writing, they regarded this area as most important in grades eight and nine. When asked whether they would give more weight to fostering reading comprehension or to offering access to literature, few teachers

---

[10] One contextual remark on the school system: the German speaking countries in Europe distinguish among three to four types of schooling in lower secondary with different exit exams, aiming at either professional training or university entrance, with an increasing prominence of the higher academic track in recent years. For a more differentiated account of TAMoLi, see Katrin Böhme et al., "Leseverstehen und literarische Bildung: Welche Schwerpunkte setzen Lehrpersonen in ihrem Deutschunterricht und welche Texte wählen sie aus?," *Leseforum* 3 (2018): 1–23, https://www.leseforum.ch/sysModules/obxLeseforum/Artikel/642/2018_3_de_boehme_et_al.pdf; Dominik Fässler et al., "Student Reading Motivation and Teacher Aims and Actions in Literature Education in Lower Secondary School," *RISTAL–Research in Subject Matter Teaching and Learning:* 118–39, https://doi.org/10.23770/rt1828.

prioritized access to literature (12), while most teachers were in favor of balancing the two (65). Thus, within our sample it can be expected that literature is frequently present in the classroom. Further evidence is provided by an online documentary, where teachers indicated in a period of several months what texts they read: literary texts were more frequent than pragmatic genres and presumably also were brought in to enhance reading comprehension.[11]

What are major aims with regard to literature education? In our questionnaire, we distinguished between student- and content-oriented purposes.[12] The teachers in our sample put a strong emphasis on supporting personal development through literature. Aims that can be connected to student orientation were much more supported than those connected to disciplinary practices around literary texts. Teachers agreed that students should be able to identify with fictional characters as well as to take a critical stance toward them; they stressed the importance of dealing with ethical and social matters. Besides this, they affirmed that learners should develop a positive attitude toward reading and enjoy it. However, more content-oriented aims had considerably less support, including knowledge of stylistic means or of traditions, epochs, or important authors. The question whether students should have aesthetic experiences with literary texts only just reached agreement in the mean. The teachers' choice of text fit these priorities. For grades eight and nine, literary texts that deal with sociopolitical issues were frequently brought in, as were texts that fit the life experiences of fifteen- to sixteen-year-olds—for example, novels from youth literature. Canonical texts that were commonly read in German lower secondary classrooms until the 1980 s and 1990 s seem to have given way to a more individualized choice of text that puts more emphasis on contemporary literature and fits presumed students' interests. When comparing students' preferences to teachers' choice of text with regard to themes and genres, we found less overlap than we first expected. Particularly with regard to students' interests for leisure reading, differences were strong: students would go for immersive reading experiences outside school—for example, reading fantasy or science fiction. However, our results confirm that when it comes to reading at school, teachers and students shared a conception of litera-

11 Steffen Siebenhüner et al., "Unterrichtstextauswahl und schülerseitige Leseinteressen in der Sekundarstufe I: Ergebnisse aus der binationalen Studie TAMoLi," *Didaktik Deutsch* 47 (2019): 44–64.

12 We followed the model of paradigms in the literature curriculum mentioned above (Witte and Sâmihăian, "Is Europe Open to a Student-Oriented Framework for Literature?"); see Irene Pieper, Katrin Böhme, and Andrea Bertschi-Kaufmann, "Professionelle Orientierungen im Literaturunterricht: Welche Ziele verfolgen Lehrkräfte in der Sekundarstufe I?," in *Wissen und Überzeugungen von Deutschlehrkräften: Aktuelle Befunde in der deutschdidaktischen Professionsforschung*, ed. Frederike Schmidt and Kirsten Schindler (Berlin: Peter Lang Verlag, 2020), 47–72.

ture education that gives some priority to dealing with challenges of growing up and adolescence and with socially critical issues. Students agreed that such themes should be tackled in the literature class.[13] This seems indicative of a shared perception of the potential of literature in communicative contexts such as the classroom. It also points to professional beliefs of the teachers concerning the role of literature as a contributor to personal development in a societal context.

As a researcher and teacher educator, I consider this shared conception of literature education as a strong potential. At the same time, it strikes me as noticeable that aims around close reading and textual analysis did not have much support among the teachers in our sample. From interviews with teachers, we learned that the stricter curricular demands are considered obligatory. Teachers more or less regularly articulated a conflict with the priorities they set as committed professionals, since these curricular requirements may hinder the experiences with literature that they would like to make room for.[14] And, indeed, the often-ritualized technical approaches to literary texts that one may find in classroom data (and textbooks) seem far removed from the form of engagement one would expect in the frame of personal development. These technical approaches may well remain separated from the individual resonance a piece of literature may have caused in the learner-reader.

At the same time, there is evidence that approaches stressing a personally engaged encounter with literature may also miss out on the ambitious aims connected to a concept of *Bildung* via literature. At least two scenarios deserve attention.[15] First, the literary text may serve as a stimulus or source for a lively encounter with or discussion of a theme of interest and relevance, but the chal-

---

13 Siebenhüner et al., "Unterrichtstextauswahl," 58; Andrea Bertschi-Kaufmann et al., "Literarische Bildung in der aktuellen Praxis des Lese- und Literaturunterrichts auf der Sekundarstufe I," in *Ästhetische Rezeptionsprozesse in didaktischer Perspektive*, ed. Daniel Scherf and Andrea Bertschi-Kaufmann (Weinheim and Basel: Juventa, 2018), 144.

14 Irene Pieper, "L1 Education and the Place of Literature."

15 We currently reconstruct video data with a focus on how subject matter is established in the literature classroom and can assume that these scenarios are not exceptions. For scenario 1, see Simone Depner, Nora Kernen, and Irene Pieper, "Gegenstandskonstitution und literarisches Lernen im Unterrichtsgespräch: Die Videostudie im Projekt TAMoLi–Texte, Aktivitäten und Motivationen im Literaturunterricht der Sekundarstufe I," in *Schulische Literaturvermittlungsprozesse im Fokus empirischer Forschung*, ed. Christian Dawidowski et al. (Berlin: Lang, 2020), 141–62. For scenario 2, see Irene Pieper and Daniel Scherf, "'Was 'ist' der Text?' Beobachtungen zu Bronskys Scherbenpark in einer neunten Gymnasialklasse," in *Aufgaben- und Lernkultur im Deutschunterricht: Theoretische Anfragen und empirische Ergebnisse der Deutschdidaktik*, ed. Christoph Bräuer and Nora Kernen (Berlin: Lang, 2019), 137–54.

lenging potential of the literary text as a possibly disturbing piece of art does not enter the stage at all. Second, the personally engaged approach to literature may become just as ritualized as the disciplinary treatment sketched above. Students may well be expected to perform as involved readers and take the role assigned to them happily, but quite as happily they may go back to "work" and explore how a character is constructed, what symbols are brought in, and the like.

The first scenario points to the risk that the potential of literature is not fulfilled but instead is brought down to some more or less interesting starting point or content. Such a fairly straightforward approach would not engage any complex hermeneutics, and the literary text could easily be replaced by any other medium offering a storyline or attractive theme. Of course, in such a scenario, valuable insights into major ethical or sociopolitical issues could be achieved, but it would not be literature that makes the difference. The capacity to offer new and surprising insights by stimulating imagination and reasoning is missed.

The second scenario is more complex. It points to the mechanisms of teaching and learning in the classroom and the positions that the various actors are assigned and assign to each other. Interaction in the literature classroom relies on practices that are not invented anew every morning but that guarantee accountability. The different actors will often adapt to expectations and cooperate. The respective practices are not neutral to power relations that the system has brought about. School is not an option for students but an obligation; literature as any other part of the curriculum is not a free choice. Within this frame, an imperative like "take the protagonist's perspective and tell us what you would do in her situation" may lead to an answer that makes sense exactly within this frame. But would it be indicative of any stance a person would take outside the classroom? This, of course, we cannot know, and rather than regretting the limits of education, I would hold that it is an essential contribution of literature education to offer an environment where students can learn and, at best, experience that literature may help them reflect on the self and others and stimulate a critical attentiveness to the broader question of how we see the world, how we would like to live, or even how we would want society and politics to develop.

Assessing Potentials with Literature

Following the line of thought proposed above, we can expect a consensus in literature education among practitioners, curriculum designers, and teachers that literature should relate to the life experiences of the student-readers, encourage an engaged encounter, and allow for approaching themes of shared interest. But how can a merely functional use of literature that subordinates the literary text under a superficial concept of student orientation be avoided? According to Juliane Köster, three characteristics of literature deserve attention: (1) literature as a medium that allows for perceiving life, (2) literature as a medium for reflecting upon life, and (3) literature as an intensifier of experience.[16] All three characteristics work within the specific mode of literary communication: rather than documenting real life experiences, literature offers a world that is as different from the world around us as it is related to it.

1) The potential of literature in education is to move beyond the familiar and open new horizons that surpass what the learners already know, think, and expect. Perceiving life through literature includes moving beyond the limits of personal experience. This capacity is stressed by approaches which focus upon the role of intercultural and world literature at school. Given our diversified and globalized societies, the literatures of the world have a lot to offer for learning about the other and for an understanding across cultural and linguistic differences. With texts from the literary canon, differences in time, place, and circumstances are also already noticeable on the surface. The task for teachers is to offer a path which first detects the themes that relate to the students' questions and experiences, so that a basis is established to move beyond. Particularly with texts from literary history, much will depend on overcoming the challenges students nowadays experience when aiming at understanding eighteenth- or nineteenth-century literary and poetic language. Schiller's ballads "Der Taucher" ("The Diver") or "Die Bürgschaft" ("The Pledge"), which are commonly read in German high schools in grades seven and eight, will be fascinating to students at the age of about fourteen, when they grasp the radicality of addressing the question of justice, authority, and tyranny.[17] However, as teachers from all forms of secondary schooling experience, this potential also needs to be raised to the level of text comprehension–with the remarkable side effect that students from various linguistic backgrounds share the experience of difference, and that students with German as a second language may master the tools of meeting the linguistic challenges even better.

The way literature addresses life may be far more direct with children's and youth literature of the present. Here again, professional expertise will have to take into account whether the respective texts–often novels in the paradigm of

---

16 Juliane Köster, "Literatur und Leben–aus der Perspektive des schulischen Gebrauchs von Literatur," in *Der Begriff der Literatur: Transdisziplinäre Perspektiven*, ed. Alexander Löck and Jan Urbich (Berlin: de Gruyter, 2010), 327–43. For Köster, these characteristics are key functions of literature which should be explored in education. My elaborations benefit from these distinctions and elaborate upon them in order to meet my slightly different focus.

17 I will refer to "The Pledge" again below. Both ballads can be found in German and English on the website of Robert Godwin-Jones, School of World Studies, Virginia Commonwealth University, http://germanstories.vcu.edu. The website translates the title of "Die Bürgschaft" as "The Hostage."

realism–offer challenging content. Since their fictional character is less obvious, a reading mode that benefits from the fictional "as if" is more demanding to establish. Thus, professionals and teachers-to-be may wonder: should they choose a novel where a protagonist is bullied by his classmates because of being overweight if they have a student in class who has a similar problem? Literature that relates less directly to the life experiences of students may often be more stimulating for a meaningful exchange among learners about challenges they face or find worth considering.

2) Reflecting upon life may thus be more fruitful if students encounter a somehow distant world through literature. A ballad like "The Pledge" presents a scene that is certainly far removed from a real-life scenario for today's students. Still, the plot involving friendship and loyalty is–once grasped–both moving and stimulating. After a dramatic quest by Damon (the main protagonist, who had intended to kill the tyrant), both he and his friend are rescued. What a relief. But what to do with the final plea of the king–whom we had known as the tyrant–to join the same two friends he was ready to have executed shortly before? What has happened to his power in the course of events? How is his change motivated? Does it mean the end of tyranny? The reflective reading mode is not limited to a purely intellectual approach. Rather, it is best when it balances an affected encounter with literature and thus moves beyond an experiential and potentially immersed reading.[18] In education, it should be part of the didactic design to create pathways in literature that allow for both. At best, such a reflection may lead to an even more intense encounter with the drama that is told in Schiller's "The Pledge." However, to mediate between reflection and reading experiences can be particularly demanding in teaching.

3) Such a balance is also required concerning literature as an intensifier of life. Köster–drawing on Proust–refers to the potential of literature to mediate particularly strong experiences because it can condense what in real life will be stretched out. In "The Pledge," a story of the end of tyranny is told in twenty stanzas; the audience presumably follows the dramatic line of events, shares the anxieties of the protagonist as well as the relief that the friends are saved, witnesses the king's change, and all in about ten minutes. Such an experience of the ballad is not without presuppositions: it depends on imaginative participation in what is poetically enacted. The denseness which opens up a complex fictional world is achieved via poetic means. Thus, the way literature allows for perceiving of life is strongly related to an experience of form. To trace the respective means not on a merely technical level but in relation to the impact on readers and listeners helps understand how the strength of a literary effect is achieved or a literary argument

---

[18] Thomas Zabka, "Literary Studies: A preparation for Tertiary Education (and Life Beyond)," *Changing English* 23, no. 3 (2016): 227–40, https://www.tandfonline.com/doi/full/10.1080/1358684X.2016.1203618.

shaped. Taking into account the aesthetic construction also leads to more demanding questions and more differentiated interpretations. The utopian or parabolic character of "The Pledge" requires an attention that moves beyond the storyline and discovers the keys to an exemplary reading that may lead to discussions of the principles presented. Thus, the potential of literature to provoke our thinking about the world around us is based on the complexities of the textual worlds that need to be explored. The challenge for teachers is to take rhetoric into account in such a way that students are enabled to grasp the link between form and effect, between poetic means and meaning, and to sense that understanding that link is worth the effort.

Challenging Relations between Literature and Education

Explorations of contemporary literature education show a determination to focus on the students and their presumed interests. Literature is considered an important source for personal development, and there is evidence that it features regularly as part of language education. Teachers aim at tackling questions that are prominent in students' environments, including perceptions of society and socio-political challenges. For a considerable time, a direct route from literature to moral education has been left behind. However, another functional approach to literature also needs to be avoided, which is the subordinating of literature to learners' current perspectives and thematic interests. Such an instrumental approach misses out on the potential of literature to move beyond the actual and stimulate personal development by offering new insights and provoking different perceptions of what has been known or perceived so far.

The classroom is not a neutral context for dense encounters with literature. Of course, it differs considerably from the literary salon of the nineteenth century. Still, it is a key place for students to experience literature as a source for reflections on the world around us, reconsider the familiar, and dare new perspectives. Much depends on the professional competences of teachers in the everyday routines of classroom work. Unleashing the power of literature in education needs to be based on thorough encounters with literary texts from the perspective of learning, encounters that move far beyond a general perception of their potential attractiveness and detect their stimulating, even disturbing character. Strong literary texts will always surprise the expert reader at some stage because of a uniqueness that is part of their literariness. Perhaps the strongest potential of the literature classroom is its capacity to allow for surprises that the student-readers bring about. Experienced teachers often have developed a listening attitude that enables them to build on these unexpected perceptions of the students, never mind whether they are still in primary school or on their way to their finals. Much of those teachers' enthusiasm about literature in education relies on the related experience that the limits of the classroom are momentarily suspended, and that it is not only the personal development of the students that is at stake with the arts in education.

Resetting Baselines for an Earth-Centered Moral Education

Darcia Narvaez

The Setting

Over the course of the past ten thousand years or so (about 1 percent of human genus history), one part of humanity has disconnected from the web of life to an increasing degree. Novelist Daniel Quinn pointed out (famously, in his novel *Ishmael*) that the problematic "Taker" culture was described in the Genesis story of the Fall.[1] Metaphorically, by eating from the tree of the knowledge of good and evil, the Takers took on godlike power to make decisions of life and death for other-than-human entities (specifically through agriculture–that is, clearing the land, exterminating "pests," hoarding food for humans alone, and so on.). We can observe now how the hubris of Taker culture–also known as civilization, now armed with the powers of science and technology–has manipulated, disemboweled, and toxified the earth, considering itself entitled and leading us to the multiple ecological crises we face (for example, global warming, species extinction, pandemics), with an abysmal end in sight.

The question I address in this chapter is what should moral educators do in the face of such a destructive culture, one that is destroying not only humanity's habitat but also the integrity of every ecosystem and that of the planet? The answer: we must examine human baselines, better understand human development, and re-adopt ancestral approaches to living a good life.

Quinn names the alternative to Taker culture "Leaver" culture, representative of nomadic foraging cultures the world over, who move with natural systems as members of the biocommunity, considering themselves no more important than nonhumans. As the most common culture of human ancestry, representing 99 percent of human genus existence, their common culture and capacities make a more appropriate baseline for determining the goals and methods of moral education. Using the baseline of humanity's 99 percent in my work, I have ad-

1 Daniel Quinn, *Ishmael* (New York: Bantam, 1992).

dressed the neurobiology of morality and the vitality of nature-centered morality.[2] Although both terms may sound foreign to Western-educated minds, they appear to be the only way to restore species-typical human potential and mitigate planetary disaster.

Civilization's Metaphors and Baselines

Western religion and academic scholarship tend to focus on the last one percent of human genus existence–civilization–ignoring six million years of human evolution, experience, attitudes and behaviors.[3] It should be no surprise that moral education does the same thing. It's as if human beings outside of written history are and were ignorant, even worthless. Yet it is civilization that has led to unfathomable widespread destruction of life on the planet. Instead of understanding how life outside civilization was vastly different in human capacities and worldview (for example, not anthropocentric), many scholars project backwards, using evolutionary arguments (at least those of natural selection) to argue that everything we see today is adaptive–it is natural selection at work. This is a specious understanding of evolution that uses a foreshortened view of human genus existence, missing essential baselines.[4]

Various problematic assumptions guide Western culture, typically rooted in confining metaphors of genetic dominance in human nature as well as human distinctiveness and superiority to nature. Civilized cultures make humans a priority, creating anthropocentric institutions, policies, and practices. Civilization's self-congratulatory orientation is embedded in various root metaphors that imbue thinking implicitly, without awareness,[5] such as "progress is linear," "abstract thinking will solve all problems," and "innovation is always good," especially for overthrowing traditions: "The assumption that equates change with progress, which is held by most Western thinkers as well as by elites in other cul-

2 Darcia Narvaez, *Neurobiology and the Development of Human Morality: Evolution, Culture and Wisdom* (New York: W. W. Norton, 2014).

3 Tracy Henley, Matthew Rossano, and Edward Kardas, eds., *Handbook of Cognitive Archaeology: A Psychological Framework* (London: Routledge, 2019).

4 Markus Christen, Darcia Narvaez, and Eveline Gutzwiller, "Comparing and Integrating Biological and Cultural Moral Progress," *Ethical Theory and Moral Practice* 20 (2017): 55; Darcia Narvaez, "In Search of Baselines: Why Psychology Needs Cognitive Archaeology," in Henley, Rossano, and Kardas, *Handbook of Cognitive Archaeology*, 104–19; Darcia Narvaez and David Witherington, "Getting to Baselines for Human Nature, Development and Wellbeing," *Archives of Scientific Psychology* 6, no. 1 (2018): 205–13.

5 Chet A. Bowers, *Mindful Conservatism: Rethinking the Ideological and Educational Basis of an Ecologically Sustainable Future* (Lanham, MD: Rowman & Littlefield, 2003).

tures who have been educated in Western universities, leads to viewing the loss of intergenerational knowledge and networks of mutual aid as a necessary part of becoming modern."[6]

This view of tradition has only accelerated with the forced spread of capitalism:

> All that "community" implies–self-sufficiency, mutual aid, morality in the marketplace, stubborn tradition, regulation by custom, organic knowledge instead of mechanistic science–had to be steadily and systematically disrupted and displaced. All of the practices that kept the individual from being a consumer had to be done away with so that the cogs and wheels of an unfettered machine called "the economy" could operate without interference, influenced merely by invisible hands and inevitable balances.[7]

The goals of globalization (also known as, colonialism) are to rid traditional societies of their ceremonies, rituals, myths, mutual aid, and networks of solidarity, so that the members can take up commodified versions of what they once had for free–so that a profit can be made and they are no longer "poor." Of course, this is a narrow view of wealth. Economic wealth comes at the great irreplaceable cost of ecological and social wealth.[8] What social wealth is lost?

> These traditional sources of authority include mythopoetic narratives that may be the foundation of a cultural group's moral codes, intergenerational knowledge that carries forward an understanding of the limits and possibilities of the bioregion, wisdom of elders and mentors, and forms of knowledge that come from direct experience of negotiating relationships in everyday life.[9]

Preconquest traditional knowledge, documented to be over a hundred and fifty thousand years old among the San Bushmen,[10] involves respectful relations with the rest of the biocommunity. Biocommunity relations that are respectful and intelligent require generations of knowledge based on observation and experience

---

[6] Chet A. Bowers, *Revitalizing the Commons: Cultural and Educational Sites of Resistance and Affirmation* (Lanham, MD: Lexington, 2006), 26.

[7] Kirkpatrick Sale, *Rebels against the Future: The Luddites and Their War on the Industrial Revolution: Lessons for the Computer Age* (Boston: Addison Wesley, 1995), 38.

[8] David Korten, *Change the Story, Change the Future* (Oakland, CA: Berrett-Koehler Publishers, 2015).

[9] Bowers, *Revitalizing the Commons*, 28.

[10] James Suzman, *Affluence without Abundance: The Disappearing World of the Bushmen* (New York: Bloomsbury, 2017).

passed between generations.[11] Carolyn Merchant[12] describes how the organismic views of sacred nature were replaced in European cultures in the last millennium with the mechanistic view of the world, where nature became dead and stupid, with its most distressing illustration being René Descartes's vivisecting a dog to demonstrate that it was only a machine–showing how a worldview can shape interpretation of events (that is, animal shrieks are only those of a machine). Despite theoretical science's move to dynamism, children still are taught a mechanistic worldview where they learn to treat animals, plants, and even people as commodities, less alive than the market system of capital whose well-being is a priority.

Existing Approaches to Moral Character Education

Civilized moral education, like other parts of Western culture, adapted to the takeover of human lives by industrialism, capitalism, and colonialism. Those that have trouble with such an inhumane system are helped to "adjust" to it by other professionals, namely, psychologists.[13] Similarly, today's moral education typically shapes children for the dominant sociopolitical structure–to dominate the natural world, respect privatization of the commons, and accept inequality.

Civilized moral education swims in Westernized metaphors. Along with anthropocentrism, mechanism, and dualism come the normalized assumptions regarding hierarchy, coercion, and punishment–none of which are part of 99 percent of human history.[14] As Bowers points out,[15] even critical pedagogists, such as Paulo Freire, adopted Westernized concepts like the progress metaphor, took the individual as the basic unit of society, and emphasized the importance of youth learning critical thinking to overthrow customs of the prior generation. Critical pedagogists who do not address the ecological crisis also assume with recent Western views that humans are superior and separate from nature (anthropocentrism). Being stuck in these and other metaphors that emerged in the last few hundreds of years leads to a limited moral education that does not foster our human

---

11 Greg Cajete, *Native Science: Natural Laws of Interdependence* (Santa Fe, NM: Clear Light, 2000).

12 Carolyn Merchant, *The Death of Nature: Women, Ecology, and the Scientific Revolution* (New York: Harper & Row, 1983).

13 David W. Kidner, *Nature and Psyche: Radical Environmentalism and the Politics of Subjectivity* (Albany: State University of New York Press, 2001).

14 Darcia Narvaez, "The 99%–Development and Socialization within an Evolutionary Context: Growing up to Become 'A Good and Useful Human Being,'" in *War, Peace, and Human Nature: The Convergence of Evolutionary and Cultural Views*, ed. Douglas Fry (New York: Oxford University Press, 2013), 643–72.

15 Bowers, *Revitalizing the Commons.*

capacities, instead cultivating a human nature that stands apart from the rest of the natural world, from ancestral wisdom, and from concern for multiple generations ahead.

Even apart from the underlying worldview of Westernized schooling, there are faults in the predominant pedagogy. As Westernized education does generally, discussions of morality move too quickly into abstractions, reasoning, and right thinking, leaving behind the cultivation of moral *being*, *manner*, and *virtue*. Moving children into abstractions too soon (before adolescence) can lead them to habitually ignore (or never learn to attend to) the nuance and individuality of situations, which is critical for virtuous behavior. Along with undercaring for the psychosocial neurobiological development of the young child, the result is that morality becomes a set of clothes put on a dysregulated body, which under stress can easily throw off the outfit.[16]

Thus, moral education is still guided by dualistic philosophical concerns for intellect, continuing a focus on reasoning. The judgment-action gap refers to the fact that people verbalize levels of reasoning that underlie their judgments in hypothetical dilemmas but that are not reflected in their own behavior.[17] James Rest[18] identified additional components beyond reasoning and judgment alone that are required for moral action to successfully take place. Along with judgment, moral behavior requires perception and sensitivity (noticing and interpreting events), motivation to take up the action judged to be most moral, and action capacities for completing that action. Failure in any of the four components undermines the fulfillment of the action. Criticizing the emphasis on reasoning is not to argue that extant emotivist or intuitionist approaches are any better, because they, too, are rooted in civilization's slice of life, not taking into account the full existence and fruition of our species, how capacities are shaped by early experience, and the importance of a heart-minded virtue that results in spontaneous action.[19]

Among the several fundamental flaws in typical accounts of moral development and action, I address two here: (1) an account of the developmental system

16 Narvaez, *Neurobiology and the Development of Human Morality.*

17 Lawrence Walker, "Gus in the Gap: Bridging the Judgement-Action Gap in Moral Functioning," in *Moral Development, Self, and Identity*, ed. Daniel K. Lapsley and Darcia Narvaez (Mahwah, NJ: Lawrence Erlbaum Associates, 2004), 1–20.

18 James Rest, "Morality," in *Cognitive Development*, 4th ed., ed. John Flavell and Ellen Markman, vol. 3 of *Handbook of Child Psychology*, ed. Paul H. Mussen (New York: Wiley, 1983), 556–629; Darcia Narvaez and James Rest, "The Four Components of Acting Morally," in *Moral Behavior and Moral Development: An Introduction*, ed. William Kurtines and Jacob Gewirtz (New York: McGraw-Hill, 1995), 385–400.

19 Francisco Varela, *Ethical Know-How: Action, Wisdom, and Cognition* (Stanford, CA: Stanford University Press, 1999).

for our species and its influence on holistic moral becoming; and (2) a sense of accountability to the web of life outside the human, rather than an emphasis on anthropocentrism and detachment from living on the earth. Disconnection from the web of life starts with disconnection from our human heritages and from our developmental system for raising children and for learning to live well.

Species-Typical Moral Development in Our 99 Percent

Moral development in our ancestral context was quite different. Here, I take our species's ancestral, sustainable/durable ways of being and becoming as a baseline for human development. The species-typical developmental system (evolved nest or evolved developmental niche, EDN) nurtures virtue, for without virtue the individual would not become a good community member, being less healthy, less self-regulated, and less cooperative, so less likely to survive under ancestral conditions.[20] In early life, the EDN is one of humanity's extragenetic inheritances, and for young children it includes soothing perinatal experiences, extensive breastfeeding and positive touch (no negative touch or coercion), multiple responsive adult caregivers, positive climate and social support for mother and child, self-directed free play with multiple-aged mates, and nature connection.[21] All aspects are associated with better health and cooperation, in part due to early development of the right hemisphere of the brain, which is associated with well-being, empathy, and relational capacities.[22]

Although moral neuroeducation is a lifelong endeavor,[23] it begins in the womb and with early life EDN provision, when the child's brain and body systems are being shaped by experience. Within the EDN, the child builds a sense of belonging to the community, to the species, to a living sentient world. In this case, moral education starts with learning the practices and morality of our species, those of deeply embedded sociality. Our heritage is to be nested in webs of support, keeping us feeling connected and like we belong, shaping our neurobiolog-

---

20 Narvaez, *Neurobiology and the Development of Human Morality.*

21 Barry S. Hewlett and Michael E. Lamb, *Hunter-Gatherer Childhoods: Evolutionary, Developmental, and Cultural Perspectives* (New Brunswick, NJ: Aldine, 2005); Mary S. Tarsha and Darcia Narvaez, "The Evolved Nest: A Partnership System That Fosters Child and Societal Wellbeing," *Interdisciplinary Journal of Partnership Studies* 6, no. 3 (2019), doi.org/10.24926/ijps.v6i3.2244.

22 Darcia Narvaez et al., eds., *Evolution, Early Experience, and Human Development: From Research to Practice and Policy* (New York: Oxford University Press, 2013); Allan N. Schore, *The Development of the Unconscious Mind* (New York: W. W. Norton, 2019).

23 Darcia Narvaez, "Moral Neuroeducation from Early Life through the Lifespan," *Neuroethics* 5, no. 2 (2012): 145–57.

ical functions "all the way up," including self-regulation and social skills for cooperation in a fiercely egalitarian community life.[24] Children spend childhood playing with one another in the natural world, shaping their socioemotional intelligence and capacities for a flourishing life in the locale;[25] they learn longstanding traditions that emerged from the group's interactions with the unique landscape. They observe and imitate adult activities as they grow in implicit understanding of how to live life well as fellow members of the biocommunity.

Paul Shepard provided the most insightful treatment of the developmental system of our species through adolescence, specifically, what it looked like among complex hunter-gatherers, tribes and chiefdoms, before they were subsumed by civilization.[26] He gives us a picture of a child's embodied sense of being a human being, before the self-identity focus of adolescence:

> The child of ten in the basic society of hunters and gatherers, with the virtual completion of his vocabulary and years of play behind him, has passed a second major stage of sorting out the self and the not-self. He is deeply family and home-centered and accepts formal relationships. He knows the internal organs of animals and the names of creatures and inanimate things. His muscular and sensory capacities have steadily improved. He is secure within a firm body boundary, evidence of a stable, healthy ego. He is a practical realist in the world of everyday life. He knows all the people around him in their respective roles. He is fond of familiar things. He has learned to estimate dimension and location and identify causative factors when these change in appearance and position. He has shifted from animism to animals, which has clarified his own being. His fears of the dark, of beasts, of surprise, of being lost have been ritualized in play and have kept him from straying much beyond the friendly terrain of visible environs. He is confident, practical, conversant, and happy. It is a true, loyal being. It is not accident, nor is it the design of any particular culture, that ten is the golden age of childhood. It is at this time that all the child has worked for seems to come to fruition. He is an expert in play, in factual knowledge, and the concrete.[27]

---

24 Christopher Boehm, *Hierarchy in the Forest: The Evolution of Egalitarian Behavior* (Cambridge, MA: Harvard University Press, 1999).

25 Toman Barshai, Dieter Lukas, and Andreas Pondorfer, "Local Convergence of Behavior across Species," *Science* 371, no. 6526 (2021): 292–95.

26 Paul Shepard, *Nature and Madness* (Athens: University of Georgia Press, 1982); Paul Shepard, *Coming Home to the Pleistocene*, ed. Frances R. Shepard (Washington, DC: Island Press/Shearwater Books, 1998); Paul Shepard, *The Tender Carnivore and the Sacred Game* (Athens: University of Georgia Press, 1998).

27 Shepard, *The Tender Carnivore*, 200.

Children then arrive at adolescence with body well nurtured and ready to expand into adult activities.[28] When deemed ready, adolescents are invited to initiation rites that vet them for adulthood, perhaps requiring a solo vision quest or other trials. Once they pass, they join their adult group, often by gender, and become a full community member, responsible for maintaining traditions of respect for nature's laws. Such nestedness occurs within a particular landscape of natural entities, such as animals, plants, waterways, and mountains. Generations of observing nature's patterns and seasonal cycles guide community decision-making, as maintaining these commons is critical.

Children of civilized nations follow a different path, often missing many of the evolved nest components even before conception, gestation, and birth. Instead of being immersed in a cultural tradition of embodied, connected selves, woven together through intergenerational narratives, practices, and nature immersion, civilized children often consider themselves without a cultural tradition[29] (although the youth culture created by globalization–that of consumerism and self-aggrandizement–is often the culture children hold implicitly). When these "unnested" children arrive at school, they are already less developed in terms of self-in-nature, lacking self-confidence and exhibiting various pathologies (especially in the United States). In individualistic nations, students might need to learn basic social skills–for example, how to get along cooperatively with others, how to express themselves appropriately, and how to resolve conflicts peacefully.[30] The RAVES and DEEP models were developed to address such needs in classroom settings.[31]

---

28 Colin Turnbull, *The Human Cycle* (New York: Simon and Schuster, 1984).

29 White culture is finally being studied as its own type rather than as the default for human normality.

30 Maurice J. Elias, Joseph Ferrito, and Dominic Moceri, *The Other Side of the Report Card: Assessing Students' Social, Emotional, and Character Development* (Thousand Oaks, CA: Corwin, 2016).

31 RAVES refers to an educational classroom model for moral character development: Relationships, Apprenticeship, Virtuous village of models and mentors, Ethical skill development, Self-authorship; see Darcia Narvaez and Tonia Bock, "Developing Ethical Expertise and Moral Personalities," in *Handbook of Moral and Character Education*, ed. Larry Nucci, Darcia Narvaez, and Tobias Krettenauer, 2nd ed. (New York: Routledge, 2014), 140–58. DEEP refers to Developmental Ethical Ecological Practice that includes self-authorship through self-calming practices and development of social joy and communal ecological imagination; see Narvaez, *Neurobiology and the Development of Human Morality.*

Moral Education Should Start Back at the Beginning

Here, briefly, are several components that moral education of the twenty-first century should address in order to respect our social mammalian nature, foster optimal human capacities, and turn around the march toward self-demise led by capitalist-industrial culture.

Decolonization of Mind

Students need to understand who humans are: members of the earth community. Jack Forbes put it starkly:

> The fact of our absolute, utter, complete dependence upon the earth is used by native teachers as a part of self-understanding. ... I can lose my hands, and still live. I can lose my legs and still live. I can lose my eyes and still live. I can lose my hair, eyebrows, nose, arms and many other things and still live. But if I lose the air I die. If I lose the sun I die. If I lose the earth I die. If I lose the water I die. If I lose the plants and animals I die. All of these things are more a part of me, more essential to my every breath, than is my so-called body. *What is my real body?* We are not autonomous, self-sufficient beings as European mythology teaches. Such ideas are based upon deductive logic derived from false assumptions. We are rooted [in the earth], just like the trees.[32]

Students can learn about the symbiotic nature of human life, how we would not exist without the trillions of microorganisms in our bodies that digest our food and keep us alive.[33] We are symbionts, not individuals; each of us is a community of life, an ecological system.[34]

Students can learn about humanity's deep history, how humanity's existence did not start with civilization, as is often assumed by Western scholars. Students also can learn that the hegemonic, competitive approach to life is rare and does not represent our heritage as cooperators in partnership societies.[35] Instead of encouraging young people to innovate and overturn traditions, they can be encouraged to learn the knowledge, skills, and attitudes of generations of wisdom that developed to preserve their local community commons. Alternative, durable ways

---

32 Jack D. Forbes, *Columbus and Other Cannibals: The Wétiko Disease of Exploitation, Imperialism, and Terrorism*, rev ed. (New York: Seven Stories Press, 2008), 181–82.

33 Rob Dunn, *The Wild Life of Our Bodies: Predators, Parasites, and Partners That Shape Who We Are Today* (New York: Harper, 2011).

34 Lynn Margulis, *Symbiotic Planet: A New Look at Evolution* (New York: Basic Books, 1998).

35 Riane Eisler and Douglas P. Fry, *Nurturing Our Humanity* (New York: Oxford University Press, 2019).

of functioning are still preserved among some First Nation, Native American/ American Indian, and similar groups.[36]

Understanding Human Becoming

The human species has the most immature primate offspring with the longest maturational schedule of any animal–three decades.[37] As a result, many aspects of who each of us becomes are powerfully shaped by the caregiving we receive in early life and beyond, through our malleability and scheduled epigenetic development, structurally "coupling" self-organizing systems into resulting personality and ethical capacities.[38] Neuroeducation of each person occurs prior to conception, as parents' and grandparents' experiences influence the functioning of the offspring's genes.[39] The EDN is especially important in early life, but individuals should be nested all lifelong. As Aristotle noted, young people should be mentored into good activities and relationships that foster virtue–until they can mentor themselves (which seems to be around age thirty). Students should understand that they grow and change and are building their characters by the activities in which they engage, that implicit assumptions about the world are being absorbed by their minds from the activities they choose.

Build Nature Connection

One of the most critical aspects of the evolved nest is ecological attachment–empathy, mindfulness, and partnership with the rest of the natural world.[40] Treat-

---

36 Four Arrows and Darcia Narvaez, *Indigenous Eloquence and Kincentric Flourishing: Selected Quotes and Worldview Reflections to Rebalance the World* (Berkeley: North Atlantic Books, forthcoming); Darcia Narvaez et al., eds., *Indigenous Sustainable Wisdom: First Nation Know-How for Global Flourishing* (New York: Peter Lang, 2019).

37 Ashley Montagu, "Brains, Genes, Culture, Immaturity, and Gestation," in *Culture: Man's Adaptive Dimension*, ed. Ashley Montagu (New York: Oxford, 1968), 102–13; Wenda R. Trevathan, *Human Birth: An Evolutionary Perspective*, 2nd ed. (New York: Aldine de Gruyter, 2011).

38 Humberto R. Maturana and Francisco J. Varela, *The Tree of Knowledge: The Biological Roots of Human Understanding* (Boston: Shambhala, 1998); Narvaez, *Neurobiology and the Development of Human Morality.*

39 Peter D. Gluckman and Mark Hanson, *Fetal Matrix: Evolution, Development, and Disease* (New York: Cambridge University Press, 2005).

40 Angela Kurth et al., "Nature Connection: A 3-Week Intervention Increased Ecological Attachment," *Ecopsychology*, 12, no. 2 (2020): 1–17.

ing nature as sacred and alive used to be a universal attitude.[41] Carolyn Merchant[42] charted the European shift away from this view over the last few hundred years. Changes in behavior led to changes in attitude. Mercantilism, colonialism, and capitalism were chief drivers of the change. As the wealthy and powerful took over the common lands, people were forced into slave or wage labor to feed themselves.[43] While people were displaced from the land, philosophers and scientists adopted a mechanistic, dualistic worldview, theoretically justifying the move to capitalism, technology, and "resource management." David Naveh and Nurit Bird-David show how, in contemporary times, the shift from nature partnership to nature-as-object can occur.[44] The Nyaka were hunter-gatherers who treated animals and plants in their locale as living partners. Forced by government and NGO pressure to raise animals for sale, they were visited by anthropologists years after this transformation. The anthropologists noted that the Nyaka no long treated their raised animals as persons. The animals had become objects, commodities for sale. As social psychologists have shown experimentally, behavior can change attitudes.[45] This suggests that practicing behaviors of respect toward natural entities may keep a partnership mindset alive, whereas behaviors of disrespect and dismissal promote an inegalitarian domination mindset. Angela Kurth and her colleagues' three-week experiments show how daily practices of ecological awareness can shift attitudes toward greater ecological empathy.[46]

First Nation traditions support a partnership orientation to living on the earth.[47] They include ritual and routine respect for "all our relations" in the web of life, honoring the particular landscape, animals, and plants that support the community, along with respect for the great mystery of life itself.[48] Such indigenous wisdom includes an expanded version of Rest's four component model of

---

41 David R. Fideler, *Restoring the Soul of the World: Our Living Bond with Nature's Intelligence* (Rochester, VT: Inner Traditions, 2014).

42 Merchant, *The Death of Nature.*

43 Dan Bollier, *Think Like a Commoner: A Short Introduction to the Life of the Commons* (Gabriola Island, Vancouver, BC: New Society Publishers, 2014); Karl Polanyi, *The Great Transformation: The Political and Economic Origins of Our Time*, 2nd ed. (Boston: Beacon Press, 2001).

44 David Naveh and Nurit Bird-David, "How Persons Become Things: Economic and Epistemological Changes Among Nayaka Hunter-Gatherers," *Journal of the Royal Anthropological Institute* 20 (2014): 74–92.

45 James M. Olson and Jeff Stone, "The Influence of Behavior on Attitudes," in *The Handbook of Attitudes*, ed. Dolores Albarracín, Blair T. Johnson, and Mark P. Zanna (Mahwah, NJ: Lawrence Erlbaum, 2005), 223–71.

46 Kurth et al., "Nature Connection."

47 Eisler and Fry, *Nurturing Our Humanity.*

48 Cajete, *Native Science.*

moral behavior to include the more than human. For example, ecological sensitivity includes receptivity toward communications from the natural world, awareness of interrelations, and taking the perspective of all interrelated entities (a "Council of All Beings").[49] Ecological judgment skills include using natural laws as guides for behavior and understanding consequences of potential action on all entities in the biocommunity. Ecological ethical motivation means orienting to partnership with the rest of nature, showing respect to the more than human, and attuning to the Common Self. Ecological ethical action skills include resolving conflicts and problems with all of nature in mind, and cultivating courage and generosity instead of fear and hoarding. (For a full listing of skills, see my *Neurobiology and the Development of Human Morality*).

Conclusion: Moving from Destruction to Flourishing

From the perspective of the planet, dominant cultural values and human nature are highly immoral. Increasingly, ecologically dismissive civilization, colonialism, industrialism, then capitalism have disrupted natural systems. Focused on extracting more and more from earth systems, using toxic chemicals for its activities, trying to make humans live as long as possible–all these are crimes against a living earth with other-than-human sentient agents within ecologies that have narrow ranges for maintaining well-being.

Ecological dismissiveness characterizes not only relations to other-than-humans but also child-rearing and education. The evolved system for developing our species to optimal capacities has been degraded over generations as adults have become distracted by their own insecurities and misunderstand human becoming. As a result of the narrowed values and ways of being among dominant societies, ethics also has narrowed, with character formation focused on human-to-human interaction, leaving out human-to-nature concerns in its particularities each day (for example, what is the moral thing to do when meeting a spider, when using water, when growing or harvesting food?).

It is becoming clear that returning to sustainable Indigenous wisdom, in existence for 99 percent of human genus existence, must be restored to save the human species and many others.[50] Species-normal character formation, apparent

49 John Seed et al., *Thinking Like a Mountain: Towards a Council of All Beings* (Philadelphia: New Society Publishers, 1988).

50 Four Arrows, *The Red Road: Connecting Diversity and Inclusion Initiatives to Indigenous Worldview* (Charlotte, NC: Information Age Publishing, 2020); Four Arrows and Darcia Narvaez, "Reclaiming Our Indigenous Worldview: A More Authentic Baseline for Social/Ecological Justice Work in Education," in *Working for Social Justice Inside and Outside the Classroom: A Community of Teachers, Researchers, and Activists*, ed. Nancy McCrary

in 99 percent of human genus existence, is a lifelong neuroeducation that is first provided by the evolved developmental niche. Ancestral ways of character formation, still seen among First Nations, are holistic and lifelong, as virtue is an ongoing enterprise requiring observation of wise elders, mentored practice, and regular rituals for respecting the other-than-human, "all our relations." Civilized humans need to step back and remember their heritages to restore the moral character of sustainable human communities. We can reset our baselines for human becoming and establish again an earth-centered, nature-respecting moral education.

---

and William Ross (New York: Peter Lang, 2015), 93–112; Four Arrows and Narvaez, *Indigenous Eloquence and Kincentric Flourishing*; Four Arrows and Darcia Narvaez, *Restoring the Kinship Worldview: Indigenous Quotes, Reflections, and Dialogue for Healing Our World* (Berkeley: North Atlantic Books, in press).

Contributors

Chung-Hyun Baik is Assistant Professor in Systematic Theology at Presbyterian University and Theological Seminary in Seoul, Korea.

Ashley Rogers Berner is Associate Professor and Director of the Johns Hopkins Institute for Education Policy at the Johns Hopkins University School of Education.

David S. Cunningham is Professor of Religion at Hope College, Michigan, and founding director of the Network for Vocation in Undergraduate Education (NetVUE).

Joachim Funke is Professor Emeritus of Cognitive and Experimental Psychology at the University of Heidelberg.

Charles L. Glenn is Professor Emeritus of Educational Leadership and Policy Studies in the Wheelock College of Education and Human Development at Boston University.

Robert W. Hefner is Professor of Anthropology and Director of the Institute on Culture, Religion, and World Affairs at Boston University.

Darcia Narvaez is Professor Emeritus of Psychology at the University of Notre Dame, Indiana.

Stephen Pickard is Professor and Director of Public and Contextual Theology at Charles Sturt University and Executive Director of the Australian Centre for Christianity and Culture.

Irene Pieper is Professor of German Literature Education at the Institute for German and Dutch Literature, Free University of Berlin.

Jo-Anne Reid is Professor Emeritus and Former Associate Dean for Teacher Education at Charles Sturt University, Australia.

Heike Springhart is Lecturer in Systematic Theology at Ruprecht Karls University Heidelberg and a minister of the Protestant Church of Baden in Pforzheim.

Anne W. Stewart is Vice President for External Relations at Princeton Theological Seminary.

Michael Welker is Senior Professor of Systematic Theology and Director of FIIT, the Research Center for International and Interdisciplinary Theology at the University of Heidelberg.

John Witte Jr. is Robert W. Woodruff Professor of Law, McDonald Distinguished Professor of Religion, and Director of the Center for the Study of Law and Religion at Emory University.